MODERNISM WITHOUT JEWS?

GERMAN JEWISH CULTURES

Editorial Board:

Matthew Handelman, *Michigan State University*
Iris Idelson, *Goethe Universität Frankfurt am Main*
Samuel Spinner, *Johns Hopkins University*
Joshua Teplitsky, *Stony Brook University*
Kerry Wallach, *Gettysburg College*

Sponsored by the Leo Baeck Institute London

MODERNISM WITHOUT JEWS?
German-Jewish Subjects and Histories

Scott Spector

Indiana University Press

This book is a publication of

Indiana University Press
Office of Scholarly Publishing
Herman B Wells Library 350
1320 East 10th Street
Bloomington, Indiana 47405 USA

iupress.indiana.edu

© 2017 by Scott Spector

All rights reserved

No part of this book may be reproduced or utilized in any form or by any means, electronic or mechanical, including photocopying and recording, or by any information storage and retrieval system, without permission in writing from the publisher. The Association of American University Presses' Resolution on Permissions constitutes the only exception to this prohibition.

∞ The paper used in this publication meets the minimum requirements of the American National Standard for Information Sciences—Permanence of Paper for Printed Library Materials, ANSI Z39.48-1992.

Manufactured in the United States of America

Cataloging information is available from the Library of Congress.

ISBN 978-0-253-02627-9 (cloth)
ISBN 978-0-253-02953-9 (paperback)
ISBN 978-0-253-02987-4 (ebook)

1 2 3 4 5   22 21 20 19 18 17

For all my families, in deep appreciation

Contents

Preface: Historicizing German-Jewish Subjectivity — ix

Part I. Terms of Engagement: Concepts, Methods, Polemics

1. Forget Assimilation: Subjectivity and German-Jewish History — 3

2. Modernism without Jews: A Counterhistorical Argument — 19

3. The Secularization Question: Germans, Jews, and the Historical Understanding of Modernity — 40

Part II. Troubled Cases: Canon and Genre

4. Edith Stein's Passing Gestures: Intimate Histories, Empathic Portraits — 59

5. Two Vultures: Freud between "Jewish Science" and Humanism — 86

6. Elsewhere in Austria: Jewish Writing between Habsburg Myth and Central Europe Effect — 101

Part III. "No Fixed Abode": The Place of Kafka, Friends, and Modernism

7. Max Brod's Homelands, Kafka's Patrimony — 121

8. Kafka and Literary Modernism — 137

9. The Law of the Letter: Kafka's Correspondence with Milena Jesenská — 151

Index — 169

Illustrations follow page 82.

Preface
Historicizing German-Jewish Subjectivity

German-Jewish Questions

The study of modern German-Jewish cultural and intellectual history, like the fate of its subjects, is both blessed and cursed. On the one hand, nowhere else in modern history is such a massive and consequential Jewish contribution to the general culture so widely recognized. From Moses Mendelssohn to Karl Marx and from Sigmund Freud to Albert Einstein, the Jewish contribution to secular German thought has been seen as both wide-ranging in scope and profound in impact. In fact, it is hard to imagine what contemporary civilization would look like had it not been for the participation of these and a striking number of other less celebrated but variously remarkable creators. On the other hand, historians encounter a stumbling block when seeking to discuss these creative contributions as manifestations of European Jewish culture—as well we should. How is a German text to be defined as Jewish? What relationship is to be drawn between the religious or ethnic or racial identity of the subject and the content of the contribution? Are there cases in which the Jewish origins of the author have contributed to a mystique that affected the way a text was received or that enhances our current perception of its importance to modernism?

This book is about the cultural contributions of secular German Jews, and it is also about their histories. The questions outlined above plague the cultural history of modern, secular Jewish culture, but they were also questions that preoccupied the writers themselves in distinctive ways. The formal political emancipation of Jews in the Habsburg and German Empires at the threshold of late modernity led to an unprecedented volume of recorded reflections on minority cultural identity and integration. This set of reflections betrays an explosion of conjecture about boundaries of self and community, as well as about the relationship of the individual to collectively engaged language and culture. Whether these texts hail from the lead-up to emancipation, the so-called Berlin antisemitism debate of 1879–1880, the context of late-Habsburg nationalist conflict, or the persecution of Jews in the 1930s, their starting point is dilemma. Yet these putative uncertainties might have concealed as much as they revealed. In what ways were the "dilemmas" and "crises" of German-Jewish identity at various historical moments alibis or deflections from other salient experiences? Were they sometimes platforms that enabled creative positions for people—did uncertainty have its own advantages? Can we find between the lines of these identity struggles "roads not taken" or reimaginings of self and culture that were overrun by models that later became dominant? The ultimate question of how this complex of interrogation might relate to cultural production is a key one, because it may offer the possibility of rethinking German-Jewish secular culture in relation to modernity.

Modernism without Jews? German-Jewish Subjects and Histories explores this set of problems from several angles. All of its chapters circle a constellation of related conceptual problems pertaining to the historical experience of central European Jews between the Enlightenment and the aftermath of the Holocaust and also to the ways their histories have been written. The opening gambit of this book is the admission that some of our fundamental assumptions about the reality lived by German-speaking Jews have been misleading, if not outright mistaken. Our assumptions about the experiences of emancipation and assimilation, or the relationship of Jewishness to modernism, or our understanding of a rapid and thorough process of German-Jewish secularization are all rooted in contemporary Jewish reflection and in the observations and judgments of non-Jewish Germans. Yet those articulations often misrepresent more than they expose, and they need to be interpreted in nuanced ways. One ought to be suspicious of the sometimes easy concord among the registers of German-Jewish experience, antisemitic censure, and critical historical analysis. What came to be known in Germany as the *Jewish question*—the troubled and troubling consideration of how one could be both Jewish and part of European, German, or Austrian society—is a central example of how a disturbing uncertainty was posited at the level of the self-reflecting individual, at the level of political and social debate, and finally in contemporary histories of German and Austrian life and culture. In this stark example—and there are others—we see antisemitic assumptions about Jewish integration as *problem* echoed in philosemitic texts; in Jewish subjects' own diaries, letters, and tracts; and in altered form in historians' and critics' accounts of German-Jewish lives and work.

This book argues for a return to the actual subjects of German-Jewish history and offers an approach to their study that might escape this trap of repetition. Sometimes that entails reading texts by German-Jewish authors against the grain: tracking the tensions and contradictions within writings and also the resistances of the texts to the historical contexts of their production, which can be as important as situating texts within the frame of historical conditions and authors' intentions. Each chapter is interdisciplinary, engaging deeply with the literary or philosophical character of individual writings and contextualizing these in a broad historical frame. Studies of the particularly complex cases of famous individuals, such as Franz Kafka and Sigmund Freud, perform much of this work. The goal is to offer a fresh view on the presumed contradictions, uncertainties, and paradoxes that have been seen by historical actors and later analysts alike to have underlain the project of Jewish participation in the general culture. Finally, the following chapters seek to forge new ways of thinking about the relationship of modernist creativity to these dilemmas and hence to redefine the terms of discussion of German-Jewish culture.

Assimilations: Hannah Arendt and Rahel Varnhagen

A short letter from Hannah Arendt to Karl Jaspers from 1952 reveals everything about the problem of secular German-Jewish identity—her own and that of the subject of her as-yet-unpublished second book, the Romantic *salonnière* Rahel Varnhagen.[1] She opens the door to her attention to the so-called Jewish question in spite of herself ("I always found the so-called Jewish question boring") through her friendship with the Zionist Kurt Blumenfeld, "one of those few Jews I've met who was as naïvely assimilated and as unprejudiced by his background as I was myself."[2] She defends her depiction of Rahel, gently criticized in a previous letter by her doctoral advisor Jaspers, in terms that are also telling: she suggests that Jaspers buys into a "falsification" of Rahel that was promulgated by her husband. Scholars have often noted the self-referentiality of Arendt's biography, identifying the ways Rahel reflects, mirrors, or serves as a mask for Arendt herself.[3] The psychodynamics of the exchange are interesting, in that Arendt is identifying the position of her *Doktorvater* (Jaspers's letters bear the salutation "Dear Hannah!" hers to him "Dear Most Honored") with that of Karl August Varnhagen von Ense, Rahel's well-meaning but paternalistic protector and spouse. The falsification spoken of here is not a dissimulation as such but rather an omission that purges reference to the Jewish question in general and to Rahel's association with Jews and converted Jews. Arendt confirms that Varnhagen's manipulation of Rahel's story accords with what Rahel herself would have wished. The forgery, in other words, corresponds to Rahel Varnhagen's own, self-motivated assimilation process. In Arendt's words, Rahel had to "bring about her own assimilation (that is, had to do consciously what others at a later time would have simply handed to them)."[4] This position of willed self-assimilation is not a reflection but rather a mirrored inversion of Arendt's own "naïvely assimilated" position, unprejudiced by background. Key here is a subtle twin gesture in Arendt's letter: a reinscription into the historical record of these indelibly Jewish features of Rahel Varnhagen's that have been written out of the historiographical image—falsified—by the husband Varnhagen, as could be imagined to have been Rahel's own wishes. One thing Arendt asserted at the outset, and repeatedly, was that this was not a biography in the traditional sense, because her intention was "to narrate the story of Rahel's life as she herself might have told it."[5] This apparent contradiction of the impulse to expose and to conceal the Jewishness of this life is symptomatic of an odd double movement in the whole text, one that characterizes much of German-Jewish self-expression as well as its historiography. It is a peculiarity of this "absolutely unique phenomenon" of "German-language Judaism and its history," unique (according to Arendt) even in relation to the history of Jewish assimilation. The book reflects on these very contradictions precisely because its mirrored protagonists—Rahel Varnhagen and Hannah Arendt—are bookends to that very history: Rahel from the interregnum between the end of the ghetto and the reign of German-Jewish assimilation, the Romantic era, and Arendt from the dusk of that reign. The manuscript was researched and chiefly composed on the eve of Hitler's seizure of power but framed and released after the destruction of German Judaism.[6]

Really what Arendt objected to in Jaspers's critique of her manuscript was the assumption of an organic, continuous, or "more or less unbroken tradition of Judaism" within which to contextualize Rahel. But, as Arendt says, "Judaism doesn't exist outside orthodoxy on the one hand or outside the Yiddish-speaking, folklore-producing Jewish people on the other."[7] The world that both the eighteenth-century Rahel and the twentieth-century Arendt inhabit is the same, deterritorialized Jewish existence. Rahel is fascinating for Arendt because "with utter naïveté and utterly unprejudiced, she stands right in the middle between pariah and parvenu."[8] The outsider, the upstart—the one not let in and the one petulantly climbing up the social and cultural ladder—this describes a positionality of secular German Judaism, not a content. When she speaks of "something like a 'Jewish type,'" Arendt is clear that several positive characteristics emerge from the pariah status, just barely if at all connected to the substance of Jewish tradition; the putative negative qualities ascribed to Jews "all derive from parvenu stories."[9] The content, in a word, is the dialectic of unselfconsciousness and necessitated self-consciousness she has described in herself and in her subject; a mask making and a blindness toward masks; above all, a complex and sometimes complicit interaction with antisemitic and sexist surroundings. Arendt in this letter, and indeed in the work as a whole, performs the problem of German-Jewish subjectivity and historiography.

Terms of Engagement

The terms of engagement with German-Jewish culture have had a legacy that extends beyond its immediate historiography. As Aamir Mufti has argued, the modern conceptualization of *minority* came out of the German-Jewish Enlightenment context and, with it, our ways of thinking about minor identities and the putative problem of integration.[10] Cultures accommodate myriad kinds of difference within their frames; there might have been a point where Jewish difference was on the way to being seen as a native German inflection along the lines of any number of regional distinctions or sociolects. The concepts that are central to the chapters that follow have application beyond the German-Jewish example. It is worthwhile to raise some considerations about the most important of these concepts.

This book's focus on the dual levels of German-Jewish subjects and their histories alerts attention to the illusive category of *subjectivity*. While in some sense an alternative to the fuzzier and ideologically freighted notion of identity, subjectivity has its own ambiguities. It emerges in chapter 1 as self-experience, as the intricate, complex, and self-contradictory ways that subjects experience their place in the world *in contrast to* how they are perceived by others, how they are ordered within relatively rigid external systems. Yet the Enlightenment roots of the modern idea of the subject insist not only on the integrity of individual self-experience—the discretion of self and other—but also on the dependence of these discrete subjectivities on a context of others. As one commentator has put it, one is always a subject *to* or *of* something. Subjectivity is hence a process (more than a stable, hidden object) that is constantly shifting, inconsistent, contradictory, and often other than how it perceives itself.[11] It is ideology that disciplines all this disorder into peculiar and consistent identities. Subjectivity is hence a process rather than an object, and it is a process whose inquiry begins with Enlightenment modernity, coinciding with the radical reevaluation of the place of Jews in society.

It is not so much a model of subjectivity as a question of the subject that is inaugurated by the modern—*die Moderne* in German, referring at once to the embracing condition of modernity and its specialized cultural formation in the arts and in thought.[12] If subjectivity itself, in this sense, cannot be seen apart from this self-perceived break of the contemporary West from its past and its contemporary others, pertaining to this modernity, then the special case of German-Jewish subjectivity is a particularly keen reflection of its peculiar ambivalences. *Modernism without Jews?* is a provocative rhetorical question that challenges us to reconsider the whole enterprise of German-Jewish secular culture—the creative production that people would ascribe to that field and the conceptualization of the field itself. The title is more capacious than the realm of self-conscious artistic formal innovation that it sometimes implies. The ingenious interventions of a Franz Kafka, a Joseph Roth, a Sigmund Freud, and so on, are included within its borders, and the *question* of the relationship of their peculiar innovations to the Jewish origins of their authors is central. It is, after all, the central question of secular German-Jewish studies. But it includes as well the lived experience of the masses of less articulate subjects and of those writers and thinkers rarely described as modernist, from the Catholic philosopher Edith Stein to the popular spinner of the paternalistic *Ostjude* image of the eastern European Jew, Karl Emil Franzos.

Rather than endorsing the notion shared by antisemites and philosemites that Jews have been the bearers or propagandists of modernist culture in all its forms, my focus in these pages is on how subjects come to define these categories and place themselves within or outside them. In a sense, the question of the subject and its studies and the so-called Jewish question are born as Siamese twins. Seen this way, it is not surprising that the Jewish contribution to secular culture becomes the symbolic key to thinking about the modern condition.

The notion of secularization is a freighted and a contested one, and this is particularly so in Jewish contexts. As is the case with related terms such as "modernization," the disputed nature of the question of secularization has opened up immensely rich discussions in a wide range of fields. Recent attention to the nature of secular Judaism—Jewishness without religiosity—has in some ways deflected Jewish studies from these discussions by narrowing the secular down to questions of identity, ethnicity, and culture. Other contemporary debates about secularization focus on the increasing irrelevance or, contrastingly, the persistence of faith in increasingly rationalized societies, leading to a rigid and linear conception of richly complex and dynamic processes. What processes are actually at play in the apparent disaggregation of faith from everyday life or, conversely, in the processes of imbuing or reimbuing material life with spiritual content?

"Secular" and all its linguistic variants have their origin in Christianity, emerging arguably out of a specifically Protestant eschatology.[13] This might be considered troubling to their application to other faith systems, including Judaism. The dichotomy of sacred and secular is a Christian one that arguably does not map onto traditional Jewish binaries of *kadosh* and *chol* (holy and profane), *tahor* and *tamay* (pure and impure), or other terms that may relate to the ritual and common domains or denote purity and impurity but not worlds defined by time and eschatology.[14] Historical Judaism was, many argue, a system in which the boundaries between spiritual experience and daily life were porous or even nonexistent: the temple was a civic as well as a sacred space, and so on. In this sense, the dynamic tension between the spiritual and the material in Jewish life is one that can be discussed outside the metanarratives of modernization, Westernization, and rationalization.[15]

The conceptualization of the secular in these pages thus turns away from the problem of secular Judaism to the problem complex of secularization and sacralization. This promises relief from some of the repetitions of discussions of Jewish secular identity but opens up other problems inherent in the broader secularization debate in intellectual history. The term "secularization" has been ambiguous in that it may refer to contradictory things. On one account, it describes the transition of societies (Western society in particular) from a worldview based on faith to one based in science and reason. This is the first version of the much maligned secularization thesis. Obversely, a more sophisticated edition of the secularization thesis posits the persistence of a sacral system through various worldly equivalents (e.g., the modern state and other nominally secular institutions displace a theologically based cosmogony). Western thinking about the sacred and the secular since the Enlightenment has thus been bound up in the troubled assessment of the status (or legitimacy) of the modern era itself.[16] "Sacralization" in turn may refer to myriad moments when subjects or communities invested worldly objects, routines, or practices with otherworldly content. Paired with "secularization," the term may imply the various ways modern subjects have sought to recover spiritual meaning presumed lost to secularization.

Some of the key figures discussed in this book can hardly be described with the word "secular." Some, such as Martin Buber, were key in the reconceptualization of Jewish spirituality in the early years of the twentieth century; we can say the same of poets like Else Lasker-Schüler, along with Nathan Birnbaum and other early Zionist thinkers. One chapter focuses on Edith Stein, a woman so pious that she was canonized as a Catholic saint. Unlike many discussed in these pages, Freud was a secular Jew par excellence, and yet we cannot avoid associations of the relationship of the new psychoanalytic science to, on the one hand, Jewish tradition or the Jewish origins of its founder or, on the other, a generalized Western process of abandonment of faith and its replacement by a new master code (one of the definitions of the process of secularization). Finally, the case of Franz Kafka, to which chapters 7–9 are devoted, is a complex one. With Kafka as with Walter Benjamin, the spiritual valence of the work has from its earliest critical reception been central and puzzling at the same time. It is both curious and underexamined that the debates around the secularization thesis, or the conception of a historical process of secularization and the debate about its legitimacy, were concentrated in a field of German-Jewish thinkers (with one key exception). Rather than thinking of this cultural production in terms of the secular, we may agree with Birnbaum himself that it may best be seen as the Jewish modern (*die jüdische Moderne*). And so we return to the question of modernism.

The book is organized in three major parts, each with a different mode of inquiry and substantive focus and each building on the foundation of the one before it. The first major part is titled "Terms of Engagement." In it, three major terms of analysis ("assimilation," "modernism," and "secularization") are analyzed in depth in relation to the problem complex of German-Jewish subjectivity. The second part, "Troubled Cases," presents particular case studies (Edith Stein, Sigmund Freud, and Jewish writers from Galicia and Bukovina) to explore the tendencies of these literatures to explode boundaries of genre and discipline. The third part, "'No Fixed Abode,'" presents several approaches to the work and life of Franz Kafka and his closest associates (friend Max Brod, lover Milena

Jesenská). As the literary figure discussed in this book who has made the most direct contribution to literary modernism, Kafka offers an appealing example for deeper analysis and a commanding way to tie the themes of subjectivity and historiography in relation to the sacred and the secular, belonging and alienation, self and other.

Debts

This book has been in the making for nearly two decades, gestating alongside other projects, some directly related and others seemingly very distant. It would be impossible to name all the people and institutions contributing to its development. Nonetheless, some call out for naming. I was able to pull all the disparate pieces together into a whole thanks to two major research leaves that came not only with research facilities but also with inspiring resident fellow colleagues. The first of these experiences was the invitation in 2013–2014 to reside in Vienna at the International Research Center for Cultural Studies for a second time in my career, funded by the Fulbright Foundation. A series of weekly workshop discussions and more public colloquia at the Frankel Institute for Advanced Judaic Studies at the University of Michigan was the second of these opportunities. Our very tight-knit group of colleagues in many disciplines tackled questions around secularization and sacralization, a theme that I had been honored to propose. A faculty seminar years ago funded by the Felix Posen Foundation and facilitated by Zvi Gitelman hosted my ruminations on assimilation, and a special issue of *Modernism/modernity* edited by Amir Eshel and Todd Presner launched the concern with "Jewish modernism."[17] Invitations by Mark Gelber of Ben-Gurion University of the Negev have continuously spurred my rethinking of the situation of writers of Prague, as have his thoughtful interventions. Dan Diner and the Simon Dubnow Institute of Historical Study at the University of Leipzig ignited questions of the use of German by Jews of the eastern Habsburg Empire, and those questions continued for me in a series of discussions with the stimulating group of historians engaged in the Rethinking German Modernities conferences under the leadership of Tracie Matysik, Jennifer Jenkins, and Geoff Eley.[18] Thanks are also due to the Department of Germanic Languages and Literatures and the Department of History at the University of Michigan, both of which have supported my ongoing work in so many ways.

The categories of friend and colleague merge rather than overlap. Something would be different about the chapters in this book without Crisca Bierwert, Kathleen Canning, John Carson, Geoff Eley, Hussein Fancy, Dario Gaggio, Paul Reitter, Jitka Malečková, Deborah Dash Moore, Regina Morantz-Sanchez, Rudolf Mrázek, Helmut Puff, Jacqueline Stevens, Jeffrey Veidlinger, and so many others. For their insights and their generosity, I cannot thank them enough.

Bits and pieces of the book were presented as lectures in many different venues, and in summary I thank them as follows: Cogut Center for the Humanities at Brown University; Cornell University; the Czech Center New York; University of Dresden; Hebrew University and Ben-Gurion University of the Negev; Hokkaido University in Sapporo, Japan; Jewish Community Center of Metropolitan Detroit; New York University; Northwestern University; Ohio State University; Moses Mendelssohn Center at the University of Potsdam, Germany; Stanford University; University of Vermont; University of Vienna; and Yale University. Previously published sections of the chapters are cited in notes.

Arendt's portrait of Rahel Varnhagen presents another mirrored pair: what Arendt has called the "pariah qualities" corresponds to what Rahel called the "realities of life," and each forms the basis for an aesthetic and ethical formation that includes an extraordinary sensitivity toward injustice; Arendt links this, in a passage of the letter to Jaspers discussed above, to a sense of family.[19] I cannot measure the ways my relationships to Benjamin and Natalie; Debra and Rebecca; Michael, Jennifer, and Leah; and, not least, Eric have left their imprint on the thoughts and sensibilities reflected in the following pages. To them I owe everything.

Notes

1. The letter is published in full in Hannah Arendt and Karl Jaspers, *Briefwechsel, 1926–1969*, ed. Lotte Köhler and Hans Saner (Munich: Piper, 1985), 233–238.

2. Hannah Arendt and Karl Jaspers, *Correspondence, 1926–1969*, ed. Lotte Köhler and Hans Saner, trans. Robert and Rita Kimber (New York: Harcourt Brace Jovanovich, 1992), 197.

3. See Norma Claire Moruzzi, *Speaking through the Mask: Hannah Arendt and the Politics of Social Identity* (Ithaca, NY: Cornell University Press, 2000), 48–60; and Seyla Benhabib, "The Pariah and Her Shadow: Hannah Arendt's Biography of Rahel Varnhagen," *Political Theory* 23, no. 1 (1995): 5–24. Cf. the related but different reading of Dagmar Barnouw, *Visible Spaces: Hannah Arendt and the German-Jewish Experience* (Baltimore: Johns Hopkins University Press, 1990), 30–71. See also Liliane Weissberg's important introduction to the English translation, "Hannah Arendt, Rahel Varnhagen, and the Writing of (Auto)biography," in Hannah Arendt, *Rahel Varnhagen: The Life of a Jewess*, ed. Liliane Weissberg, trans. Richard and Clare Winston (Baltimore: Johns Hopkins University Press, 1997), 3–64.

4. Arendt and Jaspers, *Correspondence*, 199.

5. Arendt, *Rahel Varnhagen*, 81.

6. Hannah Arendt, *Rahel Varnhagen: Lebensgeschichte einer deutschen Jüdin aus der Romantik* (Munich: Piper, 1981), 14.

7. Arendt and Jaspers, *Correspondence*, 199.

8. Ibid., 200.

9. Ibid.

10. Aamir R. Mufti, *Enlightenment in the Colony: The Jewish Question and the Crisis of Postcolonial Culture* (Princeton, NJ: Princeton University Press, 2007).

11. Nick Mansfield, *Subjectivity: Theories of the Self from Freud to Haraway* (New York: New York University Press, 2000), esp. 4–6.

12. See, e.g., H. Gumbrecht, "Modern, Modernität, Moderne," in *Geschichtliche Grundbegriffe: Historisches Lexikon zur politisch-sozialen Sprache in Deutschland*, vol. 4, ed. Otto Brunner, Werner Conze, and Reinhart Koselleck (Stuttgart, Germany: Ernst Klett, 1978), 93–131; and chapter 8.

13. A key text in the varied discussions of this issue is Karl Löwith, *Meaning in History* (Chicago: University of Chicago Press, 1949), discussed at length in chapter 3.

14. As pointed out to me by the scholar, and my colleague in the Frankel Institute in 2015–2016, Ariel Mayse, while it may be true that these binary pairs in historical Judaism did not have the same meaning as the contemporary sacred-secular distinction, neither did Christian counterparts in the same period; likewise, modern Judaism does sometimes speak in these terms. The periodic distinction may be more relevant than the Western Christian or even Protestant ascription of the dichotomy.

15. See the larger argument of Leora Batnitzky's *How Judaism Became a Religion: An Introduction to Modern Jewish Thought* (Princeton, NJ: Princeton University Press, 2011).

16. See Hans Blumenberg, *The Legitimacy of the Modern Age* (Cambridge, MA: MIT Press, 1983). See also chapter 3.

17. "Jewish Modernism," special issue, *Modernism/modernity* 13, no. 4 (2006).

18. Papers from these conferences appear in Geoff Eley, Jennifer L. Jenkins, and Tracie Matysik, eds., *German Modernities from Wilhelm to Weimar: A Contest of Futures* (New York: Bloomsbury, 2016). See also Arndt Engelhardt and Susanne Zepp, eds., *Sprache, Erkenntnis und Bedeutung: Deutsch in der jüdischen Wissenskultur* (Leipzig, Germany: Universitätsverlag, 2015).

19. Arendt and Jaspers, *Correspondence*, 200; Arendt and Jaspers, *Briefwechsel*, 236.

MODERNISM WITHOUT JEWS?

PART I

TERMS OF ENGAGEMENT: CONCEPTS, METHODS, POLEMICS

1 Forget Assimilation
Subjectivity and German-Jewish History

Forgetting Assimilation

In a famous lecture delivered at the World Jewish Congress in Brussels in 1966, Gershom Scholem recalled the history of German-Jewish assimilation.[1] It is an astonishing and elegant lecture—piercingly incisive, breathtaking in its synthesis. It tracks the path from the relative autonomy and integrity of a pre-emancipated Jewish community in Germany through the ambitious, idealistic, but what turned out to be fatally wrong-headed project of assimilation. This outline has come in the meantime to be known as the orthodox view of German-Jewish history. There are many brilliant insights in Scholem's lecture, "Jews and Germans," which also has its share of untenable assertions. One of the former that has been little noted is Scholem's disclaimer, early in the lecture, that his title forced him onto what he understood to be epistemologically and ontologically shaky ground: "For not all 'Germans' are Germans and not all 'Jews' are Jews" is the elegant truth forgotten by those citing the lecture, neglected in the historiography it inspired, and conveniently forgotten by Scholem himself throughout the rest of his address.[2] To speak of "the Germans" and "the Jews" in this period—the scare quotes are Scholem's—is to descend into the unsustainable realm of generalization, worthy of the coarsest antisemites. The philosophically trained Scholem did not bring himself to say that the embrace of such "questionable categories" is justified; he said that the ability properly to differentiate rather than to use gross categories has been hampered by the memory of a cataclysm executed by people who saw no use for any such distinctions. This was a sympathetic claim, perhaps, but not an intellectually persuasive one, and one has the sense that Scholem, too, is embarrassed by the lack of rigor.

To remember assimilation in the way Scholem would like—a way, that is, that would make sense of the catastrophe of German Judaism, as well as the hope of the fledgling State of Israel—it seems he had to forget the complex ways individual consciousnesses brushed against the grain of abstract collectivities. The poignancy of this gesture derives from the fact that Scholem was speaking not only as an exponent of the first generation of the orthodox school of German-Jewish historiography but also as a member of the last generation of its objects of study. When he spoke of the "emotional confusion of the German Jews between 1820 and 1920"—a confusion that he argued was essential to understand if one is to grasp the fraught phenomenon of "German Jewishness"—the listeners were aware that Scholem was one of those Jews.[3] He was both subject and object of his own analysis, and this is the key to a rhetoric that slipped easily from categories of identity that were in play for assimilated Jews and those available to post-Holocaust historians.

As historian and historical object, Scholem offers an extreme case of a tendency I want to call attention to: histories of German-Jewish culture sometimes suffer from an excess of empathy with their subjects. By an excess of empathy, I mean that scholars have assumed a problematic that one might call the German-Jewish identity crisis, as well as the categories of identity and culture that undergird it. This empathy, and these assumptions, have been the source of a scholarly production that by any relative measure must be considered large, especially in proportion to the size of the demographic group on which it focuses. This scholarly literature has been both interesting and critical. Yet I want to argue (somewhat polemically) that the limitations of these approaches have led to a kind of impasse that provocatively parallels the situation of the producers of German-speaking Jewish culture in the first third of the twentieth century.[4]

As a strategy to get beyond what has been described as a dead end in the historiography and to open up questions it has obscured so far, I suggest we begin by forgetting what Scholem chose to remember and remembering, and expanding on, what he invoked only to forget. To do so, it will be necessary to examine both the historiography and its subjects. Assimilation is a problematic both have shared. It is one, however, that needs to be subjected to critical analysis, whereas the categories and concepts sustaining it have with few exceptions been taken for granted by historical subjects as well as historians. Chief among these is the notion of identity inherent in the dominant image of assimilation.

That model of identity is one that assumes a spectrum of possible identifications running from the imagined pole of absolute Jewish identification (what Franz Rosenzweig called "dissimilation"), at one end, to complete appropriation of German identity at the other.[5] This model was always meant to be flexible in particular ways, not least because the notions of German and Jewish identification were open: "total" assimilation might mean baptism and intermarriage, or it could mean the retention of Jewish religious adherence in a purely private way. The most extreme pole of Jewish identification could likewise be understood in terms of religious orthodoxy, secular Jewish nationalism, Jewish spiritualism, or some other cultural and intellectual engagement specifically identified as Jewish. It is often (if not always) assumed that these poles reflect ideal types, and that actual individuals find themselves variously along this spectrum. The model clearly makes place for degrees of complexity; it may even have developed as a nuanced alternative to a simple binary of assimilated and nonassimilated.

Yet even allowing for all this variation, the spectrum of relative assimilation is an inadequate model and a deceptive one. As the late Amos Funkenstein showed in his 1995 essay "The Dialectics of Assimilation," the long-lived distinctions between "spontaneous" and "acquired" cultural character, accidental adaptation and essential adoption, or stable essence and assimilatory appearance are all themselves powerfully ideological instruments of segregation rather than descriptors of a cultural condition. While cultural adaptation has been uneven over time and space, it has nonetheless been universal; what is taken as authentic or traditional is often another example of dynamic interaction with external cultures.[6]

Scholem knew too much to deny this but justified his narrative by distinguishing the German influence on the pre-emancipated Jewish community—through a "barely conscious process of osmosis"—from the indelicate, programmatic force of self-conscious assimilation.[7] The latter process would come to produce a "sinister and dangerous dialectic" whereby Jews were both required to surrender their group identity and at the same time despised for the willingness and ability to do so.[8] This analysis of the double bind of the emancipation-assimilation pact is standard fare in the tradition of historiography represented by Scholem's talk. It is, therefore, all the more surprising that it is Scholem who points out what in his words "is now often forgotten"—namely, that assimilating Jews wished in some form to retain their Jewishness. While assimilation as an abstraction (or even as a social process promoted by a minority of community leaders) theoretically moves without equivocation toward the dissolution of Jewishness and total absorption of, and into, gentile German culture, individuals held on to their Jewishness "as a kind of heritage, as a creed, as an element unknowable and indefinable, yet clearly present in their consciousness."[9]

On one level, we are confronted with the paradox of the secular Jew, who, as Yosef Hayim Yerushalmi reminds us, is both a stranger and a more diverse sort of creature than this "blandly generic term" would seem to indicate.[10] On another level, Scholem's observation brings into view what his own focus on assimilation as a paradigm, a program, and a seemingly inexorable historical process obscures. In their lives and consciousnesses, actual Jews did not experience their relationship to Jewishness (or to Germanness, for that matter) in the zero-sum-game terms of the politics of assimilation. Yerushalmi, taking a skeptical stance toward the uneven and inconsistent positions of these men and women who hovered in an "undefined yet somehow real Jewishness," diagnoses their Judaism and Jewishness as contentless, "pure subjectivity."[11]

Scholem's and Yerushalmi's critiques of the secular Jew, especially the assimilated German Jew, identify the surrender of an integral Judaism as the root of an insoluble confusion, neurosis, or malaise.[12] What the study of secular Judaism needs is a sustained analysis of these troubled subjectivities and not the wholesale pathologization of the secular condition it has seen. Such a turn to interiority could help answer questions about modern German-Jewish cultural production that remain unasked by the paradigms of assimilation used by orthodox historiography—as well as by its most articulate critics.

A prominent revision of the orthodox school is represented by the provocative work of David Sorkin, who in several influential contributions has also sought to leave behind the governing concepts of emancipation and assimilation.[13] Working principally in the formative period of German-Jewish assimilation, Sorkin has argued that an internal "ideology of emancipation" was the motor driving the creation of a German-Jewish "subculture," which by its very nature was invisible to its own adherents, who only *imagined* that the process they were living through was effectually an abandonment of community. This argument, as Samuel Moyn points out, "sublates" or historicizes the orthodox view rather than repudiating it—it lifts the veil that assimilation held before its own eyes but preserves the integrity of the categories on which the ideology of assimilation depended.[14] Sorkin's explanation remains so profoundly structuralist as to leave little room for any subjectivity or indeed to allow self-consciousness at any level. As Anthony La Vopa points out, "The irony Sorkin finds is structural, not 'subjective.'"[15] Sorkin himself is explicit about this distinction at several points, arguing that "the community's invisibility [to itself] thus resulted from a disparity between ideology and social reality. Invisibility was a structural and not a subjective problem."[16] In turning to the concept of ideology, Sorkin relies on an assumption of totalized false consciousness. He recognizes that ideology requires "a coherent system of ideas and symbols" as well as an institutional foundation. Yet, perhaps understandably, he shies from what I have described elsewhere as the contradictory ways in which subjects (the actors in a process) understand themselves within an ideological system or the ways they are "given identity."[17] This seems, at first, to come down to the problematic dichotomy of structure and agency, even though many historians acknowledge that the dichotomy is a false one.[18] Structures and agents—or objective conditions and subjective consciousnesses—are so mutually entwined within the historical process that thinking about them apart from one another is senseless. Even the words "agency" and "agents" are to some degree deceptive, because they suggest a level of self-consciousness and deliberation that is in many cases beyond historical actors as they move through their world.

In focusing on the complicated and often self-contradictory subjective experiences of individuals, we are not abandoning the notion of shared historical experience, and we are not denying the possibility of writing a collective history. But the foundation of any such history must be stronger than the fictions a community told itself. A different picture emerges when historians attend to the wide range of ways in which German Jews understood themselves to be Jews and to be German.

Postassimilationist Reflections

When the novelist Jakob Wassermann (1873–1934) published his memoir, *My Life as German and Jew*, he seemed to be making a new claim for the possibilities and impossibilities contained within the categories German and Jew.[19] Resisting the notion of separate or even opposing racial, ethnic, or cultural identities, his life story and the aesthetic path of his works were laid out to avoid even the term "German-Jewish" and, in the process, to offer an alternative to the model of symbiosis. Instead, Wassermann and his work were simultaneously "German" and "Jewish," at odds with themselves, and this dialectical rather than dialogical relationship was central to the production of literature.[20] Wassermann depicts his struggle not as the highly individuated experience of an artist with a dual identity but as a universal condition. His descriptions of German identity sound more like discussions of the Jewish question, just as the tangential existence of the struggling writer is merely a sharpened reflection of everyday human existence.[21]

This memoir is made remarkable by all these border crossings, not least because of its emergence just at the moment when famously essentialized notions of German-Jewish difference were being solidified. Yet Wassermann's text also participates in these discursive processes. Identity in his book is forged by blood and climate, by insuperable tradition and by unassimilable foreign culture. Wassermann presents himself as German *and* Jew, because there are such things as Germans and Jews, collective identities that define their members as similar to all others within—yet still distinct from all those outside. As do the antisemitic and Zionist challenges to the Jewish participation in German-language culture, Wassermann takes for granted the status of his self and work as question or problem. For all its complexity, *My Life as German and Jew*, by virtue of its very appearance, perches on the crest of the tide rather than riding against it. Although Gershom Scholem identified Wassermann's text as a "cry into the emptiness, one which recognized itself as such"[22]—and which also beckoned Scholem himself to taste the substance of Palestine—it shares with Scholem's critiques a universe of terms.[23] Within this universe, one could champion or oppose assimilation, but doing either implied a silent concession to the existence of a German-Jewish identity crisis.

The generations I focus on in this chapter are ones that could be called postassimilationist. Steven Aschheim has used the term more narrowly to denote certain German Jews at the turn of the century and later, "second generation" Jewish nationalists and Zionists in particular.[24] But whether Zionist or liberal, the Jews of the generation coming of age at the turn of the century and shortly after were all in some sense postassimilationist. For them, the classic liberal-assimilationist position, with its optimism about a potentially unproblematic fusion of Jewish (private) identities with German public ones, was no longer available. As anyone who has reviewed the primary sources of the period will testify, liberal and Zionist Jews, as well as their non-Jewish counterparts from the socialists to the antisemites, had all come to argue their different positions from a shared conceptual universe that suggested a different set of assumptions from those of official assimilationist discourse.[25]

Postassimilationist Historiography

Postassimilationism can also productively be applied to our historiographical perspectives. Like other "post-" labels (poststructuralist or post-Marxist, for instance), postassimilationism should not necessarily suggest an openly antagonistic relationship to the ideology of assimilation; to the contrary, it suggests a position that clearly follows from the failed logic of its predecessor. This succession, furthermore, takes place with an extreme uneasiness about the conclusions of its forerunner yet is also dependent on it. Thus, the passage from assimilation to postassimilation might be presumed to be dialectical rather than merely successive or progressive, and some historiographical reviews and debates that are relevant to these lines of inquiry have sought to follow this path. They have sought to chart the course away from a German-Jewish historiographical literature that is more or less strictly formed along lines mirroring the ideological alternatives of Jewish identity (i.e., national, or Zionist, and liberal, or sometimes cultural, which is not to be confused with the designation of liberal internal to German Judaism), and despite their sometime disagreement, they have achieved a consensus that considers viewing these alternatives in a starkly dichotomous way as obsolete.[26]

A serious concern of a particular species plagues modern German-Jewish cultural and intellectual history. As discussed in the preface, we are faced with what must be considered the overwhelming contribution of modern German-speaking Jews to the general secular culture, from music to science to literature and the arts. But if these products are by definition secular—if they emerge, not out of specifically Jewish religious traditions, but instead within German or European cultural and intellectual ones—how are we to discuss them as Jewish cultural products at all? These questions instantly reproduce the debates of the postassimilationist period through the categories in which they are forced to work themselves out. Michael Brenner, in his excellent study of Weimar Jewish culture, avoided this problem by focusing on cultural manifestations that defined themselves specifically within a Jewish cultural sphere.[27] Yet such a strategy necessarily fails to take into account precisely those works produced by German-speaking Jews that have wielded the greatest cultural influence. Many other works have taken the contrary tack, assessing the Jewish contribution to secular, modern culture through a kind of census of great contributions, organizing authors by the arguable Jewishness of their origins. The complicity of such approaches to the problem complex of what we may call Jewish modernism is the subject of chapter 2, and there is no need to dwell on it here. But it is useful to recognize the unspoken logic of identifying even the thematically Christian aesthetic work of a Hugo von Hofmannsthal or a Gustav Mahler or the universalism or atheism of a Karl Marx, the analytic approach of a Ludwig Wittgenstein, and so on, as products of a putatively Jewish background. Scholem, in his lecture "Jews and Germans," falls into this trap when, once again forgetting his bracketed antiessentialist remark opening the lecture, he turns to the production of secular Jews—from Karl Marx and Ferdinand Lassalle to Karl Kraus, Gustav Mahler, and Georg Simmel—and argues that "even in their complete estrangement of their awareness from everything 'Jewish,' something is evident in many of them that was felt to be substantially Jewish by Jews as well as Germans—by everyone except themselves!"[28]

This only goes to show that in the postassimilationist generation, these questions and the assumptions behind them were shared by many of the subjects in question, not merely antisemites, although it was the antisemites who were the first to bring the connection of Jewish background and modern German cultural production to the forefront of a sociopolitical discussion. Jewish nationalists and Zionists famously shared many of these assumptions. But so too (if in a different way) did liberals from the turn of the century through the Holocaust.[29] Not just Scholem but so many of the Jews of nineteenth- and twentieth-century central Europe who would make powerful contributions to secular culture had a strong, if not always precise, consciousness of Jewishness. Yet deep ambivalence troubled this identity. For them, Jewishness was something neither intrinsic and inherited nor stable and capable of being taken for granted. It was a problematic: it stood for this very complex of questions rather than representing a clear and decisive answer, an identity. In other words, the very same difficulty confronting the cultural historian haunted their own relationship to Jewishness. At the same time, the overlap of the problems facing German-Jewish subjects and their historians is not precise. As Wassermann's memoir shows, many of the questions we associate with the problem of identity were apparently familiar to members of the postassimilationist generation itself. They asked themselves: How can I be both Jewish and German? What does it mean to me to be Jewish if I am not religiously observant or believing? How are the products of my creative and intellectual activity inflected by my Judaism?

Furthermore, while historians and contemporary actors share to some degree the model of assimilation as played out along a spectrum, the actual experience, or self-experience, of people in this period gives the lie to such models of self-identification. In society, German-speaking Jews made judgments about their relative acculturation, as well as that of others in various Jewish communities.

Quite a different matter was the complex way in which they imagined themselves in relation to Jewish, German, or other collective identities.

The German-speaking Jewish writer of this period with whom I am most familiar, Franz Kafka, is arguably an exceptional case, but like many exceptions, his example may highlight a condition that is more shared than commonly recognized.[30] Although his friend Max Brod argued for an understanding of Kafka as someone who moved from a distant relationship to an ever-increasing identification with Judaism and even Zionism, a careful reading of Kafka's comments on Jewish and German identity in his diaries and letters reveals, above all, a powerful ambivalence throughout. Most symptomatic may be the entry in his diary of January 1914: "What have I in common with Jews? I have hardly anything in common with myself and should stand very quietly in a corner, content that I can breathe."[31] The swift acceleration of political and social antisemitism in German-speaking society from the first decade of the twentieth century through the Shoah seems to have constricted the space for being simultaneously a German and a Jew to such a point that German-Jewish identity became less plausibly a grounded subcultural location than an occasion for the radical critique of identity itself. This, at any rate, is what Kafka's reflection anticipates. It attacks even the notion of self-identity just as it raises the question of whether this non-self-identical position is not the human condition *tout court*. This is arguably an eccentric stand to take, but it is worth noting that Kafka was not alone in exploiting a situation of "mutual impossibilities" to imagine a way "out" of identity.[32] In the aftermath of the Shoah, the explosive potential of German-Jewish subjectivity would not dissipate. To the contrary, it would be opened to full exposure. The recognition of the magnitude and existential significance of the Holocaust would bring even a man like Theodor Adorno—Jewish only by virtue of his somewhat distant father's background and never Jewishly identified during the boom years of the Frankfurt School—to increase attention to the question of Jewishness. He found himself, like Kafka before him, drawn ever more into thinking about (his) Jewish identity but in a way that offered an escape from identity as such. "Auschwitz confirmed the philosopheme of pure identity as death," he wrote in *Negative Dialectics*.[33] In Adorno's conception, heterogeneity, difference, multiplicity—in his own jargon, "non-identity"—was the principle of life, and the cultural marker for nonidentity was the Jew.[34]

Subjectivity, as I mention above, has eluded discussions of the limitations of the concepts of emancipation and assimilation, however sophisticated these analyses have been. While emancipation and assimilation are classically understood to be twin figures—the former describing the external conditions offered by the host society, the latter the Jews' internal response to those conditions—in fact, both describe abstracted structural and collective phenomena.[35] Yet post-assimilationist Jews such as those engaged in the Jewish Renaissance identified the internal question as one taking place within the consciousnesses of individual German Jews. Martin Buber spoke of "the personal Jewish Question, the root of all Jewish questions, the question that we find in ourselves, and which we must decide within ourselves."[36] Wassermann, echoing Buber from the other side of the spectrum of assimilation, used the same language, translating the Jewish question into the implied, but much sharper, term "problem" and transmuting it into something within the self: the "tragedy" of each individual Jewish life is the dualism within the self that constitutes "the most fundamental, most difficult and most important part of the Jewish problem."[37]

All of this points to a tension between an insistent postassimilationist focus on individual subjectivity and a recurrent translation of this issue into what is often understood as a failed dialogue between hypostatized collectives, Jewish and German. The irony of Scholem's well-known position that the German-Jewish symbiosis was a myth was that he himself embodied that symbiosis even as he was questioning it; the dialogue that was imagined not to have taken place was in fact the internal, ambivalent dialogue that went on within the individual subject.[38] The problem of German-Jewishness was in this as in many other senses a problem of subjectivity.

Subjectivity as Problem

The chief problem historians have, or should have, with the notion of subjectivity is related to sources. The difference between identity and subjectivity makes the latter more difficult to access, requiring a heavy reliance on interpretation and subtle forms of analysis. Subjectivity refers to the intricate, complex, and self-contradictory ways that historical actors experience their place in the world *in contrast to* how they are perceived by others or how they are ordered within relatively rigid external systems.[39] These systems (in large part discursive, as we have seen) colonize the means we have of articulating our place in the world. Thus, at the very moment that writers like Wassermann, Scholem, or Edith Stein, as we are about to see, write a memoir (or indeed even a diary or letter) to address the problem of identity, they conform to a set of rules that might as well have been laid down by the antisemitic minority.

Where are the sources for how these individuals might really have moved through German, German-Jewish, Jewish, or other cultural identifications? As has been noted, the decision to identify as German or as Jewish was obviously one that no one really had to make and that most never thought to make.[40] What is really required is a sociocultural history that traces practices as well as reflections—an everyday history of interior life.

Put differently, a particular set of methodological problems may be associated with the very sources that have seemed most suited to investigations of the German-Jewish identity crisis. Such self-reflexive texts include memoirs like Wassermann's or that of Karl Löwith, or the diaries of Victor Klemperer, or Scholem's essays on Germans and Jews, or the famous *Kunstwart* debate on the failure of the German-Jewish symbiosis.[41] In each of these examples, the conditions producing the need for writing about German-Jewish identity have governed the terms in which the problem can be articulated (as I note above, the conceptualization of the existence of a problem in the first place already concedes to these discursive conditions). Nonetheless, these all remain rich sources. They may be unable to do what they claim (that is, illustrate how German Jews felt about their identities). Instead, they provide a mass of material that illustrates the inversions, contradictions, and collusions that characterized German-Jewish identities, whether assimilated or Jewishly identified.

In chapter 4 I present an admittedly extreme example in Edith Stein, the student of Edmund Husserl who left Judaism and became a Carmelite nun, writing a "Jewish memoir" in the late 1930s.[42] Stein is well known today thanks to her controversial canonization as Saint Teresa Benedicta of the Cross by Pope John Paul II. As I discuss, the very complexity regarding German-Jewish subjectivity is closely linked to the difficulty of assimilating Stein's life and work to various other canons, such as German-Jewish studies and feminist studies. The linear model of understanding identity along a simple spectrum is indeed easier to comprehend than the dialectical one I propose, but Stein herself did not see her embrace of Catholicism and entry into the convent as an abandonment of either her Jewishness, her philosophical thought, or her feminism. The historian who asks, "How assimilated to German culture was my subject?" could, in Stein's case (and those of many other German-speaking Jewish exemplars), find a citation to support a historiographical assertion of relative assimilation. In contrast, the dialectical readings required to study subjectivity properly require a more expansive analysis. Stein's memoir, translated as *Life in a Jewish Family*, is a particularly complex document that offers an antidote to the antisemitic caricature of the Jew at the same time as it seemingly reinforces Jewish stereotypes. A dialectical structure of identification and disidentification with the figure of Jewishness in that text, I argue, resists a model of assimilation to a German-Christian context, and the memories of a Jewish family instead configure Jewishness as a primordial and authentic figure of both Christianity and Germanness. Moreover, this incipient kernel of authenticity is rediscovered in order to be worked through to a higher spiritual level of Christianity. Yet for all that, to subvert the stark dichotomies under which she was oppressed by her own historical contexts (German-Jew, Christian-Jew, and also male-female), Stein's texts, like that of Wassermann, consistently resort to a restoration of precisely these dichotomies. Her confession of Jewishness documents her spiritual enlightenment at the same time that it presages her martyrdom and canonization.

At the other end of the presumed assimilatory spectrum is Martin Buber. Raised in Galician Lemberg, Lviv in today's Ukraine, Buber made his career as philosopher, publisher, translator, and popularizer of Hasidic culture in Berlin. In each of these activities, Buber's Jewish identity undoubtedly stands out, but so, too, does his deep engagement with German culture. Jewish identification saturated all these activities, certainly, but it is just as certain that each of them represented a deep engagement with German culture. His philosophical work, like Stein's, was written in German and within a largely German phenomenological tradition; his translations of sacred texts were as much a German literary project as was Martin Luther's Bible translation. His journal *Der Jude* was a typical product of early twentieth-century urban German literary culture. Finally, literary works such as the *Tales of Rabbi Nachmann* and *Legend of the Baal-Shem* owe more to a German neo-Romantic tradition than to the font of lore from which they are collected.

His lectures for the Bar-Kochba Association in Prague (1909–1910) offer special food for thought. From the time they were delivered, these lectures have been viewed as key sources for the central European Jewish Renaissance that captured the hearts and minds of Jewish youth in the years leading up to World War I.[43] The addresses are often cited as the place where Buber's notion of Jewishness appears in its most essentialist form. Steven Aschheim, for example, cites Buber's references to a "community of blood" (rather than an external community of shared experience), "the deepest, most potent stratum of our being."[44] Yet this deepest, hidden layer of being—evoked by the suspicious metaphor of blood—cannot be seen as essentialist in any sense that parallels the contemporary *völkisch*, or racialist, uses of the term. The central figure in the lectures is not blood or even Jewish essence; it is the idea of choice. Buber exhorted the members of his youthful Jewish audience to mine this invisible stratum and to elect Judaism for themselves. Clearly, any attempt to link elective with racial belonging would have been anathema to the essentialist nationalist discourses current in the period when the Prague lectures were delivered, including those of liberal assimilationists who argued for private Jewish identities within a context of public German cultural participation. Yet it is through a literal invocation of the language of blood that the shared language of essences is ironically subverted.

These far-too-abbreviated examples are offered not to solve the problem of German-Jewish subjectivity but to present an early outline of its dimensions. Deeper and more extensive readings are required to bring out the dialectical structure that appears and reappears in a multitude of individual forms, differing as much from one another as the writings of Wassermann, Buber, Stein, Kafka, and Scholem differ among themselves. The chapters in parts II and III of this book seek to offer such readings. To be clear, getting beyond the assimilation paradigm does not necessitate dropping the categories historical actors used to define their sense of belonging, but it does require a historian's skepticism toward these categories, a sensitivity to the conditions under which they were produced, and painstaking care in following how these conditions were actually lived. Many examples of textual analysis of German-Jewish figures are compatible with these principles without entirely abandoning categories such as identity and assimilation or focusing exclusively on subjectivity. Aschheim's 1999 study of Scholem, Hannah Arendt, and Victor Klemperer, in the wake of contemporary publication of ego-documents by each of these three, explores thinkers whose positions on the assimilation spectrum seem clearly differentiated: Scholem and Klemperer are at the poles, Arendt near the middle. Yet Aschheim's readings suggest a twisted path to these positions.[45] A careful reading of his essay on Scholem, the thinker with whom we began, reveals how Scholem's "Jewish self-certitude" emerges out of a deep engagement with German culture, especially Friedrich Nietzsche (Scholem wishes at one point to write a *Judenzarathustra*), with the panoply of German vitalism (*Lebensphilosophie*), and with pronounced strains of *völkisch* nationalism.[46] What resulted from Scholem's immersion in these sources was an intricate braid in which German sources received "Jewish" readings and Jewish sources "German" ones, producing the staunch position Scholem disavowed in the "Jews and Germans" lecture and then set free into history: an ironclad binary of two incompatible and hostile principles—two "essences," as he called them, whose integration was "evil" and "impure"—"German" and "Jewish."[47]

The delicately self-contradictory and nonetheless self-affirming subjective experiences of modern German-speaking Jews might often have articulated themselves in terms of essential identities, of binary and exclusive oppositionality, and of processes like assimilation. Yet these vulgar formulas betrayed the subtle chemistry that gave them substance. They were, to put it in Buberian terms, ruined by speech, forced by the process of language to rend those fibers that could not be unraveled from one another. Does it make sense to think of this rarefied position of German-Jewish subjects in the early twentieth century as somehow illegitimate or inauthentic? Must (or can) a radically complex subjectivity be equated with false consciousness? Scholem conflated this complexity with a "destructive dialectic," a "liquidation of the Jewish substance by the Jews themselves," and he notoriously linked this process to their ultimate fate.[48] Yet the dialectics of German-Jewish subjectivities might be more justifiably, more productively, and more honestly linked to the cultural contributions that emerged from them than to their catastrophic destruction. A history of the culturally innovative generations of German Jews who called themselves or were called assimilated has to go beyond the word to capture how the individuals making up those generations lived in their world. The historical exploration of subjectivity is a search for context.

Notes

A version of this chapter was originally published as Scott Spector, "Forget Assimilation: Introducing Subjectivity to German-Jewish History," *Jewish History* 20, nos. 3–4 (2006): 349–361, and Scott Spector, "Beyond Assimilation: Introducing Subjectivity to German-Jewish History," in *Religion or Ethnicity? Jewish Identities in Evolution*, ed. Zvi Gitelman (New Brunswick, NJ: Rutgers University Press, 2009), 90–103.

1. The lecture was held on August 2, 1966, as part of the plenary session of the World Jewish Congress. Gershom Scholem, "Juden und Deutsche," *Neue Rundschau* 77 (1966): 547–562, reprinted in Gershom Scholem, *Judaica*, vol. 2 (Frankfurt am Main, Germany: Suhrkamp, 1970), 20–46.
2. Gershom Scholem, "Jews and Germans," in Gershom Scholem, *On Jews and Judaism in Crisis: Selected Essays*, ed. and trans. Werner J. Dannhauser (New York: Schocken, 1976), 71–92.
3. Scholem, "Juden und Deutsche," 28.
4. In 1996, Shulamit Volkov suggested that German-Jewish historiography had reached a "dead end" because of the persistence of two tendencies that should now be overcome or synthesized. Both the national-Zionist and liberal-ethnic approaches to Jewish history limit the connection of Jewish history/ies to European history more generally. See Shulamit Volkov, "Reflections on German-Jewish Historiography: A Dead End or a New Beginning?" *Leo Baeck Institute Year Book* 41 (1996): 309–320. The impasse I refer to here precedes the liberal or Zionist ideological moment in that it refers to assumptions about identity shared by both historiographical schools, as they were by historical actors of both ideological tendencies.
5. Franz Rosenzweig, *Gesammelte Schriften I: Briefe und Tagebücher*, ed. Rachel Rosenzweig, Edith Rosenzweig-Scheinmann, and Bernhard Casper, vol. 2, *1918–1929* (The Hague: Martinus Nijhoff, 1979), 770. The more recent revival of the term "dissimilation" has yielded inconsistent definitions, but each of these tends to bring out Rosenzweig's intended dialectical tension between the terms "assimilation" and "dissimilation" in more explicit ways, implicitly subverting the spectral paradigm. See, especially, Shulamit Volkov, "The Dynamics of Dissimilation: *Ostjuden* and German Jews," in *The Jewish Response to German Culture: From the Enlightenment to the Second World War*, ed. Jehuda Reinharz and Walter Schatzberg (Hanover, NH: Dartmouth University Press, 1985), 195–211; Shulamit Volkov, *Die Juden in Deutschland, 1780–1918* (Munich, R. Oldenbourg, 1994), esp. 53–56; David Sorkin, "Emancipation and Assimilation: Two Concepts and Their Application to German-Jewish History," *Leo Baeck Institute Year Book* 35 (1990): 17–33; and Jonathan Skolnik, "Dissimilation and the Historical Novel: Hermann Sinsheimer's *Maria Nunnez*," *Leo Baeck Institute Year Book* 43 (1998): 225–237.
6. Amos Funkenstein, "The Dialectics of Assimilation," *Jewish Social Studies* 1, no. 2 (1995): 1–14.
7. Scholem, "Germans and Jews," 73–74.
8. Ibid., 76–77.
9. Ibid., 83. The original reads, "Sehr breite Schichten der deutschen Juden waren zwar bereit, ihr Volkstum zu liquidieren, wollten aber, in freilich sehr verschiedenen Ausmaßen, ihr Judentum, als Erbe, als Konfession, als ein Ichweißnichtwas, ein undefinierbares und doch im Bewußtsein deutlich vorhandenes Element bewahren." Scholem, "Juden und Deutsche," 35.
10. Yosef Hayim Yerushalmi, *Freud's Moses: Judaism Terminable and Interminable* (New Haven, CT: Yale University Press, 1991), 9–10. Steven Aschheim speaks of the "insistence on a Jewishness that resists definition" as a "prevailing ideology of our own times, a way in which countless contemporary secular Jews approach articulating their own persistent but difficult

to locate sense of a 'Jewish self.'" See Steven E. Aschheim, "(Con)Fusions of Identity—Germans and Jews," in *In Times of Crisis: Essays on European Culture, Germans, and Jews* (Madison: University of Wisconsin Press, 2001), esp. 72.

11. Yerushalmi, *Freud's Moses*, 10.

12. The locus classicus of this critique from the culture-historical perspective is Ahad Ha'am's essay "Slavery within Freedom," in which the paradoxical position of the emancipated Jew who must justify his own Jewishness and find meaning in it is laid out. Ahad Ha'am, "Slavery in Freedom," in *Selected Essays of Ahad Ha-Am*, ed. Leon Simon (New York: Jewish Publication Society of America, 1912), 171–194. See also Paul Mendes-Flohr, "Cultural Zionism's Image of the Educated Jew: Reflections on Creating a Secular Jewish Culture," *Modern Judaism* 18, no. 3 (1998): esp. 228.

13. David Sorkin, *The Transformation of German Jewry, 1780–1840* (New York: Oxford University Press, 1987); Sorkin, "Emancipation and Assimilation"; David Sorkin, "The Impact of Emancipation on German Jewry: A Reconsideration," in *Assimilation and Community: The Jews in Nineteenth-Century Europe*, ed. Jonathan Frankel and Steven J. Zipperstein (Cambridge: Cambridge University Press, 1992), 177–198.

14. Samuel Moyn, "German Jewry and the Question of Identity: Historiography and Theory," *Leo Baeck Institute Year Book* 41 (1996): 298.

15. Anthony J. La Vopa, "Review: Jews and Germans: Old Quarrels, New Departures," *Journal of the History of Ideas* 54, no. 4 (1993): 688.

16. Sorkin, *Transformation*, 7.

17. Sorkin, "Impact of Emancipation," 187–192, esp. 187–188. See the treatment of ideology and subjectivity in relation to Slavoj Žižek and Louis Althusser in Scott Spector, "Was the Third Reich Movie-Made? Interdisciplinarity and the Reframing of 'Ideology,'" *American Historical Review* 106, no. 2 (2001): 460–484, esp. 481.

18. For an extended discussion of this issue in social theory, see Margaret Scotford Archer, *Structure, Agency, and the Internal Conversation* (Cambridge: Cambridge University Press, 2003).

19. Jakob Wassermann, *Mein Weg als Deutscher und Jude* (Berlin: S. Fischer, 1921); Jacob Wassermann, *My Life as German and Jew*, trans. S. N. Brainin (New York: Coward-McCann, 1933).

20. See Funkenstein, "Dialectics of Assimilation."

21. See Wassermann, *Mein Weg*, 69. The description here of a "German essence" consisting of "fragmentation," transition and mobility, and lack of center in relation to European cultures proper might be described as a novel form of (Jewish) "German self-hatred." Ibid.

22. Gershom Scholem, "Wider den Mythos vom deutsch-jüdischen 'Gespräch,'" in Scholem, *Judaica* 2:10 (translation mine).

23. See Scholem, *Judaica* 2:7–46. Needless to say, the differences of opinion within the shared universe of terms described here were significant and remain of historical importance; focusing on where spokesmen like Wassermann and Scholem silently agreed reveals a history distinct from that revealed by focusing on where they obviously differed.

24. Steven E. Aschheim, "Assimilation and Its Impossible Discontents: The Case of Moritz Goldstein," in Aschheim, *In Times of Crisis*, 65.

25. La Vopa, "Old Quarrels, New Departures," esp. 693–694.

26. Besides the Volkov essay cited above, see Evyatar Friesel, "The German-Jewish Encounter: A Reconsideration," *Leo Baeck Institute Year Book* 41 (1996): 263–275; and Evyatar Friesel, "Jewish and German-Jewish Historical Views: Problems of a New Synthesis," *Leo Baeck Institute Year Book* 43 (1998): 323–336.

27. See Michael Brenner, *The Renaissance of Jewish Culture in Weimar Germany* (New Haven, CT: Yale University Press, 1996).
28. Scholem, *On Jews and Judaism in Crisis*, 82.
29. Steven E. Aschheim eloquently and persuasively tracks the liberal-assimilationist adoption of essentialist terms in "Assimilation and Its Impossible Discontents," 64–72.
30. The example of Kafka is useful as a reminder that the problematics of German-Jewish assimilation as they unfolded in the nineteenth and early twentieth centuries included German-speaking Jewish Austrians, who had no hesitation in identifying themselves as German-Jews (*Deutschjuden*), or in some cases simply Germans, even as they felt themselves to be in a situation different from that of Germans from the Reich to the north.
31. Franz Kafka, *Tagebücher in der Fassung der Handschrift*, ed. Hans-Gerd Koch, Michael Müller, and Malcolm Pasley (New York: S. Fischer, 1992), 622.
32. In a letter to Max Brod in reference to the writing of Karl Kraus, Kafka writes that the German-Jewish writers of his generation "lived between three impossibilities. . . . The impossibility of not writing, the impossibility of writing German, the impossibility of writing differently." This literature, "impossible from all sides," is in fact the only possibility left for literature. Franz Kafka and Max Brod, *Briefe, 1902–1924* (New York: Schocken, 1958), 337–338. See also Scott Spector, *Prague Territories: National Conflict and Cultural Innovation in Franz Kafka's Fin de Siècle* (Berkeley: University of California Press, 2000), 89–92.
33. Theodor W. Adorno, *Negative Dialectics*, trans. E. B. Ashton (New York: Seabury Press, 1973), 362.
34. Ibid. See also Martin Jay, *Adorno* (Cambridge, MA: Harvard University Press, 1984).
35. See Otto Brunner, Werner Conze, Reinhart Koselleck, eds., *Geschichtliche Grundbegriffe: Historisches Lexikon zur politisch-sozialen Sprache in Deutschland*, vol. 2 (Stuttgart, Germany: Ernst Klett, 1978), 153–197, esp. 178–185. The classic literature on these concepts is large, and there are quite a few overviews and critiques, including Todd M. Endelman, "Continuities and Discontinuities in Constructions of Jewishness in Europe, 1789–1945," in *The Construction of Minorities: Cases for Comparison across Time and around the World*, ed. André Burguière and Raymond Grew (Ann Arbor: University of Michigan Press, 2001), 127–146; and Sorkin, "Emancipation and Assimilation," 17–21.
36. Martin Buber, *Drei Reden über das Judentum* (Frankfurt am Main, Germany: Rütten and Loening, 1916), 27 (translation mine).
37. Wassermann, *My Life as German and Jew*, 75. The dualism here is the coexistence of twin senses of superiority and inferiority; Buber elsewhere identifies dualism as the essential nature of the Jew.
38. Paul Mendes-Flohr appears to share this view. Citing Gustav Landauer, Hermann Cohen, Buber, and Rosenzweig, he argues that the imagined symbiosis or cultural dialogue between Germans and Jews was less at issue than "an inner Jewish dialogue—of a dialogue within the souls of individual Jews as well as between themselves." See Paul Mendes-Flohr, *German Jews: A Dual Identity* (New Haven, CT: Yale University Press, 1999), 93.
39. There is no room here for a discussion of theories of subjectivity that would be expansive enough to be satisfactory; the shorthand of identity as more fixed and perceptual in contrast to a more open, complex, and experiential subjectivity is overly schematic if also useful for us in this context. Nick Mansfield's concise statement is useful here: "Subjectivity is primarily an experience, and remains permanently open to inconsistency, contradiction and unself-consciousness. Our experience of ourselves remains forever prone to surprising disjunctions that only the fierce light of ideology or theoretical dogma convinces us can be homogenised into a single consistent thing." Nick Mansfield, *Subjectivity: Theories of the Self from Freud to*

Haraway (St. Leonards, Australia: Allen and Unwin, 2000), 6–7. Mansfield usefully reviews twentieth-century theoretical models of subjectivity. I am personally deeply influenced by Michael P. Steinberg's densely historicized and subtly complex account in *Listening to Reason: Culture, Subjectivity, and Nineteenth-Century Music* (Princeton, NJ: Princeton University Press, 2004): 4–17.

40. Samuel Moyn, "German Jewry and Identity," 301.

41. These examples are drawn from very different, if tellingly linked, moments of perceived crisis of German-Jewish relations. The *Kunstwart* debate about Jewish integration into German culture began in 1912 with Moritz Goldstein's provocative essay "Deutsch-jüdischer Parnaß" (German-Jewish Parnassus), which challenged the German-Jewish assimilationist ideal and suggested that the overwhelming contribution to German culture by Jewish writers was made by these writers not as Germans but as Jews. See Moritz Goldstein, "Deutsch-jüdischer Parnaß," *Der Kunstwart und Kulturwart* 25 (1912): 281–294. Assertion or questioning of the so-called German-Jewish symbiosis in Wassermann's and Scholem's texts cited above is also trackable in Karl Löwith, *Mein Leben in Deutschland vor und nach 1933: Ein Bericht* (Stuttgart, Germany: J. B. Metzler, 1986); and Karl Löwith, *My Life in Germany before and after 1933: A Report*, trans. Elizabeth King (Urbana: University of Illinois Press, 1994), as well as in the recently celebrated diaries of Victor Klemperer—especially Victor Klemperer, *Ich will Zeugnis ablegen bis zum letzten*, ed. Walter Nowojski (Berlin: Aufbau, 1996); and Victor Klemperer, *I Will Bear Witness: A Diary of the Nazi Years, 1942–1945*, trans. Martin Chalmers (New York: Random House, 1999).

42. Elsewhere I have offered a detailed reading of this extraordinary life and work and the complex relations of these to each other and to surrounding historical contexts. Scott Spector, "Edith Stein's Passing Gestures: Intimate Histories, Empathic Portraits," *New German Critique* 75 (Fall 1998): 28–56.

43. The published, albeit reworked, lectures are in Martin Buber, *On Judaism*, ed. Nahum Norbert Glatzer (New York: Schocken, 1967). I offer a more detailed discussion of the texts in Spector, *Prague Territories*, 147–151.

44. Aschheim, "Assimilation and Its Discontents," 70.

45. Steven E. Aschheim, *Scholem, Arendt, Klemperer: Intimate Chronicles in Turbulent Times* (Bloomington: Indiana University Press, 2001).

46. Ibid., 9.

47. Ibid., 23.

48. Scholem, "Once More: The German-Jewish Dialogue," in Scholem, *On Jews and Judaism*, 68–69.

2 Modernism without Jews

A Counterhistorical Argument

Modern

Sometime around 1877, while beginning work on what would become the opera *Parsifal*, Richard Wagner was sent an anonymous pamphlet attributed to a "significant Jewish voice." The pamphlet prophesied the inevitable victory of "the modern world" over the old, "orthodox" one, in spite of the power and elegant rhetoric of conservative forces:

> Modern journalism and Romanticism have utterly conquered the freethinking Jewish and Christian worlds. I include the freethinking Jewish world—for in fact German Jewry is working so forcefully, so colossally, and so tirelessly on the new culture and science that, consciously or unconsciously, the majority of Christendom is being led by Jews.[1]

Wagner could not have agreed more ("How true!") and quoted the pamphlet at the opening of his vociferous and explicitly antisemitic attack on "the new culture" (not yet called modernism).[2] His salty attack itself had the concise and apt title "Modern," and in it he reiterated and condensed opinions he had long expressed: "modern" was fleeting and arbitrary, moved by whimsy rather than deep necessity, and was linked to *Mode* (fashion), to the base manifestations of the new materialist civilization, to France, and to the Jews—and hence foreign to both the German spirit and to art itself.[3] Wagner's radical artistic program rejected the modern present even as it shared modern culture's rejection of traditionalism—but instead of "the modern," Wagner spoke of revolution and the future.[4]

It is not my intention to rehash the debates among latter-day Wagnerites and their detractors concerning the degree and importance of the composer's antisemitism and its relationship to his art. Still, the most extreme of these defenses—arguing that Wagner's statements on Jews and culture either were not particularly hateful or were simply consistent with ideas current when he was writing—miss the centrality of the figure of the Jew in the edifice of Wagner's rhetoric on the art of the future.[5] Whatever he might have felt about real, existing Jews (his antipathy toward his rival Meyerbeer notwithstanding), the absence or presence of Jews is key to the structure of Wagner's arguments about the value of this or the other art and the historical trajectory of art.

I suggest that it is not for nothing that this early formulation of antisemitic antimodernism agrees so readily with its concurrent philosemitic modernist triumphalist counterpart. Both depend on a story of emancipation, assimilation, and integration in which presence immediately becomes omnipresence and participation becomes hegemony (of a surreptitious kind), leading to the emergence of modernism. But this emergence is not as linear as it sounds. To return to the passage quoted above, the Jews are won over to or conquered by the modern, the triumph of which constitutes the illicit conquest of the German Christian population by the Jews. A bracketed phrase betrays that this conquest is especially nefarious because the vanquished are not even aware it has happened; neither, it seems, are the victors. To demonstrate this invisible truth, the writer points out that hardly a newspaper or other publication is produced in Germany that is not "directly or indirectly" in Jewish hands. The philosemitic and promodernist argument is in this case (as in others) dependent on the twin premises that modernism is Jewish, and yet that modernism's Jewishness is somehow hidden and needs to be revealed. A recurring strategy for making this invisible Jewishness visible again concerns what seems to be a dialectic of Jewish presence and absence, by posing a counterfactual or counterhistorical hypothesis: Suppose Jews were absent from modern culture. How would it look then? Wagner pursues this precise tactic. In "Judaism in Music" he had already made a claim both for the total jewification of modern art (employing the unlikely and repugnant term *Verjudung* that the Nazis would make familiar three-quarters of a century later) and that "the Jews have not produced a single true poet."[6] Without Jews, the modern culture industry, as Wagner understood it in his own time, would vanish or transform itself completely; art, on the other hand, would be unaffected. So in this incipient instance of modern German cultural antisemitism—an only half racialist Jew-baiting with one foot in the illustrious past and one in the formidable future of Christian German Jew hatred—and in this attack on Franco-Jewish modernism *avant la lettre*, a rhetorical strategy emerges that will come into its own after Wagner's death. This rhetoric poses the questions: You want to know how the Jews have spoiled the modern world? What's Jewish about *die Moderne*?[7] What's wrong with the Jewish modern? And responds: Take them away, and you'll see!

There are reasons for me to begin a chapter that looks back at Jewish modernism with this reminder of the moment when Wagner anticipated it; of course, as I pointed out above, in his own view he was diagnosing the present and dreaming of a different future. The object to be traced here is specific to German-speaking central Europe, and it is a figure that has been particularly powerful there, although significant aspects of the figure will be more broadly familiar. I call this *jüdische Moderne* (Jewish modern) a figure and expressly avoid discussing it as a catalogue of authors or works. To think of Jewish modernism in a topical way, as though there were a specific corpus or prescriptive formal definition captured by the term, seems futile at best (if not ominous). There can be no literary history of Jewish modernism. Perhaps, though, there is a history to be told about a discourse on Jewish modernism in German-speaking central Europe. Even that discourse is not singular, prescriptive, or consistent but may perhaps better be characterized by its operation than by its contents. If this is the case, then the question cannot be what is or was Jewish modernism, but what work does and did the figure Jewish modernism do for its users. This is not to warn students of modern Jewish culture that to invoke this figure is to play with fire but rather to consider how one might think with Jewish modernism, engage it on the multiple levels on which it has functioned, without being swept in its tide. If, as in the Wagnerian example, Jewish modernism is a complex field of self-contradictory tensions and inversions, its story cannot simply be narrated but can perhaps best be captured by representing a constellation of moments in its elastic life.

From Jewless City to Jewish Modern

"Modernism without Jews" borrows from another title familiar to German and Jewish studies readers. Hugo Bettauer's 1922 novel and the generally faithful 1924 Hans Karl Breslauer film adaptation were both called *Die Stadt ohne Juden* (*The City without Jews*).[8] Bettauer was born to a Jewish family as Maximilian Hugo Bettauer but became a convert and a Protestant, although his real faith was in progressive secular rationalism. He was a publicist, journalist, and writer of a score of rapidly published popular novels, the best selling of which was to be *The City without Jews*. His writing, in other words, was a prime example of the burgeoning popular culture industry in the era of the Weimar Republic. Bettauer's easy-reading tale is set in the not-so-distant future (its German subtitle is "a novel from the day after tomorrow"), and it is clearly a light-hearted satire rather than the warning toll of catastrophe that it has been made out to be. *The City without Jews* bases itself on the premise, meant to be somewhat absurd, that in a time of financial and cultural crisis not unlike the mid-1920s, the parliament of Austria passes a measure expelling the country's Jews. A unifying melodrama involving the separation of the young Jewish hero Leo Strakosch from his gentile beloved and his maneuvers to reverse the order ties together a series of scenes displaying the cultural anarchy that the absence of Jews in Vienna unleashes: we witness the anarchic collapse of the stock market and of consumer culture, among other hallmarks of modern life. Strakosch, meanwhile, moving through Vienna in disguise as the bearded Frenchman Henry Dufresne, puts out a series of pamphlets calling for the reversal of the expulsion and signed by the "League of Truthful Christians," leading to a parliamentary vote on repeal, which he ingeniously rigs, and the Jews are welcomed back into the city.

We may see Wagner's text and Bettauer's (and Breslauer's film even more starkly) as bookends of German-Jewish modernism in several ways. Once again, this term cannot refer to a particular kind of modern culture that is Jewish but rather refers to a complex discourse linking an origin of authorship to the modern in a network of self-contradictory but compelling ways. These bookends reflect one another in an apparently inverted way—but inversion seems to be integral to the discourse I am describing. Just as Wagner was able to introduce the essay "Modern" with a (presumed) philosemitic text understood to be by a Jew, Bettauer's and Breslauer's enlightened works conjure the utopian fantasy of Jewish absence to refute antisemitism. As with all inversions, elements remain intact and often enough identical in both versions: today's viewers of Breslauer's film will be struck by the persistence of horrific antisemitic stereotypical caricatures throughout, which is the case in the book as well; a simple analysis of character types in the film shows that the rudest portrayals and greatest number of such portrayals are of Jews, while the pan-German antisemites and others are represented at worst as a bit dim. Granted, the young Jew Strakosch is a romantic hero, but one who vanquishes the antisemites at the price of proving their central theses: there is a Jewish conspiracy, and modernity is in the hands of the Jews. He slips back into Austria in disguise, passing as a Christian. Another inverted twin of this film, Fritz Hippler's Nazi propaganda feature *The Eternal Jew* (1940), employs passing as a primary trope in persuading the audience of the invisible, infiltrating, alien presence. A famous dissolve sequence, from the faces of a group of bearded Polish Jewish men in kaftans to the same men groomed as Westerners, dissolving then to a cocktail party of cultivated Berlin Jews, gives visual form to the conflicting notions of Jewish passing and essential difference, ineradicable separateness and total infiltration and saturation.[9] In *The City without Jews*, Leo Strakosch reveals himself in a scene that inverts Hippler's dissolve. At the moment the ban on Jews is lifted, he tells the story of how he has been responsible for this happy turn of events, all the while clipping and shaving the beard of his Christian-French alter ego and revealing himself to be the "handsome, smooth-faced" young hero.[10] Of course, one could protest, the inversion is meant to reverse the meaning of the antisemitic narrative, but this example shows how in spite of these admitted intentions, the inversion proves the rule: the Jew has passed and has infiltrated, he has used the sham popular mechanisms of democracy to further his own ends, and he has done so through deception and dissimulation—and his primary personal motive, after all, is the desire for an Aryan woman.

The City without Jews seems not to be able to help but compulsively name and confirm every tenet of antimodernist antisemitism. An interesting case of this involves the propaganda surrounding the film's distribution, in which great efforts were made to mark the film as a vehicle of enlightened anti-antisemitism that was coming from rational German Christians. Bettauer's and the film's antisemitic opponents naturally aimed first to expose that this was really a propaganda piece generated by a Jewish culture industry, and they did not have to scratch the surface of the production very hard to find more than a few participants who were Jewish according to their own criteria (not least, of course, Bettauer himself). Interestingly, though, this drama is inscribed in the book and film themselves, with the question of pseudepigraphy embodied in the propaganda leaflets signed by the nonexistent organization League of Truthful Christians, which the audience knows is not a league or truthful or Christian but the fabrication of a single, lying Jew.

Even more than with other works, today one cannot write about *The City without Jews* without placing it within a dense historical context that foregrounds its afterlife and confounds where else it might be placed in relation to its own past, present, and future. Its eccentric fantasy of the elimination of Jews from a central European country—the absurdity of the thesis in its time is impossible to reproduce today—must seem to every contemporary reader or viewer a shockingly frank prophesy of the Nazi final solution rather than an "amusing" satire of the Austrian Christian Social past and contemporary pan-German antisemitic rhetoric.[11] Within two years of the film's release, Hugo Bettauer was murdered in his office by a fanatic with Nazi ties, making the link of the 1922 text and its author to the Nazi violence of the future impossible for latter-day readers to disaggregate. Bettauer's subtitle was "a novel from the day after tomorrow," but the English translation of a few years later changed the subtitle to "a novel of our times," making the author of the satirical future fantasy for the American public of 1926 "first and last a realist, an accurate and astute observer."[12] The film's rediscovery and reconstruction in 1991 was the object of an extremely heavy investment of effort led by Filmarchiv Austria and leading to the publication of a 487-page documentation volume accompanying the release of the digitally restored and reconstructed film, making this relatively minor production one of the most-documented German-language films from the interwar period, the powerful scholarly interest in Weimar film history notwithstanding.[13]

While the rediscovery of the film produced a flurry of scholarly interest in its wake, the example of Hugo Bettauer had long been seen to offer a dense case study of the complex of Jewishness and Jewish self-hatred or antisemitism in relation to modernism, modernization, and modernity. "The Bettauer case" (*Der Fall Bettauer*) was in fact the title of one scholar's attempt at synthesizing Hugo Bettauer's biography, historical contexts, and literary texts. Ironically but significantly, a lead article of the same title graced the front pages of the antisemitic serial *Der Weltkampf* (World struggle) by its editor, no less an ideologue of the National Socialist movement than Alfred Rosenberg.[14] The Nazi propagandist and the German studies scholar share more than a title, though. They both find Bettauer of interest as a symptom of his time (just as retrospective observers would call *The City without Jews* a *Zeitdokument*, or documentation of its time).[15] Bettauer was not only a prolific writer of popular fiction; he was also a tireless publicist for sexual enlightenment. He edited a publication designed to popularize freethinking and open discussion of issues regarding sexuality titled *Him and Her*.[16] He was an outspoken campaigner for the decriminalization of homosexuality and pushed the envelope of censors by testing the boundaries of permissible publication of erotica. All this led to a widely publicized indecency case, itself a product of the cultural politics of the Austrian battle between progressive socialists and antisemitic Christian Socials. Bettauer's assassination by a right-wing dental student in 1925 was clearly a result of this sensationalism, but the trial of the murderer became no less a sensation: like so many fanatic right-wing murderers of Weimar Germany, Otto Rothstock got off with a remarkably light sentence, hailed by many on the right as a moral hero. "The Bettauer case" hence refers to an immensely ramified exemplar that includes these two sensational court cases, played out in public with richly overdetermined meanings. The articulation and interpretation of these strands of meaning is an objective shared to a remarkable extent by the two "Bettauer case" texts, one German studies and one Nazi. Both concern themselves with the network of new mass-culture texts, including pulp novellas, popular sex education, erotica, scandal, and sensationalism. For both writers, this was a modernity infused and obsessed with Jewishness.

The epigraph to the Filmarchiv Austria documentation volume is a one-page condensation of a 1956 article by Harry Zohn, called "The City without Jews" and, recalling Bettauer's "strangely prophetic book from the year 1922, a sort of inverted utopia describing Vienna without Jews and the subsequent collapse of the economic and cultural life of the city." Zohn goes on to ruminate on present-day (1956) Vienna, the relatively peripheral if not fully nonexistent Jewish population of the city, and attribution of the "provincialism of daily life, the brutalization of taste, the reduction of cosmopolitanism of the city" to the decimation of its Jewish population.[17] Steven Beller's 1989 *Vienna and the Jews*, a chief history of the Jewish cultural presence in Vienna in the period of high modernism, cites the same source, using the same strategy: also deploying the term "prophetic" to describe the 1924 novel, he summarizes Bettauer's fantasy of a city stripped of contemporary popular culture (but not the opera), essentially stagnant and uneventful, and he determines that, "for anyone who has been to Vienna in the 1980s, there are remarkable similarities between what Bettauer foresaw and what the present city is like."[18] Bettauer is an apt introduction to Beller's book, certainly, since it is no exaggeration to reduce Beller's thesis to the crudest reading of *The City without Jews*: Viennese modernism was and is Jewish, whether visible or not (and mostly, it seems, it was). The awkward similarity of this central thesis to that of the modernists' contemporary antisemitic critics occurs to Beller, but he does nothing to suggest what we are to do with this similarity or how we are to account for the recurrence of this pattern.[19]

The link has not been lost on all readers. Sir Ernst Gombrich, invited by the Austrian Cultural Institute to contribute to a 1996 seminar, "Fin de Siècle Vienna and Its Jewish Cultural Influences," took the occasion to resist the given topic, "the Jewish influences on the visual arts."[20] Focusing particularly on Beller's thesis on the Jewish character of "Vienna 1900," Gombrich expressed his objection as succinctly as possible: "I am of the opinion that the notion of Jewish Culture was, and is, an invention of Hitler and his fore-runners and after-runners."[21] Among these fore- and after-runners, Gombrich seems to have counted his fellow Vienna Jews Stefan Zweig (who calculated that nine-tenths of nineteenth-century Viennese culture had been the property of Jews) and George Steiner (who attributed "most of the innovations" of the twentieth century to Viennese of Jewish extraction).[22] Gombrich is baffled by such claims and in his lecture refutes the apparently insuperable nonlogic of (Austro-)Jewish modernism by tracing his own intellectual genealogy—naming the fathers of the Vienna School of art history, including Franz Wickhoff, Alois Riegl, Max Dvořák, and Julius von Schlosser—and certifying that none of these were Jewish. Beyond the macabre resemblance of this method to the Nazi requirement of producing baptismal certificates of four grandparents, this moment in Gombrich's very sound lecture also frankly adopts the despicable practice of racial identification and cultural attribution that he condemns. Unlike those he critiques, though, Gombrich is acutely aware of the processes of adoption and inversion mentioned above and that these inversions prove the rule of antisemitic antimodernism rather than performing a reversal. In his own, pithier phrase, "Even if you turn a myth on its head, you do not get the truth."[23]

The perspicacious Viennese cultural critic Hermann Bahr (allow me to abstain from identifying him as a Jew or a non-Jew)—early diagnostician if not founder of such latter-day historiographical principles as Secession, fin de siècle, and modernism, actually—could not resist this observation in his portrait of Vienna:

> The real Jew has no power in the city of Vienna. Unfortunately. It could use some of his diligence, his industriousness, his earnestness. But the city has always defended itself against him. It does not want the competence, greatness, and strength of Jewry. But the Jew who does not want to be one, who betrays his race by leaving it, the one who plays something he is not, he is Vienna's kin. The artificiality of these fugitive beings who, emptied of all past, crave to cloak themselves in any present and any future, who are no more than shells of men ready to spout off something different every day, who are capable of being nothing but appearing anything—these have always allured the Viennese. He finds himself in such people. If we take the term in this way, it can be

said that Vienna is jewified [*verjudet*] through and through. It was so before the first Jew arrived.[24]

It seems that, to be the first both to identify literary modernism as a critical category and to designate turn-of-the-century Vienna as the modernist cultural capital par excellence, Bahr could not but invoke Jewish modernism. Here the myth is turned not so much on its head as inside out: Vienna is a city so jewified that its Jewishness preceded the Jews, just as a latent Vienna modern anticipated modernity.

Jüdische Moderne

Jewish modernism is clearly a potent historical figure that calls for study, and at the same time it seems to have been immensely difficult to employ any variant of this figure without reproducing, more than analyzing, the problem complex to which it refers. The point here is not simply a methodological one (e.g., how to find a way of studying the discourse of Jewish modernism without merely reproducing it). What kind of problem is Jewish modernism?

In German, the term "Jewish modernism" coincides not only with "Jewish modernity" but also with "modern Judaism." *Die Moderne* had a special ring at the turn of the century, referring at once to a new age and an avant-garde art; "Die jüdische Moderne" was the title of an important lecture given by early Zionist Nathan Birnbaum in Vienna and published in 1896.[25] Birnbaum seems to have been the one to have coined the term "Zionism," a decade before this lecture, but by the turn of the century his place in the movement was all but utterly eclipsed by the hero of political Zionism, Theodor Herzl. Birnbaum, at much the same time as Herzl, began to dream of a Jewish state in Palestine in light of what he saw as the failed project of assimilation. But Birnbaum stood among those self-proclaimed cultural Zionists who emphasized the spiritual renewal of Judaism through the Zionist venture, their internal rejection of the abject state of assimilated Jewishness, and consciousness-raising among Jews in the diaspora. The term "Jewish modern" in his lecture plays two apparently contrary functions. It is used as a disdainful term for assimilationist Jews who consider themselves forward thinking (modern), but it also stands for Judaism at a moment of reorientation; the plea of the essay is for the Jewish modern to appreciate that what is needed is an independent national existence.[26]

Birnbaum's figure of *die jüdische Moderne*, not unlike other aspects of his thought, ultimately proved too confusing—too complex, ambivalent, and even self-contradictory—for his contemporary audience.[27] "Jewish modernism" was hence overtaken by the term "Jewish Renaissance," which was favored by other cultural Zionists in the same period, particularly Martin Buber and Ahad Ha'am.[28] While the linkage between Renaissance and modernity is not unfamiliar, the former figure unambiguously emphasized a return to Jewish spiritual roots. "The modern," as Birnbaum himself suggested in one way he used the term in his lecture, seemed to imply a rejection of the past, of tradition, of history. As Wagner's essay of that title already showed, the root "modern" was weighed down by its own baggage in the German and German-Jewish context. But it is precisely that complexity that Birnbaum wanted to capture and that indeed the term "Jewish Renaissance" did not wish to dispose of: the relationship between historical consciousness and creative innovation was meant to be neither oppositional nor simply complementary.[29] Rather, figures of history, tradition, memory, and the past, on the one side, and of modernism, modernity, and radical innovation, on the other, constituted poles of a field of tension, sets of axes within a single apparatus.

It was both the strength and the weakness of the term *jüdische Moderne* that it stood for too many things at once, and the same must be said of the meager translation "Jewish modernism." It would be a mistake to bracket the historical debates around the Jewish modern as somehow referring to something other than what students of modern Jewish culture do when they refer to Jewish modernism, because its intended referent was internal to Jewish culture. The different meanings of the term, from an aesthetic modernism leaning toward abstraction, commodified mass cultural organs and their products, a condition in the secular world putting pressures on a Jewish community struggling for continuity, and the intrinsic refashioning of that community itself, were all part of a single complex. One user of the term, for instance, defines it as "a series of disjointed efforts to renew traditional ideational, social, and textual patterns broken by the uneven encounter with Western culture."[30] As in both the antisemitic and Jewish uses of the concept so far, this definition establishes a distinction of Jews and Western culture (or else there would be no "encounter") and also allows one to think about specifically Jewish engagements in terms of the guiding forms of modernism; at the same time, the special investment of these specifically Jewish engagements in orientalism, primitivism, spiritualism, and so on, in turn informed modernism.[31]

Of course, the antinomies of Jewish modernism were not inscribed only in the sideline voices of Nathan Birnbaum and the creative adherents of a Jewish Renaissance, but mainstream Zionism itself emerged in this very context and nourished it as well.[32] Not only Birnbaum's *jüdische Moderne* but Herzl's *Altneuland* (Old-new land; 1900) was infused with all the principle features of the texts discussed above: the paradoxes of tradition and innovation, the destiny of essential character and the promise of a radical break from it, and discomfort with a present modernity above all. This is not to repeat the thesis that Zionist and certain contemporary antisemitic discourses shared a lexicon with their common antiliberalism, cult of youth, and so on.[33] All the manifold (including the now forgotten) branches of the fin-de-siècle Zionist imaginary shared this play of past, present, and future, as well as the dialectical presence and absence fantasies present in the above texts of Wagner, Bettauer, and Bahr.³⁴ Zionist writings, youth movements, international congresses, and the like further nourished these discourses in turn, setting on a grand stage, as it were, fantasies of a Jewish withdrawal from European modernity and the inauguration of a different future utopia, just as their relentless critiques of assimilation echoed those of Wagner's successors. Zionism was nothing if not Jewish modernism in all these senses.

Clearly the complexity of the relations between the figures of modernism and of Jewishness stems in no small part from the famously ambiguous status of modernism itself, as well as its relationship to modernity on the one hand and popular culture on the other.³⁵ The discourse on Jewish modernism in the German-language context, I am arguing, encompasses these very tensions, giving them specific form. While this discourse is surely one that took familiar form over the course of the last half of the nineteenth century and remained intact through the first half of the twentieth, the Jew and so-called Jewish question already played central roles in German Enlightenment discourse, representing, as it were, the tension between universalism and particularity.³⁶ But the German (including German-speaking Austrian) eighteenth and early nineteenth centuries were not haunted by a discourse on Jews until the mid-nineteenth century; by the 1880s onward, the culture was saturated by it. While it would be too much to claim that to speak of *die Moderne* after Jewish emancipation was to speak of Jews, a linkage of these figures in the period cannot easily be dismissed. It is hence a somewhat counterhistorical exercise to seek to reconstruct a German discourse on the modern—let us call it modernism—purged of reference to Jews, Judaism, or Jewishness. This is odd because modernism, in at least one of its principal contemporary versions, stood for a presumed anticontextualism as well as an antihistoricism; it famously made a claim for aesthetic autonomy.³⁷ This is a contradiction at the core of the whole notion of Jewish modernism. There is no reason to rehash a difficult discussion of aesthetic autonomy here or to evaluate the difference between the program and practice of art for art's sake; my concern is rather with the relationship of programmatic modernism and its histories (or criticisms). We have seen how antisemitic and philosemitic programmatic statements on the modern seem to bear an unshakeable rhetorical kinship with German and Jewish studies treatments of them, so that in some cases they are structurally identical. Similarly, certain critical methodologies such as the American postwar New Criticism shared distinct elective affinities with aestheticist formalism, such that our contemporary critical discourse on modernism developed in a mutually reflexive relationship to it.³⁸ In other words, if German-Jewish studies cannot help but posit a modernism as inexorably Jewish as the antisemites', there is also an insufficiently historicized criticism of modernism that is stripped of these associations. This modernism without Jews is not a history of

German modernism freed from its antisemitic discursive associations; rather, it is a disavowal.

De Man's Literary Modernity without Jews

Paul de Man's influential essay "Literary History and Literary Modernity" would seem to be an account of modernism without Jews; in its sly use of the term "literary modernity" it seems to be able to do even without "modernism."[39] De Man's essay, at its core an exegesis of one of Nietzsche's short pieces from *Untimely Meditations*, became exemplary for a generation of literary critics (although not historians) interested in a modernism that was neither a static descriptor of literary history nor a self-cannibalizing category of aesthetic formalism free of context. De Man sees the category (again, modernity rather than modernism) emerging as ideological weapon, theoretical problem, and promising link between theory and praxis.[40] This discussion of modernism leads provocatively to a lucid statement about the textuality of history: that intensive textual interpretation is true historical work and that historical phenomena are texts in other guise.[41]

While influential, de Man's essay is often misunderstood. Many readers see it as casting (or recasting, after Nietzsche) an ironclad binary of history and the modern.[42] That binary is the starting point rather than de Man's own polemic—the presumed opposition of history and the modern is what he took to be obvious, modernism's own self-mythology. In Carl Schorske's words, the modernists "all broke, more or less deliberately, their ties to the historical outlook central to the nineteenth-century liberal culture in which they had been reared."[43] The opposition between "history" and "modern" is established in de Man's text (and in his reading in Nietzsche's) only to be broken down: modernism's concern for futurity implicates it at once in the "chain" of history; its self-consciousness entails reflection, even as it demands a spontaneity at odds with such reflection:

> Considered as a principle of life, modernity becomes a principle of origination and turns at once into a generative power that is itself historical. It becomes impossible to overcome history in the name of life or forget the past in the name of modernity, because both are linked by a temporal chain that gives them a common destiny.... *Modernity and history relate to each other in a curiously contradictory way that goes beyond antithesis or opposition.* If history is not to become sheer regression or paralysis, it depends on modernity for its duration and renewal; but modernity cannot assert itself without being at once swallowed up and reintegrated into a regressive historical process.... Modernity and history seem condemned to being linked together in a self-destroying union that threatens the survival of both.[44]

De Man very clearly identifies the relation between history and modernity in Nietzsche's text with the trope of *aporia*. This figure, which in classical rhetoric signified the moment of real or feigned undecidability between two mutually contradictory positions presented by a speaker (from the Greek for "impassable"), was a privileged one for practitioners of deconstruction. For a reader like de Man, this prime trope of doubt and undecidability points to the paradox wherein the conditions of possibility of something like the modern are also the elements blocking its existence.[45] Nietzsche does not so much argue for modernity against history (the Nietzschean Now against historicist reflection), according to de Man, but rather his own text is caught in the aporia of reflection and immediacy, of history and the modern. This reading is persuasive. Still more interesting than its accuracy is its mirrorlike identical inversion of the position of Walter Benjamin familiar to so many in German studies: the dialectical image, frozen in a lightning-moment in which the then and the now, history and the modern, coincide.[46] De Man does not mention Benjamin in this essay, and the latter's presence lingers in implication only. The aporetic in de Man's usage could be seen in contrast to the dialectical; of course the former term is the one that emerges from literary criticism, rhetorics, or tropology; dialectics is the historical concept. By insisting on the aporetic rather than dialectical relation of the terms "reflection" and "spontaneity" (or "history" and "modern"), de Man, with Nietzsche, refuses the primacy of history while insisting on keeping it braided with the modern within a single knot. If that knot does not bear the name Jewish modernism, that is so in part because of the conspicuous absence not only of Benjamin but of other prime subjects of German(-Jewish) studies whose projects describe the collision of reflection and spontaneity (i.e., Freud), or history and modernization (e.g., Marx).

The deconstructionist taste for aporia—if anyone indulged in it more often and more idiosyncratically than de Man, it was Jacques Derrida—reminded these thinkers' critics of the accusation of moral relativism. That is certainly a debate that is too expansive and too distant from this discussion of Jewish modernism to be included here. Yet it is worth mentioning that this criticism reached its most fevered pitch around an affair involving issues very close to those I have been discussing. Attackers of a wide range of theoretical work in literary criticism came to claim that this critical work was tainted and could not be seen without reference to the historical fact of the author's collaboration with the occupying German regime during World War II. A particularly influential report by Jon Wiener in *The Nation*, for instance, specifically cited de Man's "Literary History and Literary Modernity" as evidence of the objectives of "deconstruction," which were to "[free] literature from context and history."[47] But de Man's claim in this essay was precisely not that history should be ignored in the name of aesthetic autonomy; rather, he asserted that intense scrutiny of the text on its own terms would constitute historical work. Real formalism—the rejection of history and context of the New Criticism, for example—he attacked ruthlessly.[48]

At the center of the controversy was a piece a twenty-one-year-old de Man had written on the subject of "Jews and contemporary literature."[49] It cannot be disputed that de Man, in this one-page contribution, enlists antisemitic discourse, but the question of how he engages it has been the object of some discussion. For the major thrust of the article is without doubt contrary to the central thrust of the Nazi antisemitic view of the role of the Jews in modern culture: the accusation about a penetrating Jewish presence in modern culture is a "lapidary judgment," a product of "vulgar antisemitism," or even a "myth" spread in part by the Jews themselves; but modern European culture, far from being "jewified" (*enjuivé*, the standard contemporary translation of *verjudet*), was healthy at its root, not fundamentally affected by the relatively minor Jewish participation, and indeed, an imagined solution to the Jewish question involving the Jews' isolation from Europe would "not entail, for the literary life of the West, deplorable consequences."[50] A complex case, to be sure—blatantly antisemitic discourse deployed in a way that undermines the ideology? To interpret this appalling text, readers have to contextualize it, historicize it, in different ways: the immediate context of de Man's collaborationist activity and his apparent resistance to contribute to this special issue of *Le Soir* on Jews and literature, for instance. Some readers focus on de Man's involvement in a group on the antifascist and democratic left not long before this moment. For critics, the future doctrines of de Man's literary theory would be as crucial a context as those more immediate to this text.[51]

For our purposes, it is salient that this 1941 de Man, like exterminationist antisemites of his time no more or less than the murdered Hugo Bettauer, posits a European modernity without Jews as a rhetorical strategy. We have come full circle back to Wagner's essay "Modern" a century before: both imagine a modern popular sphere (for de Man the "phony and disordered existence of Europe since 1920"[52]) rife with Jewish influence, and both determine that this Jewish sphere has not touched true art. And so, in de Man's writing, another pair of bookends—at one end, modern literature without Jews, at the other, a literary modernity that sublates history and leaves both Jewishness and antisemitism unspoken. Jewish presence or absence, history and the modern, face one another in an impassable encounter—an aporia.

Counterhistories of Jewish Modernism

The subtitle of this chapter, "A Counterhistorical Argument," has several competing implications. This is necessarily so, in light of the similarly concurrent and conflicting strands of Jewish modernism itself. Some of the reference points of Jewish modernism and counterhistory map onto one another neatly: the Zionist Jewish *Moderne* immediately concerned itself with the self-conscious effort to remake Jewish destiny by resisting its own lachrymose history—instead of being subjected by history, the new, creative, and activist Jews would reauthor themselves. David Biale embodied the term with new life in his study of Gershom Scholem, in which he suggested that the revival and reinterpretations of the Jewish mystical tradition rewrote the story Judaism told itself about its own rationalist and legalistic core.[53] While the Zionist "muscle-Jew"[54] and his counterpart student with Franz Rosenzweig's *Star of Redemption* under his arm might have had little to say to each other, both were Jewish modernists in their own way. Both embraced the innovative and even redemptive moment that came in an engagement with a Jewish historical essence that was also a refusal: they each insisted on identifying with a Jewish essence that other Jews would have found alien. This complex pattern of identification and disidentification with history—closely linked to a focus on the redemptive inauguration of a utopian future—is not far at all from the contemporary discourses on Jewish modernism by self-identified non-Jewish Germans. These Jewish modernisms, as we have seen, entailed their own versions of counterhistory, imagining what various modernisms and modernities would look like if purged of the historical presence of Jews. To be clear, my argument is not that all these different discourses are in concord, describing a same or similar *Moderne*, Jewish in one and the same way. Rather, to regard all these preoccupations as part of a landscape, to stand back and blur the eyes, is to draw out a field of tension among figures of self and other, past and future, text and author. This murky and ambivalent field is covered, as it were, by the name "Jewish modernism" rather than denoted by it.

Technically speaking, a counterhistorical argument is a rumination about the succession of past events that relies on a counterfactual premise—for example, "if Hindenburg had not appointed Hitler chancellor of the Reich in 1933," "if the Jews had not been emancipated," or "had the Weimar Constitution not included the Emergency Powers provision . . ." While historians have traditionally espoused skepticism regarding the legitimacy of counterhistorical arguments, implicitly many if not most historical arguments rely on such premises. Some years ago an interest in counterfactuals and history surfaced, marked by a flurry of conference panels and publications.[55] While eccentric imaginary historical experiments are a staple of a genre of popular counterfactual history, professional historians are more comfortable with counterhistorical arguments based on realistic premises.[56] Upon examination, many historical arguments use implicitly counterfactual reasoning: in asserting the association of Viennese modernism and its Jews, for instance, Beller in his *Vienna and the Jews* must silently imagine what that modernism would have looked like without them. German-Jewish studies, no matter how patently historical, hence often resorts to premises that might be as extravagant as the statement "if turn-of-the-century Vienna had no Jews." To analyze the Jewish influence on the work of a Kafka, a Freud, a Marx, or a Gustav Mahler does suggest, after all, that their work would have to have been essentially different if they were *not* Jews.

I wonder if a counterhistorical exercise of precisely this extravagance would not be useful to flesh out this historiographical dilemma and its consistent entanglement with the problematics of Jewish modernism. Generations of scholarship, invective, and silent public opinion have culled meaning from the relationship of texts like "On the Jewish Question," *Moses and Monotheism*, and so on to the facts of the Jewish origins of their authors' families.[57] There is no use disputing that many deep insights into these and a great many works more remote to Judaism have been made on the basis of this contextualization. But what if it were now to be discovered that these artists and thinkers, or one of them, did *not* actually have Jewish origins, that this had just been assumed on the basis of a later manipulation of the historical record or a mistake? Too much of a stretch, surely, to imagine, but it must be confessed that a text like either of the two mentioned *could* be authored by someone with no discernable Jewish origins and, in that case, would have to be interpreted differently. We could perform this eccentric experiment in another way, no less stark: what if the author of the *Genealogy of Morals*, Friedrich Nietzsche, were the son not of a Lutheran minister but, like Marx, of a convert from Judaism? From an intellectual historical perspective, it is an absurd premise—the life of Nietzsche would have been utterly different had this been the case, the environment informing the oeuvre completely different, the professional training and trajectory impossible. Yet we can say with certainty that if this were the case, and we had before us the text *Genealogy of Morals*, shelves of its interpretation would be saturated with references to the author's relationship to his Judaism, the Jewish education or popular knowledge informing the text, Jewish self-hatred, the context of antisemitism, and so on. And voilà! Suddenly we have a cornerstone of the canon of Jewish modernism.

Cultural historians (including me) are convinced that texts, figures, and ideas are embedded—they have a relationship to their given historical contexts and are unthinkable without them. Writers like de Man offer the possibility of unthinking this truism. What is called the autonomy of the text or of art can really be seen as a willed assertion, a hypothesis: *what if* texts, works, or figures could be understood outside the presumed overdetermined contexts of their authorship?[58]

My question in this chapter is somewhat different: How are we to historicize Jewish modernism? How is it to be defined, and how can it even be invoked without immediately falling into the traps set by its own violent history? A common strategy for historicizing a concept, movement, or work calls for an excavation of an author's origins and intentions, but the difficult case of Jewish modernism shows that there are reasons to take a step back from this model of contextualization. The constellation of disparate historical moments I have organized here under the rubric Jewish modernism is intended to bring these reasons into relief and to provide a context of a different sort—one that helps situate an elusive object that is not a body of work or a register of authors but a way of thinking about oneself and one's place in relation to the past, the future, and creativity.

Notes

A version of this chapter was previously published as Scott Spector, "Modernism without Jews: A Counter-Historical Argument," in "Jewish Modernism," special issue, *Modernism/Modernity* 13, no. 4 (2006): 615–633. Copyright © 2006 Johns Hopkins University Press. Reprinted with permission by Johns Hopkins University Press. Special thanks for our conversations are due Ross Chambers, Amir Eshel, Anton Kaes, Johannes von Moltke, Todd Presner, and Eric Rentschler.

    1. Quoted in Richard Wagner, "Modern," in *Richard Wagners Gesammelte Schriften und Dichtungen*, 3rd ed. (Leipzig, Germany: Hesse and Becker, 1898), 10:54.

    2. Brigitte Hamann claims provocatively that Wagner had used the term "Jewish modernism" (*die jüdische Moderne*) already in "The Artwork of the Future" (which would have been November 1849), but errors in her citation make this difficult to track. See Brigitte Hamann, *Hitlers Wien: Lehrjahre eines Diktators* (Munich: Piper, 1996), 112, 595n83. The same errors are reproduced in the English translation; see Brigitte Hamann, *Hitler's Vienna: A Dictator's Apprenticeship*, trans. Thomas Thornton (New York: Oxford University Press, 1999), 78, 418n71. I find no direct use of the term in available versions of Wagner's essay.

    3. The locus classicus for this observation is Wagner's 1850 essay, "Judaism in Music," but the explicit and polemical antisemitism of this and other essays can be read as contexts for the aesthetic program in the essays "Art and Revolution," "The Art Work of the Future," and others. In "Judaism in Music," the most often cited piece in regard to Wagner's programmatic antisemitism, the author assumes a recognizably alien relationship of Jews to European art; much later essays like "Modern" and "What Is German?" express the more nefarious linkage of Jews to modern German culture that is particularly relevant to my inquiry.

    4. See, e.g., Richard Wagner, "Die Kunst und die Revolution," in *Richard Wagners Gesammelte Schriften und Dichtungen*, 3:8–41; Richard Wagner, "Das Kunstwerk der Zukunft," in *Richard Wagners Gesammelte Schriften und Dichtungen*, 2:42–177; Richard Wagner, "'Zukunftsmusik': An einen französischen Freund (Fr. Villot) als Vorwort zu einer Prosa-Übersetzung meiner Operndichtungen," in *Richard Wagners Gesammelte Schriften und Dichtungen*, 7:87–137; and Richard Wagner, "Deutsche Kunst und Deutsche Politik," in *Richard Wagners Gesammelte Schriften und Dichtungen*, 8:30–124.

    5. In short, a neutral position identifies and historicizes an antisemitic strain in the sociocultural critique essays, usually focusing particularly on "Judaism in Music," and brackets the question of a relationship between these opinions and the artistic work. See, e.g., Dieter Borchmeyer's excellent summary in Ulrich Müller and Peter Wapnewski, *Richard-Wagner-Handbuch* (Stuttgart, Germany: Alfred Kröner, 1986): 137–161. Many lengthy studies avoid discussion of this element and, when they do cursorily handle it, tend to dismiss it. See, e.g., Curt von Westernhagen, *Wagner: A Biography*, trans. Mary Whittall, 2 vols. (Cambridge: Cambridge University Press, 1978). Some treatments deal with the problem at length but ultimately apologetically, considering antisemitic attitudes to be discrete artifacts of Wagner's milieu— one source, for instance, equates his views on Jews with those of Marx and Benjamin Disraeli. See L. J. Rather, *Reading Wagner: A Study in the History of Ideas* (Baton Rouge: Louisiana State University Press, 1990), 114–217. Many even argue that the "Judaism" essay was nothing more

than a personal attack on Meyerbeer (who is not named in the essay). Since T. W. Adorno's *Versuch über Wagner* (Frankfurt am Main, Germany: Suhrkamp, 1952), various studies have tried to relate the antisemitism of the essays to the content, form, imagery, or score of the music dramas; see, especially, Marc A. Weiner, *Richard Wagner and the Anti-Semitic Imagination* (Lincoln: University of Nebraska Press, 1995); and David J. Levin, *Richard Wagner, Fritz Lang, and the Nibelungen* (Princeton, NJ: Princeton University Press, 1998). Wolf-Daniel Hartwich offers a reading of this relation that goes furthest beyond looking for Jewish allegory in the dramas; see Wolf-Daniel Hartwich, *Romantischer Antisemitismus: Von Klopstock bis Richard Wagner* (Göttingen, Germany: Vandenhoek and Ruprecht, 2005), 205–258.

6. Richard Wagner, "Das Judenthum in der Musik," in *Richard Wagners Gesammelte Schriften und Dichtungen*, 5:84–85. The later term for "jewification" would drop the umlaut.

7. The German term *die Moderne* encompasses the aesthetic movements of modernism (*Modernismus*) as well as the broader experiences of modernity; the emergence of the term coincides with the movement of modernism, however. See Hans Ulrich Gumbrecht, "Modern, Modernität, Moderne," in *Geschichtliche Grundbegriffe: Historisches Lexikon zur politisch-sozialen Sprache in Deutschland*, ed. Otto Brunner, Werner Conze, and Reinhart Koselleck (Stuttgart, Germany: Ernst Klett, 1978), 4:120–126.

8. Hugo Bettauer, *Die Stadt ohne Juden: Ein Roman von übermorgen* (Vienna: Gloriette, 1922); Hugo Bettauer, *The City without Jews: A Novel of Our Time*, trans. Salomea Neumark Brainin (New York: Bloch, 1926).

9. Eric Rentschler has been the clearest on the "strange territory of the Nazi dissolve," which in his argument establishes a kinship between oppositional figures, transforming the communal rejection of a Jewish other into an interior monologue. See Eric Rentschler, *Ministry of Illusion: Nazi Cinema and Its Afterlife* (Cambridge, MA: Harvard University Press, 1996), 161.

10. Bettauer, *Stadt*, 216; Bettauer, *City*, 187.

11. Bettauer himself wrote in 1922, "I have written an amusing book that, through a series of harmlessly and novelistically assembled vignettes, offers a cinematic picture of what Vienna would look like without Jews." His inspiration to do so, to be sure, was an encounter with a scrawled graffito, "Hinaus mit den Juden!" (Jews out!), and his subsequent "playful fantasy" of what would really happen if the Jews were suddenly to accept the "polite" invitation. Hugo Bettauer, "Bettauer über seinen Roman," *Die Börse* (Vienna), July 13, 1922, p. 16.

12. *New York Evening Post*, cited in the flyleaf of Hugo Bettauer, *The City without Jews*, cited in Beth Simone Noveck, "Hugo Bettauer's Vienna, 1918–1925," in *Jura Soyfer and His Time*, ed. Donald G. Daviau (Riverside, CA: Ariadne Press, 1995), 370, 383n17.

13. Guntram Geser and Armin Loacker, eds., *Die Stadt ohne Juden*, film and text ed. (Vienna: Filmarchiv Austria, 2000).

14. Murray G. Hall, *Der Fall Bettauer* (Vienna: Löcker, 1978); Alfred Rosenberg, "Der Fall Bettauer: Ein Musterbeispiel jüdischer Zersetzungstätigkeit," *Der Weltkampf: Halbmonatsschrift für die Judenfrage aller Länder* 2, no. 8 (1925): 337–351. There are many such parallels. The title "Index of Jewish authors" (*Verzeichnis jüdischer Autoren*), for instance, marks the title page of the standard reference work *Bibliographia Judaica*, ed. Renate Heuer (Munich: Knaur, 1981), but a search for it by this subtitle may lead the researcher to the Nazi reference manual, with the difference that the latter was a secret document for internal bureaucratic use. See Nationalsozialistische Deutsche Arbeiter-Partei, ed., *Verzeichnis Jüdischer Autoren: Vorläufige Zusammenstellung des Amtes Schrifttumspflege bei dem Beauftragten des Führers für die gesamte geistige und weltanschauliche Erziehung der NSDAP und der Reichsstelle zur Förderung des deutschen Schrifttums*, 3rd ed. (Berlin: Nationalsozialistische Deutsche Arbeiter-Partei, 1939).

15. See Noveck, "Bettauer's Vienna," 384n18, which cites Hans Habe, *Ich stelle mich: Meine Lebensgeschichte* (Vienna: Kurt Desch, 1954), 111.

16. The original name is *Er und Sie: Wochenschrift für Lebenskultur und Erotik*. Five editions of the weekly journal were published in 1924 between February 14 and March 13 before cessation of publication. For an original take on the significance of the journal, see Britta McEwen, *Sexual Knowledge: Feeling, Fact, and Social Reform in Vienna, 1900–1934* (New York: Berghahn Books, 2012), 144–174.

17. Harry Zohn, "Die Stadt ohne Juden," *Das Jüdische Echo* 4, no. 5 (1956): 14, quoted in Geser and Loacker, *Die Stadt ohne Juden*, 7 (translation mine).

18. Steven Beller, *Vienna and the Jews, 1867–1938: A Cultural History* (Cambridge: Cambridge University Press, 1989), 6.

19. See ibid., 5. Beller ridicules the trend of scholarship on fin-de-siècle Vienna that treats assimilated (apparently including converted or baptized and children or grandchildren of converted or baptized) Jews as other than Jewish, although such approaches are possibly "praiseworthy." On the same page, he names the objection that considering all these people and works Jewish reiterates the Nazi practice, but he dismisses it, apparently on the basis of Jewish cultural predominance. The compelling argument throughout Neil Levi's *Modernist Form and the Myth of Jewification* (New York: Fordham University Press, 2014) expounds forcefully along the lines I have set out here, although he may not have recognized the kinship. I am, indeed, not arguing that Beller's argument is problematic because it reiterates antisemitic discourse but rather that the structure of Jewish modernism in both antisemitic and philosemitic fantasy calls for analysis. Again, this strikes me as very much in line with Levi's project (see pages 12–13).

20. Emil Brix, "Preface," in Ernst Gombrich, "The Visual Arts in Vienna c. 1900: Reflections on the Jewish Catastrophe," *Occasions* 1 (1996), https://gombricharchive.files.wordpress.com/2011/04/showdoc28.pdf.

21. Gombrich, "The Visual Arts in Vienna." Gombrich was responding to Beller's article "Was bedeutet es 'Wien 1900' als eine jüdische Stadt zu bezeichnen?," *Zeitgeschichte* 23, nos. 7–8 (1996): 274–280.

22. Gombrich, "The Visual Arts in Vienna."

23. Ibid.

24. Hermann Bahr, *Wien* (Stuttgart, Germany: Krabbe, 1906): 69 (translation mine).

25. See Mathias Acher [Nathan Birnbaum], *Die jüdische Moderne: Vortrag gehalten im akademischen Vereine "Kadimah" in Wien* (Leipzig: August Schültze, 1896).

26. Acher, *Jüdische Moderne*, 38, reprinted in Nathan Birnbaum, *Die jüdische Moderne: Frühe zionistische Schriften* (Augsburg, Germany: Ölbaum, 1989), 39–82.

27. Birnbaum's Zionism floated from an emphasis on territory in Palestine to "present-work" focusing on the welfare and education of Jews in the diaspora or exile (*Golus*) to a return to religious orthodoxy. More than one commentator has seen in this complexity or even inconsistency the source of his relatively low status in the Zionist pantheon (in spite of apparently having coined the movement's name). See Henryk Broder, "Nicht alle Wege führen nach Jerusalem: Nathan Birnbaum—von der Geschichte vergessen," in Birnbaum, *Frühe zionistische*, 7–15; see also Leo Herrmann, *Nathan Birnbaum: Sein Werk und seine Wandlung* (Berlin: Jüdischer, 1914).

28. For a detailed discussion, see Inka Bertz, "Jewish Renaissance—Jewish Modernism," in *Berlin Metropolis: Jews and the New Culture, 1890–1918*, ed. Emily Bilski (Berkeley: University of California Press, 2000), 164–188. A key essay was Martin Buber, "Jüdische Renaissance," *Ost und West* 1, no. 1 (1901), now in translation as "Jewish Renaissance" in *The First Buber: Youthful Zionist Writings of Martin Buber*, ed. Gilya G. Schmidt (Syracuse, NY: Syracuse University

Press, 1999), 30–34. See also Mathias Acher [Nathan Birnbaum], "Die jüdische Renaissance-bewegung," *Ost und West* 2, no. 9 (1902): 577–584; Asher D. Biemann, "The Problem of Tradition and Reform in Jewish Renaissance and Renaissancism," *Jewish Social Studies* 8, no. 1 (2001): 58–87; Michael Brenner, *The Renaissance of Jewish Culture in Weimar Germany* (New Haven, CT: Yale University Press, 1996); and Delphine Bechtel, *La Renaissance culturelle juive en Europe centrale et orientale, 1897–1930: Langue, littérature et construction nationale* (Paris: Belin, 2002).

29. See two important studies that, in their different ways, work through the tensions of historical consciousness or memory and the resistance to it in Jewish consciousness: David N. Myers, *Resisting History: Historicism and Its Discontents in German-Jewish Thought* (Princeton, NJ: Princeton University Press, 2003); and Yosef Hayim Yerushalmi, *Zakhor: Jewish History and Jewish Memory* (Seattle: University of Washington Press, 1982), 81–103.

30. Zachary Braiterman, *(God) After Auschwitz: Tradition and Change in Post-Holocaust Jewish Thought* (Princeton, NJ: Princeton University Press, 1998), 6.

31. A similar result, from the opposite direction, was achieved by Noah Isenberg in *Between Redemption and Doom: The Strains of German-Jewish Modernism* (Lincoln: University of Nebraska Press, 1999), which consists of case studies of three Jewish contributors to the German modernist canon (Kafka, Arnold Zweig, and Walter Benjamin) and a case study of the Jewish-themed film *Der Golem*. The "strains" of Isenberg's subtitle refers at once to the thoroughly distinct and often contradictory ways Jewish and German identifications worked among these authors and in these texts and to the difficult tensions among them.

32. Besides the personal alienation from Birnbaum, Herzl's political Zionism was perennially at odds with cultural as well as spiritual Zionist streams informing the general movement calling itself the Jewish Renaissance.

33. This was first and most forcefully argued by George L. Mosse, "The Influence of the Volkish Idea on German Jewry," in *Germans and Jews: The Right, the Left, and the Search for a "Third Force" in Pre-Nazi Germany* (New York: Howard Fertig, 1970), 77–115. I also mean here something much broader than what I describe elsewhere as a "complicity of discourse"; see S. Spector, *Prague Territories: National Conflict and Cultural Innovation in Franz Kafka's Fin de Siècle* (Berkeley: University of California Press, 2000): 115–120.

34. In this I strongly agree with the thesis that fin-de-siècle aesthetic modernism and Zionist thought share not only a common context but much more. See Michael Stanislawski, *Zionism and the Fin de Siècle: Cosmopolitanism and Nationalism from Nordau to Jabotinsky* (Berkeley: University of California Press, 2001).

35. Hans-Ulrich Gumbrecht's conceptual history of the German terms is helpful, as it both systematizes and historicizes their deployments. See Gumbrecht, "Modern, Modernität, Moderne," 93–131. See also Susan Stanford Freeman, "Definitional Excursions: The Meanings of Modern/Modernity/Modernism," *Modernism/Modernity* 8, no 3 (2001): 493–513.

36. The centrality of Moses Mendelssohn and Salomon Maimon and their relationships to Christian German enlighteners is well known and documented. A more intricate argument for the centrality of the Jew to this tradition is Michael Mack, *German Idealism and the Jew: The Inner Anti-Semitism of Philosophy and German Jewish Responses* (Chicago: University of Chicago Press, 2003).

37. The bibliography on modernism is large, and discussions of aesthetic autonomy are many and complex, including many treatments of turn-of-the-century aestheticism or symbolism. Concise programmatic discussions of modernism focusing on this feature include Maurice Beebe, "What Modernism Was," *Journal of Modern Literature* 3, no. 5 (1974): 1065–1084; and Joseph Frank, *The Widening Gyre: Crisis and Mastery in Modern Literature* (New Brunswick, NJ: Rutgers University Press, 1963), 10.

38. Astradur Eysteinsson, *The Concept of Modernism* (Ithaca, NY: Cornell University Press, 1990). See especially pages 12–14 ("Outside History") for the view that some of the claims of modernists such as aestheticists corresponded to the purist views of formalists and New Critics.

39. Paul de Man, *Blindness and Insight: Essays in the Rhetoric of Contemporary Criticism*, 2nd ed. (Minneapolis: University of Minnesota Press, 1983), 142–165.

40. Ibid., 142–143.

41. Ibid., 165.

42. This misreading of the essay is widespread, and the assertions of de Man's hostility to history are equally broad; the more nuanced, and also more accurate, position is laid out in Frederic Jameson, *A Singular Modernity: Essay on the Ontology of the Present* (London: Verso, 2002), 106–110.

43. Carl E. Schorske, *Fin-de-Siècle Vienna: Politics and Culture* (New York: Knopf, 1980), xviii.

44. De Man, *Blindness*, 150–151 (emphasis added).

45. "An aporia is a rhetorical figure of doubt in which the conditions of possibility of an event or concept are, paradoxically, its own conditions of impossibility resulting in an interpretive impasse or moment of undecideability." Martin McQuillan, *Paul de Man* (London: Routledge, 2001), 87.

46. See Walter Benjamin, *Gesammelte Schriften* (Frankfurt am Main, Germany: Suhrkamp, 1977), 5:566–567, 5:1034–1035. The difficult problem of the dialectical image is not exactly a historical or narrative model in the sense that dialectics in classical Hegelianism and Marxism have been, in that it freezes a dialectical moment rather than moving forward; it is also different from de Man's aporia in that it freezes the then and the now together in an active and spontaneous way rather than at an aporetic impasse. Frequently, Benjamin's messianic revisions of Western Marxism are explained, again, by resorting to his German-Jewish background. A symptomatic example that is expressly relevant to the problematic explored in this chapter is Robert Alter, *Necessary Angels: Tradition and Modernity in Kafka, Benjamin, and Scholem* (Cambridge, MA: Harvard University Press, 1991).

47. Jon Wiener, "Deconstructing de Man," *The Nation* 246, no. 1 (1988): 22–24. On page 22 he cites and mocks de Man's assertion about the textuality of wars and claims this represented a more extreme antihistoricist interpretation of literature than the New Criticism. On page 23 he cites the essay again, paradoxically claiming that it is "full of references to a hidden past."

48. De Man, "Form and Intent in the American New Criticism," in De Man, *Blindness*, 20–35.

49. Paul de Man, "Les Juifs dans la Littérature actuelle," *Le Soir*, March 4, 1941, reprinted in Paul de Man, *Responses: On Paul de Man's Wartime Journalism, 1939–1943*, ed. Werner Hamacher, Neil Hertz, and Thomas Keenan (Lincoln: University of Nebraska Press, 1989), 45. A translation by David Lehman is published as an appendix to Lehman's *Signs of the Times: Deconstruction and the Fall of Paul de Man* (New York: Simon and Schuster, 1991), 269–271.

50. Jacques Derrida, "Like the Sound of the Sea Deep within a Shell: Paul de Man's War," trans. Peggy Kamuf, in Hamacher, Hertz, and Keenan, *Responses*, 142.

51. See Hamacher, Hertz, and Keenan, *Responses*.

52. Derrida, "Like the Sound," 143.

53. See David Biale, *Gershom Scholem: Kabbalah and Counter-History* (Cambridge, MA: Harvard University Press, 1982). Amos Funkenstein provides a different take on Jewish counterhistory—one that could be related to those discussed here in a more complicated way but that did not focus in particular on the period of high modernism. See Amos Funkenstein, *Perceptions of Jewish History* (Berkeley: University of California Press, 1993), esp. 36–49; and

David Biale, "Counter-History and Jewish Polemics against Christianity: The *Sefer toldot ye-shu* and the *Sefer zerubavel*," *Jewish Social Studies* 6, no. 1 (1999): 130–145.

54. For a contextualization of the contemporary Zionist term "muscle-Jew," attributed to Max Nordau, see Todd Samuel Presner, *Muscular Judaism: The Jewish Body and the Politics of Regeneration* (London: Routledge, 2007).

55. The conference of the American Historical Association in 2006 in Philadelphia featured an association-sponsored roundtable titled "Not Just a 'Parlour Game' Anymore: Counterfactual History in the Historical Mainstream." In 2004, the professional organ of the association published an article on the issue of counterfactual history and created an online forum for a discussion. See Martin Bunzl, "Counterfactual History: A User's Guide," *American Historical Review* 109, no. 3 (2004): 845–858. The general direction of these discussions seems to be not only to diagnose the phenomenon of the resurgence of counterfactual history but to consider what its appropriate methods, boundaries, and applications are. Richard Ned Lebow, in "What's So Different about a Counterfactual?" *World Politics* 52, no. 4 (2000): 550–585, argues that counterfactual historical arguments are not inherently different from factual ones, although the examples he reviews are logically deficient in his view. An influential collection to this field was Niall Ferguson, ed., *Virtual History: Alternatives and Counterfactuals* (New York: Macmillan, 1997). On the level of popular history, examples are Robert Cowley's edited series *What If? Eminent Historians Imagine What Might Have Been* (New York: Putnam, 2001–2002) and his earlier volume focusing on military history, *What If? The World's Foremost Military Historians Imagine What Might Have Been* (New York: G. P. Putnam's Sons, 1999); Steve Tally, *Almost America: From Colonists to Clinton: A "What If" History of the United States* (New York: HarperCollins, 2000); and a veritable spate of fantastical books with titles such as *Roads Not Taken*, *History That Never Was*, *The Way It Wasn't*, and *Alternate History Stories*.

56. See Bunzl, "Counterfactual History," 848.

57. Karl Marx, "Zur Judenfrage" [On the Jewish question], in *Karl Marx–Friedrich Engels Gesamtausgabe* [Karl Marx–Freidrich Engels complete works] (Berlin: Dietz, 1982), 2:141–169, 2:648–667; Sigmund Freud, *Der Mann Moses und die monotheistische Religion* [Moses and monotheism] (Frankfurt am Main, Germany: Fischer, 1999). Some classic examples of the literature that analyzes these include Isaac Deutscher, "The Non-Jewish Jew," in *The Non-Jewish Jew and Other Essays*, ed. Tamara Deutscher, 25–41 (London: Oxford University Press, 1968), and Yosef Hayim Yerushalmi, *Freud's Moses: Judaism Terminable and Interminable* (New Haven, CT: Yale University Press, 1991).

58. Distinct but related hypotheses are posited by Roland Barthes and Michel Foucault in essays assessing the problem of authorship. See R. Barthes, "The Death of the Author," in *Image, Music, Text*, ed. and trans. Stephen Heath (New York: Hill and Wang, 1977), 142–148; and Michel Foucault, "What Is an Author?" in *Language, Counter-Memory, Practice*, ed. Donald F. Bouchard, trans. Donald F. Bouchard and Sherry Simon (Ithaca, NY: Cornell University Press, 1977), 124–127. These texts could be said to be not only well known but widely influential, as is de Man's essay, which was published close to the time these essays came out in English translation. Nonetheless, that influence does not seem to have extended to Jewish and German studies treatments of Jewish modernism. The problematic of authorship is a central strand of the discourse complex I have been discussing under this rubric. For the discursive complex of Jewish modernism, it seems important to remember Barthes's old claim that, in writing, "everything is to be *disentangled*, nothing *deciphered*." See Barthes, *Image, Music, Text*, 147.

3 The Secularization Question
Germans, Jews, and the Historical Understanding of Modernity

Is Secularization (Jewish) History?

When historians grapple with a notion we call the secularization thesis of history, we sometimes mean more than one thing. First (let us call this one secularization I), there is the idea that science and reason come gradually to displace myth, theology, and blind faith in a linear fashion from the Renaissance and Enlightenment to the modern world. The twentieth century, with its fascisms and genocides and holocausts, put to rest that particular idea of progress. Another, more subtle and complex version of the secularization thesis came to take its place after World War II (secularization II). Is the modern world really something completely new in its break from theology, faith, and myth? Or are modern, presumed rational institutions simply replacements of theological categories, in different guise? On this view, in place of the Lord we vest authority in the sovereign (king, president, what have you); in place of commandments we have civil codes and laws, the nation or polity is a just a copy of the community of faith, and so on. Carl Schmitt (1888–1985) articulated a particularly incisive version of this thesis during the embattled Weimar Republic and labeled it "political theology."[1] Political theology—once again in intellectual currency, owing to the traction of Giorgio Agamben and other contemporary theorists—is certainly a slippery concept and one that entails several convening genealogies as well as different parameters. A particular discussion emerged out of the seed that Schmitt planted, and this is the stream I am concerned with here—it led from a reflection on politics to one on history and on the nature of modernity.

This journey began in the postwar period, when Karl Löwith (1897–1973) applied the notion not to state theory and the legitimation of sovereignty but to the philosophy of history—to our whole approach to understanding the mechanics of human action over time.[2] Moving backward through the pantheon of writers and theorists of history from Jacob Burckhardt to Karl Marx to G. W. F. Hegel, through the Enlightenment to the Middle Ages to antiquity, and ending with the biblical view of history, Löwith saw an endless repetition of Christian eschatology.

The most pointed response to this view came from the philosopher and literary critic Hans Blumenberg (1920–1996), whose book-length rejoinder made clear what was at stake already in its title, *The Legitimacy of the Modern Age*.[3] The philosopher Jacob Taubes (1923–1987) was another central interlocutor, from his dissertation *Occidental Eschatology*, published proximate to Löwith's study, through his public pronouncements and private correspondences with Schmitt and Blumenberg. Beyond these key players we must also consider the contributions of German thinkers who remained in their places of former exile, especially across the Atlantic: Leo Strauss (1899–1973), Hannah Arendt (1906–1975), Theodor W. Adorno (1903–1969), Ernst Kantorowicz (1895–1963), and others.[4] The lively arguments that ensued among German-language philosophers, historians, cultural critics, political thinkers, and other intellectuals were taken to be important, because they had to do with the *legitimacy* of our democratic modernity, the very thing that the Nazis had completely obliterated and yet that now, after 1945, had to be reimagined.

This history of thinking about secularization as history is graced by a poignant and unspoken paradox. It is a particularly strange and uncommented aspect of this discussion that it was advanced almost exclusively by a group of intellectuals who were, by Nuremberg-decree definition (Nazi so-called racial law), Jews. Some did not think of themselves as Jews and were in fact Christians (Blumenberg, Löwith), and others were completely secular to the point of atheism, but all were identified as racial Jews by the Nazi regime and suffered persecution.[5] There is a single, very important exception in the jurist Carl Schmitt—a Catholic who strongly and controversially supported the Nazi regime—and this exception is another point that raises interesting questions. Is there something to be made of this salient, if prominently ignored, fact?

If we are speaking of a paradox, it is in part because the whole idea of the secularization thesis seems to be rooted in Christian notions of hierarchy and of time—the idea of progress itself is taken to be a translation of the theological eschatology, or necessary movement forward to the End of Days, Second Coming of Christ, and so on. Even the distinction of sacred and secular itself does not seem to have a clear parallel in the Jewish tradition.[6] And yet none of these thinkers strays from the script of (Christian) secularization, discusses his or her secular Judaism, or—and this is oddest of all—even seems to notice that the whole secularization thesis is emerging out of this fragmented remainder of the tremendous contribution to civilization that was German-Jewish culture and that had been, for all intents and purposes, extinguished.

My title is "The Secularization Question" to refer to this unspoken question of the relationship of Jewishness to the notion of secularization itself by invoking that noxious notion of the Jewish question that had plagued German and Jewish history since Jewish emancipation. *Die Judenfrage* was meant to be shorthand for the question or problem (*Frage* means both of these things) of Jewish presence in majority non-Jewish society. The famous "final solution" (*Endlösung*), or plan to exterminate European Jewry, was a direct response to this question or problem (*Lösung* means "solution" or "answer"). It is for this reason proper and understandable that the term, current in German since early Enlightenment and the promise of Jewish emancipation and integration, virtually disappeared from use in postwar discourse. That it recurs from time to time (without scare quotes or the modifier "so-called") in academic usage is particularly problematic, but that is not immediately relevant here. Rather, my question is whether some of the contents of the complex Jewish question might have been shuffled to the unspoken shadows of other discussions and debates, particularly the one about secularization.

In tracing the German-language discussions of secularization as a historical process, we begin to detect something like a dialectic of Jewish presence and absence such as that explored in chapter 2. The juxtaposition of history and the modern implicated the Jew in myriad and contradictory ways in the German-language discourse on modernism. On the most intuitive level, exploring the Jewish investment in the secularization thesis would be expected to lead to a linear connection, whereby endorsement of secularization I (the gradual displacement of theology with science) would render the Jewish question moot. But the Nazi sacralization of politics and the twentieth-century evidence of the error of that model of history was absolutely apparent. The challenge of secularization II—the displacement model articulated already by Schmitt in the 1920s—came to be understood, through Blumenberg most clearly, as the promise of Enlightenment, or, as he put it, the *legitimacy* of modernity. Jews were just as important in articulating the complexities of the road from Enlightenment to totalitarianism (in the famous words of Frankfurt School quasi-Jews Theodor Adorno and Max Horkheimer, the "dialectic of Enlightenment") as they were to the defense of Enlightenment and of modernity.[7] Blumenberg avoids the loaded terms for modernity that were associated with Jewishness—*die [jüdische] Moderne*—to such a degree that *Neuzeit* (as his title has it) strikes one as a placeholder for them. Not naming the modern becomes another way of leaving Jewishness unspoken.

Löwith and the Meaning of "Meaning"

The postwar discussion of secularization has been discussed in depth, largely conducted on the field of political theory (the rightful heir of the jurist Schmitt's political theology, one could argue). The context of philosophy of history is in all events not the most immediate to most of these discussions. This despite it being the territory explicitly claimed by the philosopher Karl Löwith as he wrote from his exilic home in Hartford, Connecticut. For Löwith, the moderns represent an inconsistent and inauthentic mélange of pagan and Christian impulses. What is more, in Löwith, "Christian" is—uncharacteristically for the time—Jewish and Christian (instead of the commonplace current jargon "Judeo-Christian," Löwith invokes an innovative "Hebrew-Christian" hybrid). At other times, our inheritance is a hybrid of Hebrew prophecy and Christian eschatology.

The object of Löwith's criticism is the very thing for which he offers a genealogy—to wit, the philosophy of history, defined as the "systematic interpretation of universal history in accordance with a principle by which historical events and successions are unified and directed toward an ultimate meaning."[8] From the Enlightenment moment in which Voltaire "invents" this philosophy of history in the modern sense, the principle of teleology orients itself no longer to divine providence but now to the will of man and human reason. Löwith identifies the postwar moment in which he writes his study as one that has suffered the dissolution of belief in reason and progress, leaving the philosophy of history homeless. Is this reference to the homelessness of the discipline on Löwith's first page also his earliest, unspoken reference to the exile, the refugee, the Jew? What is the relationship between this vision of universal (providential or world-historical) movement and the particular position of the persecuted minority?

Virtually never does Judaism appear explicitly in the fraught history of secularized historical thinking, except in Marx, who emerges not as a Hebrew-Christian but, in spite of himself, as a Jew:

> It is only in Marx's "ideological" consciousness that all history is a history of class struggles, while the real driving force behind this conception is a transparent messianism which has its unconscious root in Marx's own being, even in his race. He was a Jew of Old Testament stature, though an emancipated Jew of the nineteenth century and even anti-Semitic. It is the old Jewish messianism and prophetism—unaltered by two thousand years of economic history from handicraft to large-scale industry—and Jewish insistence on absolute righteousness which explain the idealistic basis of Marx's materialism. Though perverted into secular prognostication, the *Communist Manifesto* still retains the basic features of a messianic faith: "the assurance of things to be hoped for."[9]

Meaning in History seems to be a self-contradictory book in that it sets out to reveal the falsity of any search for overarching meaning in the movement of history. The meaning it exposes, in other words, is that there is no such meaning; if anything, it means something that the Western consciousness has so consistently returned to the fantasy of a forward movement of humanity. The structure of Löwith's work is meant to counter the teleological impulse by moving backward. In beginning with Burckhardt, he occupies at first the most secular of historians: the reactionary (or antirevolutionary, in all events), the historicist who, so early, resisted the pull of the master narrative of the philosophy of history.

But historicism itself is implicated in Löwith's secularization narrative, which sees both Hegel and the nineteenth-century historicists as secularizations of a theological historicism already apparent in the Christian reflections on history from the antique to the medieval period. An irony in Löwith's text is that, in rejecting the autonomy of modernity by exposing the inauthenticity of its narrative of secularization, it makes its own secularization thesis about these historical narratives.

Yet the exposure of the philosophy of history as a redressed eschatological narrative does not serve the same purposes as it does for Schmitt when interrogated more fully. As Jeffrey Andrew Barash has explicated in detail, the political implications of this book are, quite contrary to the case of Schmitt, progressive, delegitimating of the decisionist gesture.[10] The broader position from which this springs becomes explicit in Löwith's much later essays on Martin Heidegger and existentialism.[11] Löwith argued that decisionism, not only in Schmitt but in Heidegger and others, was an ultimately nihilist surrender that ironically depended on an uncritical assimilation of assumptions of the historicist positions it sought to delegitimate.[12]

Barash has also uncovered an unpublished letter to Leo Strauss from early 1933 that exposes the paradoxes of Löwith's peculiar antihistoricist historicism (in contrast to Strauss's oddly obverse method, as I explore below). Löwith argues that he wants his critique to proceed "utterly ahistorically . . . on the foundation of a radically historical consciousness."[13] By the beginning of the postwar period, Löwith and Strauss were to share the experience of persecution and exile. They were separated not only by religion but by discipline.

Leo Strauss, or Jewish People's Theological-Political Problems

Unlike Löwith, Leo Strauss was born to an orthodox Jewish family in 1899 in rural Germany. Turning to Zionism as a teenager, he went to gymnasium and university in nearby Marburg, attracted in part by the neo-Kantian Jewish philosopher Hermann Cohen (1842–1918), who also plays a part in my larger story about the Jewish history of secularization theory.[14] In 1922, Strauss went on to study in Freiburg when Edmund Husserl and his precocious assistant Martin Heidegger were there.

The Strauss work I focus on in this constellation of contributions to secularization theory is *Natural Right and History*, published in 1953 as a compilation of lectures delivered at the University of Chicago concurrent with Löwith's book in October 1949.[15] "Natural right" and "history" are far-from-complementary poles of Strauss's analysis throughout the lectures, which betray an undisguised anxiety about the degree to which modern philosophy is prepared to stand up to the tide of moral relativism he sees rising around him. That relativism is identified very strongly in the term "history," understood as German historicism (Weberian sociology is also implicated)—the nineteenth-century movement advocating local and contingent contexts of meaning as against universal and absolute truths ("natural right"). In the lectures, he dwells on modern natural right theory in Thomas Hobbes and then contrasts it to the classical notion of natural right, on his account, in Plato.

Later, Strauss's controversial work on Machiavelli (1958) argues that what he would call "anti-theological ire" in the political thinker leads to modernity.[16] This, too, is a secularization thesis: the birth of modern (instrumental) politics is the decisive break leading to modernity. The reason to focus on natural right, though, is the way it is set against German historicism (relativism): it sets reason, or the secular, on the side of the philosophical and pagan Athens and the religious (revelation) on the side of Jerusalem. What really needs to be explored here is what Strauss calls the "theologico-political predicament." In one sense, this central term for Strauss constitutes something like his own, somewhat different version of political theology; it is the term he uses in his 1965 preface to the republication of his 1930 dissertation on Spinoza's critique of religion to describe his position as a young author writing it during the Weimar Republic.[17] The theological-political problem, or conflict between the worldview of faith and revelation against that of reason and philosophy, has been seen as the core of Strauss's oeuvre and the key to a reflection on secular existence that takes Judaism merely as an example.[18] The problem for Strauss relates ultimately to legitimacy: "Is political authority to be grounded in the claims of revelation or reason, Jerusalem or Athens?"[19] While the theologico-political problem has sometimes been identified as a synonym for political theology, his rephrasing as a question, and other syntactical uses in Strauss's work, suggests a very different perspectival focus.

While my interest is really this postwar moment of historico-political reorientation, Strauss's remarks prefacing the Spinoza book (written chiefly between 1925 and 1928) foreground the centrality of the 1920s and 1930s as the setting in which the rules of the game that will be played out in coded fashion after the war are laid out. Michael A. Rosenthal demonstrates this in spades in a rich essay comparing the responses of Schmitt, Strauss, and the influential neo-Kantian Hermann Cohen to the Spinozist tradition in Weimar Germany.[20] Schmitt sees Spinoza at the root of the Weimar Republic's failure as a state representing the mythical unity of people and sovereign idealized in Hobbes's *Leviathan*. Instead, the republic's respect for pluralism has hobbled unity and authority. Hermann Cohen in some sense confirms Schmitt's suggestion that the pluralistic liberalism at the heart of this failure is a Jewish invention, according to Rosenthal, and both thinkers (differently) detest Spinoza.[21] Strauss, according to his extensive 1965 preface to the Spinoza book, at any rate, did not see the crisis of Weimar liberalism in the 1920s, but he did see, as did Schmitt, that the liberal state is not neutral.

What was the problem of Weimar liberalism for Jews, according to Strauss? It more or less accords with David Sorkin's idea of the delusion of the first generation of emancipated Jewry, a "subculture invisible to itself":[22] German Jews interpret a solution to the theologico-political predicament as a call to assimilate and be accepted and integrated, but the main body of Germany rejects this model. Here is a direct historical link of the crisis of the republic—the constitutional question as well as the question of liberalism in conflict with an image of the nation—to the Jewish question. Hence, according to both Schmitt and Strauss, the modernization of the state qua Weimar liberalism is deeply flawed, and its flaws are both Jewish in origin and fatally dangerous to Jews.

Blumenberg, or the Legitimacy of Secularization

The real challenge to Löwith's *Meaning in History*, however, was not to come for more than a decade after its publication, when Hans Blumenberg presented a paper at the Seventh German Philosophy Congress in 1962 titled "Secularization: Critique of a Category of Historical Illegitimacy," which was to become the first part of his master work, *The Legitimacy of the Modern Age* (1966). Löwith reviewed the work in the *Philosophische Rundschau* in 1968, and Blumenberg responded to Löwith's critiques in his revisions in the 1968 edition of *The Legitimacy of the Modern Age*.[23] Blumenberg and Löwith were respectful adversaries, possibly even friends, and although they were not of the same generation, as Nuremberg-decree Jews they shared a fate of persecution during the National Socialist era. Neither, as I mention above, was Jewish (Löwith was said to have been assumed to be a Protestant theologian,[24] and Blumenberg was explicit about the "shock" he experienced when organized into this category—he was permitted to write the valedictorian's speech at the gymnasium from which he graduated far ahead of the next best student but not to deliver it). He survived the war in the contingent and arbitrary ways of all survivors, escaping from a labor camp and waiting out the war in exile. The only explicit identification with this experience I could find in Blumenberg—in his long correspondence with Schmitt, for instance, it is never mentioned, although I wonder if it can be found in the extensive correspondence with Taubes[25]—was to the lost decade of intellectual work, to which he attributed his lifelong obsessive work habits. At any rate, Blumenberg's return to Germany and to the German academy was never in question. Years later, he was in fact dumbfounded (or at least feigned shock) when Hans Jonas (the German-Jewish philosopher who had also studied with Heidegger and who left Germany after the war) refused to consider his offer to replace him in his chair in philosophy at Marburg.[26]

Blumenberg is not the most transparent writer in the German language, and that seems deliberate.[27] His argumentation is plodding as a result of a combination of philosophical precision that recognizes very fine shades of nuance at every turn, on the one hand, and an extraordinarily weighty demonstration of breathtaking erudition on the other. Löwith's style, in comparison, while certainly both intellectually careful and learned, aims for the utter transparency and accessibility of an American college teacher of the mid-twentieth century. But at heart, Blumenberg's investment in the argument turns on the possibility of a relative autonomy, in a substantial rather than a functional way, of the Enlightenment moment from its medieval and theological precursors. He is willing to concede that the story modernity tells itself about a radical break from the theological is a self-deception and that so many of the categories that Löwith and Schmitt and other proponents of the secularization thesis critique as inauthentically original are beholden to theological models: the force of progress to providence, the teleology of progressive history to Christian eschatology, and so on. But over the course of many pages and examples, he illustrates the subtle difference between identifying this movement as a *transposition* of sacred concepts into presumed secular ones and recognizing that they are really *reoccupations* of those positions. The repetition is hence one of function, not of substance. In later parts of the book, Blumenberg argues for the authenticity or legitimacy of the modern gesture of *self-assertion*.

The question of which modernity was at stake for Blumenberg would seem to be an unanswerable one—certainly, it is not a question that would have made sense to Blumenberg himself. In 1987, shepherded into theoretical reassessments of critiques of the Enlightenment via an excellent English translation and lucid translator's introduction, the book was understood as invested in the ontology of knowledge: "Although *The Legitimacy* touches on many subjects its main aim is to rehabilitate the principles of inquiry that were meant to govern modern science."[28]

Others noted that Blumenberg shared with Löwith more than he rejected, in that both "think that the legitimacy or illegitimacy of the modern age is something that can be decided at the level of the history of ideas without consideration of other factors (political, economical, social, etc.)."[29] Setting aside the methodological issue for a moment, Blumenberg was also very private, if not reclusive, and it would be both difficult and somehow pointless to seek a political motive behind the intellectual project, to be sure. But is it reasonable to wonder about how the potential political implications of the work mesh with the historico-political background of its production? The ingeniously organized reoccupation hypothesis would seem to rescue modernity, if in a fragmentary way, from the claim of total self-delusion, deception, illegitimacy. Richard Rorty in his review in the *London Review of Books* notes that Blumenberg's "self-assertion" rehabilitates "all the things which Heidegger despised about the 20th century: its proliferating curiosity, its urge for technical mastery, its refusal to be interested in something larger than itself which contains it and makes it possible, and its consequent orientation toward an unknown future." The Romantic attack on Enlightenment conflates the latter's arrogant claims of self-foundation with the legitimate ideal of self-assertion.[30] The rethinking (rather than abandonment) of the secularization paradigm, in other words, defended against the modern, antiliberal currents that conspired against the last German democracy.

More important, perhaps, is that Blumenberg's reoccupation hypothesis offers a *nonessentialist* model of the historical secularization process, even as it allows for the logic of substitution that grounds the conventional secularization thesis and its close relatives. This refuted directly Schmitt's commitment to what Pini Ifergan cites Schmitt as defining (ambiguously) as a "historical identity," an essential or essentializable position to which he was deeply committed.[31] In his correspondence with Blumenberg, Schmitt questioned why the former even needed the concept of secularization.[32] Yet the biggest unanswered questions about Blumenberg's attack on the secularization theorists emanate from the question itself. That is to say, must the secularization thesis delegitimate modernity at all? Hegel's system itself was a frank secularization, and its origin in Christian eschatology was its power.[33] But Blumenberg's resistance to speculative philosophy is as strong as his allergy to Romantic antimodernism.[34] More to the point, what about the spate of Romantic modernist accounts to emerge in the interwar period and their legacies? Where is Ernst Bloch's narrative of secularization, where are Buber, Rosenzweig, Benjamin?[35] The German-Jewish radical impulse to harness the secularization narrative and perform a kind of political resacralization was, for reasons that may also be identified with the resistance to political theology, equally anathema to Blumenberg, who leaves these virtually unmentioned.[36]

In his parry with Löwith and the secularization theorists, Blumenberg might have won the battle but lost the war. His responses to Löwith always seem a step ahead of the latter, with more persuasive arguments, more evidence, and a more satisfying degree of subtlety, no doubt because of the ambivalence that inheres in his antiessentialist solutions. His rediscovery in the theory-seeking 1980s promised renewed interest in a writer whose works were declared comparable only to Jürgen Habermas's "for both path-breaking originality and widely recognized importance."[37] Yet unlike thinkers of the Frankfurt School and others of his caliber, his work did not yield a subdiscipline of inheritors of a project divided between its own philosophical and historical demands. As a deflating epigraph put it, "As a philosophical program, the intellectual enterprise initiated exactly thirty years ago with *The Legitimacy of the Modern Age* remains unfulfilled."[38]

A full investigation of the hidden Jewish question behind the contemporary debates on secularization as a historical process would have to look at the work of the Frankfurt School thinkers—especially but not exclusively Adorno—in a detailed way. In some ways, however, the contributions of Hannah Arendt may be even more important. Some of that work has already begun. A key text is *The Human Condition*, in which Arendt espouses a perspective on the "unworldly worldliness" of the modern age. Arendt is cited in Blumenberg's original text, although, as Elizabeth Brient thoroughly analyzes, he either misconstrues or deliberately distorts her categories; her appraisal of modernity in relation to the Western past and especially in contrast to antiquity is more pessimistic.[39] Samuel Moyn has offered a reading of Arendt's response to the political theology of Schmitt in what may seem at first an unlikely source: her reflections on the emergence and evolution of notions of civic freedom in *On Revolution*.[40] Arendt thus puts her own account of secularization at the very center of her political hope for the future. A third source that might be particularly promising is Arendt's early work on the Jewish Romantic salonnière Rahel Varnhagen (the first book after Arendt's dissertation, originally intended to be submitted for her habilitation, the degree after the doctorate required for professors).[41] As I discuss in the preface, this book is a complicated case that signals a kind of self-reflection at the same time as it posits a model of German-Jewish secularization. It stands as an example of the specific content of German-Jewish assimilation marshaled to the debate on the Jewish question on the eve of the National Socialist seizure of power (when all but two chapters had been completed) and then to the postwar discourses on secularization, coinciding with the book's release.

Finally, we need to return to Carl Schmitt, whose notion of political theology was the engine that got the secularization train rolling after the war ended. In some ways he seems the outlier in the large group I am discussing, not only because he was the only one who could not be defined as a Jew under the Nuremberg statutes but because his focus was on legal theory in a way that distanced him, more than any of these others, from the problem of history. But Schmitt, in spite of his association with National Socialism, was in dialogue with many (actually almost all) the Jews and quasi-Jews involved in the secularization debates—he was in literal correspondence with many of them. The secret to where he fits within an inquiry into the shadow of the Jewish question in the postwar debates on secularization lies in the relationship of his work during the Weimar and National Socialist periods to the Jewish question itself. Luckily, that inquiry has been done by Raphael Gross, and his findings along with the boisterous discussion inaugurated in its wake can be the foundation of further inquiry.[42] Gross's work definitively changed the various ways readers were for a long time able to compartmentalize Schmitt's involvement with National Socialism and scattered remarks of apparent antisemitic nature from his innovative and remarkable legal imagination. Instead, Gross demonstrates, each of the key concepts Schmitt introduced—not only the ones grounding the political theology thesis but also "the enemy," "nomos," and others—were dependent on the figure of the Jew and the long shadow of the Jewish question. This complex figuration, which Gross attributes to the particular minority Catholic milieu in which Schmitt was raised, identified the Jewish with a modernity that was minoritizing to Catholics (the Jews' enthusiastic adoption of a Protestant model of *Bildung* at the catastrophic expense of a Catholic-based education system). At the same time, the young Hegelian suspicion of Jews' insurmountable particularism merged with Catholic counterrevolutionary theory to create the consummate enemy, a convergence of disparate and partially contradictory streams of thought.[43]

It is important to stress that I am not aiming to find a secret strand shared by these authors and to attribute that strand to their varied, hidden, crypto-, or quasi-Jewishnesses. The moment of debate around the historical concept of secularization is one that was conditioned by several different historico-political contexts: reflection on the failed pluralistic republic when its founding ideas found gestation; reflection on the failed Reich, with its own failed solutions; and, not least, an incipient democratic future that had not yet taken form and that needed to take a different form from those states and societies of the past.

Questions that govern this study need to be refined in future inquiry. Is secularization a site of contesting the emancipation-assimilation pact? Does the Jewish question in fact lurk behind this fraught reconsideration of the original contribution (self-assertion), of reason, of the Enlightenment legacy and its relationship to Christian theology? What is the secularization thesis about? What was at stake for the participants in the debate, and what did their experience as "Jews" in the racial state have to do with it?

Some of the thematic fields that these questions have provoked are intriguing and need to be understood together. First, there is the overarching question of the legitimacy of *modernity* and with it, an assessment of the Enlightenment project for human beings to make a just polity for themselves. This was explicitly on the minds of many engaging in these early debates, from Löwith and Blumenberg to Strauss and Arendt. Related to this is the question of the possibility of getting beyond the paradoxes of modernity and Enlightenment that have wrought more, rather than less, violence against individuals and groups. The contributions of the Frankfurt School in this sense did not merely shatter idols of nineteenth-century faith in reason and humanity but rather opened new fields of imagining the future.

Missing in not all but in much of the analysis of secularization is its other side, the *sacralization* or *resacralization* that it so often simultaneously implies and produces. In the historical context of Germany in proximity to National Socialism, any reflection on secularization must be seen as responding in some sense to the sacralized politics of the movement and the regime. Again, this response is not at all consensual: Walter Benjamin's famous essay on the work of art in the age of mechanical reproducibility attacked the problem early on by seeking a theoretical alternative to aestheticized politics, whereas historian Hans Rothfels argues that National Socialism is, rather, a radical extension of the secularization process.[44]

These examples remind us that the secularization debates encompassed very liberal and very conservative positions, extreme even, from apologies for National Socialist dictatorship (Schmitt) and the arguable sympathy for aspects of the National Socialist worldview that the part-Jewish Hans Rothfels held even as the regime excluded him, to the conservatism of an Ernst Kantorowicz, whose famous *The King's Two Bodies* speaks immediately to the debate on political theology even though he did not engage in the theoretical discussion directly, to conservative liberalism (Strauss, Arendt), and to the progressive gambit from Löwith (liberal) to Taubes (far left) to the Frankfurt School authors.

As in all vital debates, these ideological differences were far more apparent to any of the discussants than was the common ground from which their positions sprang. What did the actors think was at stake? The historian Peter Eli Gordon has reminded readers that the dispute was really an older, philosophical one within Kantianism, an internalist, philosophical discussion related to neo-Kantianism and questions of subjectivity. This is useful. For Blumenberg in particular, and probably also Taubes, the stakes were explicitly and primarily philosophical; the legitimacy of modernity did have broad implications, but I do not argue that these were coded politico-cultural concerns. If Blumenberg were before us, he would identify with these philosophical stakes and barely recognize the ones about emergent democratic subjectivity, anti-antisemitism, and so on. But to confess this is not to say that this is all that is going on in the debate and that, especially in historical retrospect, we cannot read within it high-stakes questions of democratic subjectivity in post-Holocaust Germany.

Notes

1. Carl Schmitt, *Political Theology: Four Chapters on the Concept of Sovereignty*, trans. G. Schwab (Chicago: University of Chicago Press, 2005). The concise definition of the problem is best quoted in its full context: "All significant concepts of the modern theory of the state are secularized theological concepts not only because of their historical development—in which they were transferred from theology to the theory of the state, whereby, for example, the omnipotent god became the omnipotent lawgiver—but also because of their systematic structure, the recognition of which is necessary for a sociological consideration of these concepts. The exception in jurisprudence is analogous to the miracle in theology. Only by being aware of this analogy can we appreciate the manner in which the philosophical ideas of the state developed in the last centuries." Ibid., 36.

2. Karl Löwith, *Meaning in History* (Chicago: University of Chicago Press, 1949). Löwith equally concisely states on page 1 that the "philosophy of history is, however, entirely dependent

on theology of history, in particular on the theological concept of history as a history of fulfillment and salvation."

3. Hans Blumenberg, *Die Legitimität der Neuzeit* (Frankfurt am Main, Germany: Suhrkamp, 1966).

4. Others that could be counted in this discussion include Eric Voegelin, also a refugee from Nazism, and the German-Jewish philosopher Hans Jonas, both of whom made careers in the United States as exiles and both of whom remained there.

5. Pini Ifergan refers to the first two of these as representative of the understudied category of "residual Jews." See P. Ifergan, "Karl Löwith and Hans Blumenberg: 'Neither Jewish nor German,'" unpublished paper, https://www.academia.edu/19862741/Karl_Löwith_and_Hans_Blumenberg_Neither_Jewish_nor_German_ (accessed February 1, 2017). One I mention above, whose view of Western (secularized) eschatology ties it explicitly to Hebraic sources, is Jacob Taubes, whose dissertation, "Abendländische Eschatologie," also emerged briefly after the war, in 1947. Jacob Taubes, *Abendländische Eschatologie* (Bern: Francke, 1947). Taubes had extensive correspondence with others discussed here, notably Blumenberg and Schmitt. David Ratmoko's preface situates Taubes's work in the triad with Schmitt and Löwith in the following way: Schmitt's notion of political theology and Löwith's philosophy of history are both active in the work (indeed, Löwith and Taubes read each other's work); Schmitt ultimately (and infamously) opts for the notion of an authoritarian *katechon*, a divine legitimation of power that restrains apocalypse, whereas Taubes sees its revolutionary potential. Löwith in his turn is also critical of the secularization of eschatology, failing to see the distinction of the spiritual, apocalyptic, and potentially redemptive tradition from an imperial, *katechontic* one. See David Ratmoko, "Preface," in *Occidental Eschatology*, by Jacob Taubes (Stanford, CA: Stanford University Press, 2009), xv–xvii.

6. I use "seem to," rather than "has" or "does not have," because this is a more complicated question than I first thought. As my colleague Ariel Mayse pointed out to me, the traditions interweave and overlap in ways that complicate identifying our notion of secular and secularization as emergent from Christian categories, and while it is true that these dichotomies are foreign to traditional Judaism, they would be unfamiliar to premodern Christian thought as well. The interventions of Leora Batnitzky and Talal Asad are relevant to this observation. See Leora Faye Batnitzky, *How Judaism Became a Religion: An Introduction to Modern Jewish Thought* (Princeton, NJ: Princeton University Press, 2011); and Talal Asad, *Formations of the Secular: Christianity, Islam, Modernity* (Stanford, CA: Stanford University Press, 2003).

7. See Max Horkheimer and Theodor W. Adorno, *Dialectic of Enlightenment* (New York: Continuum, 1995).

8. Löwith, *Meaning*, 1.

9. Ibid., 44.

10. See Jeffrey Andrew Barash, "The Sense of History: On the Political Implications of Karl Löwith's Concept of Secularization," *History and Theory* 37, no. 1 (1998): 69–82. The explicit critique of Schmitt's decisionism had emerged already in 1935 in a text Löwith published under a pseudonym with the title "Politischer Dezisionismus," republished in a slightly different version as "Der okkasionelle Dezisionismus von Carl Schmitt," *Sämtliche Schriften* 8, no. 57 (1984): 32–71, and as "The Occasional Decisionism of Carl Schmitt," trans. G. Steiner, in *Martin Heidegger and European Nihilism*, ed. R. Wolin (New York: Columbia University Press, 1995), 137–169.

11. Karl Löwith, "Heidegger: Problem and Background of Existentialism," *Social Research* 15, no. 3 (1948): 345–369; Karl Löwith, "Nature, History, and Existentialism," *Social Research* 19, no. 1 (1952): 79–94; Arkadiusz Górnisiewicz, "Karl Löwith and Leo Strauss on Modernity, Secularization, and Nihilism," in *Modernity and What Has Been Lost: Considerations*

on the Legacy of Leo Strauss, ed. Arkadiusz Górnisiewicz and Pawel Armada (South Bend, IN: St. Augustine's Press, 2010), 99.

12. Barash phrases this irony succinctly: "For these three authors [Schmitt, Heidegger, and Friedrich Gogarten] the decline of the historical process disqualified it as a source of normative values, necessitating radical decision in the face of nothingness. And yet it is precisely in their attempts to break with Marxian and liberal assumptions concerning the movement of history that the decisionist theories show their profound dependence on these assumptions and, from Löwith's standpoint, on a long heritage of reflection on historical meaning originating in Christian eschatology, of which these assumptions are the secularized expression." Barash, "Sense of History," 80.

13. Ibid., 75–76. The letter on which Barash reports, dated January 8, 1933, was found in the Leo Strauss archive, Special Collection Research Center, University of Chicago Library.

14. Cohen had stopped teaching regularly at Marburg by the time Strauss studied there, and Michael Zank states that Strauss never met Cohen personally, although the pull of this towering figure in Jewish philosophy is undeniable. Zank, "Introduction," in *The Early Writings (1921–1932)*, by Leo Strauss, trans. and ed. Michael Zank (Albany: State University of New York Press, 2006), 6. A key work here is Hermann Cohen, *Religion der Vernunft aus den Quellen des Judentums* (1919; repr., Frankfurt am Main, Germany: J. Kauffmann, 1929).

15. Leo Strauss, *Natural Right and History* (Chicago: University of Chicago Press, 1953).

16. Leo Strauss, *Thoughts on Machiavelli* (Chicago: University of Chicago Press, 1958); Leo Strauss, *What Is Political Philosophy? And Other Studies* (Chicago: University of Chicago Press, 1988), 44.

17. Leo Strauss, *Spinoza's Critique of Religion* (New York: Schocken, 1965), 1.

18. See Heinrich Meier, *Leo Strauss and the Theologico-Political Problem*, trans. Marcus Brainard (Cambridge: Cambridge University Press, 2006); see also Steven B. Smith, "Leo Strauss: Between Athens and Jerusalem," in "The Thought of Leo Strauss," special issue, *Review of Politics* 53, no. 1 (1991): 75–99. Strauss's essay that appeared in *Commentary* decades later was drafted at the same postwar moment as Löwith's book; see Leo Strauss, "Jerusalem and Athens: Some Introductory Reflections," *Commentary*, June 1, 1967, https://www.commentarymagazine.com/articles/jerusalem-and-athens-some-introductory-reflections.

19. Leo Strauss, "Preface to Hobbes politische Wissenshaft," in *Jewish Philosophy and the Crisis of Modernity*, ed. Kenneth Hart Green (Albany: State University of New York Press, 1997), 453–456.

20. Michael A. Rosenthal, "Spinoza and the Crisis of Liberalism in Weimar Germany," *Hebraic Political Studies* 3, no. 1 (2008): 94–112. See also Benjamin Lazier, "On the Origins of 'Political Theology': Judaism and Heresy between the World Wars," *New German Critique* 3, no. 105 (2008): 143–164.

21. Rosenthal, "Spinoza and the Crisis," 102. The key Cohen text for Rosenthal here is Hermann Cohen, "Spinoza über Staat und Religion, Judentum und Christentum," in *Jüdische Schriften*, vol. 3, ed. Bruno Strauss (Berlin: Arno Press, 1924), 290–372.

22. David Jan Sorkin, *The Transformation of German Jewry, 1780–1840* (Detroit, MI: Wayne State University Press, 1987), 140.

23. The standard account of the debate has become that offered by Blumenberg's English translator, Robert Wallace, in "Progress, Secularization and Modernity: The Löwith-Blumenberg Debate," *New German Critique*, no. 22 (Winter 1981): 63–79. See also Robert Wallace, "Introduction to Blumenberg," *New German Critique*, no. 32 (Spring–Summer, 1984): 93; and Robert Wallace, "Translator's Introduction," in *The Legitimacy of the Modern Age*, by Hans Blumenberg, trans. Robert M. Wallace (Cambridge, MA: MIT Press, 1985), xi–xxxi.

24. See Górnisiewicz, "Karl Löwith and Leo Strauss," 94.

25. Hans Blumenberg and Carl Schmitt, *Briefwechsel 1971–1978 und weitere Materialien*, ed. Alexander Schmitz and Marcel Lepper (Frankfurt am Main, Germany: Suhrkamp, 2007); and Hans Blumenberg and Jacob Taubes, *Briefwechsel 1961–1981 und weitere Materialien* (Berlin: Suhrkamp, 2013). In the fierce and protracted debate with Carl Schmitt, Pini Ifergan contends, "Schmitt contrived to trap Blumenberg in his own problematics and compelled him to take part in the theological debate over the enduring presence of Christianity in the political-public sphere." Pini Ifergan, "Cutting to the Chase: Carl Schmitt and Hans Blumenberg on Political Theology and Secularization," *New German Critique*, no. 111 (2010): 157. Thus, Blumenberg was relegated to the side of the debate against Schmitt populated by Christians that objected to Schmittian political theology. See also Ifergan's discussion of Schmitt's notion of identity in relation to secularization (161). This is the clearest contrast to what I am calling Blumenberg's antiessentialist alternative formulation.

26. Pini Ifergan quotes (but unfortunately does not cite) the letter from Jonas and the response from Blumenberg in "Neither Jewish nor German," 3–4.

27. See Elizabeth Brient, *The Immanence of the Infinite: Hans Blumenberg and the Threshold to Modernity* (Washington, DC: Catholic University Press, 2002), esp. 6–8. This opacity applies as much to Blumenberg's theoretical agenda as it does to the even more remote political background to his work. Brient does much to illuminate what is at stake in the work and to put it in dialogue with Hannah Arendt's account of modern worldliness.

28. Laurence Dickey, "Blumenberg and Secularization: 'Self-Assertion' and the Problem of Self-Realizing Teleology in History," *New German Critique*, no. 41 (Spring–Summer 1987): 152. Tracie Matysik phrases her similar point in a way that does more to suggest its culture-political content: "Blumenberg's motivation was to defend elements of European rational-philosophical and scientific thought against prevalent secularization theses that found modern concepts to be often unacknowledged repetitions of theological categories." T. Matysik, "Hans Blumenberg's Multiple Modernities: A Spinozist Supplement to *Legitimacy of the Modern Age*," *Germanic Review* 90 (2015): 23.

29. Elías José Palti, "In Memoriam: Hans Blumenberg (1920–1996), an Unended Quest," *Journal of the History of Ideas* 58, no. 3 (1997): 508–509. The charge that Blumenberg was working, in spite of himself, squarely in the tradition of German idealism was made already by Martin Jay in his review of the English translation: Martin Jay, *History and Theory* 24, no. 2 (1985): 183–196, esp. p. 194.

30. Richard Rorty, "Against Belatedness," *London Review of Books* 5, no. 11 (1983), https://www.lrb.co.uk/v05/n11/richard-rorty/against-belatedness.

31. Pini Ifergan, "Cutting to the Chase," 161.

32. Blumenberg and Schmitt, *Briefwechsel 1971–1978*.

33. See Robert B. Pippin, "Blumenberg and the Modernity Problem," *Review of Metaphysics* 40, no. 3 (1987): 540.

34. Ibid.

35. Any discussion of these together as a single, and singularly secular-German-Jewish, strain of intellectual history is beholden to the influential work of Michael Löwy. See especially Michael Löwy, *Redemption and Utopia: Libertarian Judaism in Central Europe* (Stanford, CA: Stanford University Press, 1992).

36. See Martin Jay, "Review: *The Legitimacy of the Modern Age* by Hans Blumenberg; Robert M. Wallace," *History and Theory* 24, no. 2 (1985): 192–193: "Perhaps because Blumenberg is so sensitive to the debunking function of the secularization thesis, he underestimates its possibly legitimating role in the hands of those who want to preserve the emancipatory moment in the pre- and even counter-Enlightenment past for radical purposes in the present."

37. Wallace, "Introduction to Blumenberg," 93.
38. Palti, "In Memoriam," 524.
39. Hannah Arendt, *The Human Condition* (Chicago: University of Chicago Press, 1958); Elizabeth Brient, "Hans Blumenberg and Hannah Arendt on the 'Unworldly Worldliness' of the Modern Age," *Journal of the History of Ideas* 61, no. 3 (2000): 513–530; Brient, *Immanence of the Infinite*, 74–93.
40. Hannah Arendt, *On Revolution* (New York: Viking, 1965); Samuel Moyn, "Hannah Arendt on the Secular," *New German Critique*, no. 105 (Fall 2008): 71–96.
41. Hannah Arendt, *Rahel Varnhagen: Lebensgeschichte einer deutschen Jüdin aus der Romantik* (Zurich, Switzerland: Piper, 1981).
42. Raphael Gross, *Carl Schmitt and the Jews: The "Jewish Question," the Holocaust, and German Legal Theory*, trans. Joel Golb (Madison: University of Wisconsin Press, 2000).
43. Gross, *Schmitt and the Jews*, esp. 9–13, 226–229.
44. Walter Benjamin, "The Work of Art in the Age of Mechanical Reproduction," in *Illuminations: Essays and Reflections*, ed. Hannah Arendt, trans. Harry Zohn (New York: Schocken, 1968). For more on Rothfels, see, e.g., Christiane Blume, "Transformationen eines Historikers—Hans Rothfels' Weg aus dem Dunstkreis der Volksgeschichte zur leuchtenden Symbolfigur der Nachkriegshistoriografie," *H-Soz-Kult*, September 28, 2004, http://www.hsozkult.de/article/id/artikel-525. Richard Steigmann-Gall argues, pace Rothfels, that the Nazis sacralized the state through their own nefarious secularization and sacralization program. See Richard Steigmann-Gall, *The Holy Reich: Nazi Conceptions of Christianity, 1919–1945* (New York: Cambridge University Press, 2003).

Part II
Troubled Cases: Canon and Genre

4 Edith Stein's Passing Gestures
Intimate Histories, Empathic Portraits

Canons and Contexts

In a mass at Saint Peter's Square on October 11, 1998, Pope John Paul II elevated the Jewish-born philosopher, nun, and Holocaust victim Edith Stein, from that point on Sister Teresa Benedicta of the Cross, to sainthood.[1] The announcement reawakened the controversy surrounding Stein's 1987 beatification, which relied on a definition of her murder at Auschwitz as a martyrdom of Christian faith, a declaration reiterated in the announcement of her elevation. On both occasions, the debate was described as a question of appropriate memorialization, or of "Stein's proper place in history."[2] Yet this was not the beginning of the dilemma of identifying the proper context for the Edmund Husserl student whose writings spanned phenomenology, feminism, theology, hagiography, and mysticism. The recurring debate points, rather, to a persistent and difficult problem of the negotiation of subject positions and contexts that remained salient throughout Stein's own works and life and that lingers today.

We begin at the end. At the Breslau railroad yard on August 7, 1942, as German soldiers on their way to the Russian front were waiting for their train to be refueled, they had a passing encounter with the prisoners on board a freight train bound for Auschwitz. The report of one of the soldiers asserts that the train had originated in Holland and that when the sliding doors were opened they revealed a squalid interior, with a huddled mass of people penned within, including a woman in a nun's habit. In this report the nun exchanges words with the soldier; indeed, she is the only passenger represented as having a voice. She speaks first of the miserable conditions in the car and then looks to Breslau in the distance and says, "This is my home. I'll never see it again.... We are going to our death." The shaken soldier asks whether the others know this terrible secret. The peaceful figure shakes her head—it is better that they remain in ignorance. They are in darkness, she is in light; they are squatting on the floor, she is standing; they are "listless," she is pensive and composed.[3]

In this, as in other accounts of the last days of Edith Stein, the philosopher and Carmelite nun is portrayed in a manner that would pave the way toward her canonization: "resigned" and "composed," "the glow of a saintly Carmelite radiat[ing] from her eyes," a "heavenly atmosphere" emanating from her

Christian faith and insight, prepared for whatever would come while those around her were ignorant and frightened, comforting and resolved among a mass of confused and despairing victims. "Every time I think of her sitting in the barracks [of the Dutch detention camp]," reads another testimony, "the same picture comes to mind: a Pietà without the Christ."[4]

These portraits of Edith Stein already point to the potential controversy of her canonization. A paradigmatic image of the historical Jewish tragedy, the crowded freight car on its way to the death camps, has become a Pietà without a Christ; the story of the deportations and exterminations is diverted into a narrative of Catholic salvation and the making of a saint.[5] The pope's beatification of Stein in Cologne in 1987 met resistance on a number of levels but most pointedly because it rested, as beatifications in the absence of miracles must, on the definition of her extermination at Auschwitz as a Christian martyrdom.[6] The terms used by opponents are telling: the Catholic appropriation of the Shoah, the "Christianization" or even "universalization" of the Holocaust.[7]

The figure of Edith Stein is problematic in still other ways that might be particularly useful to broader inquiries of Jewish history and German-Jewish identity, and yet this problematic status has impeded such consideration. Indeed, her inclusion on the list of central German-Jewish cultural figures of the twentieth century has been disputed on the basis of her embrace of Catholic faith and entrance into the Carmelite order. Similarly, while her status as the first German woman to serve as a professorial assistant in philosophy and her continued engagement with the woman question might suggest her inclusion in another canon, that of contemporary feminist history, the evident essentialism in her writing on the status of woman has apparently encumbered that move, while the same engagement has been troubling for those Catholic writers who read her feminist biblical interpretation as unorthodox.[8] Intellectual historians and literary critics who might be interested in the work of one of Husserl's most promising students have not known what to do with a phenomenology that moved seamlessly into Catholic theology and mysticism.

I suggest that it is not accidental that Stein's status is problematic in each of these very different ways; furthermore, this uneasy status is itself useful for addressing questions of identity politics that may be of interest to contemporary observers. This is an argument not for revising our canons to include more marginal elements but instead for highlighting how an exceptional, idiosyncratic figure can call for a rethinking of categories of subjectivity, canonicity, and contextuality that the focus on representative German-Jewish figures may well obscure. In Stein's case, as I argue in chapter 1, an analytic framework placing her between the poles of assimilation and Jewish communal identity is utterly useless. How subjects are situated in—and situate themselves within—historical contexts is obviously a central issue for the cultural historian, and yet the complexity of those processes is stunningly underexamined. It is worthwhile to bring the critical interest in identity (in this case, Stein's self-identification as a Jew or as a martyr for her "unbelieving" people) back to the culture-historical study of contextualities: how does a subject's consciousness of her placement within history work to inflect or control contexts of reception? How do historical actors work to inform or to trouble the future memory of themselves?[9] While the term "passing" is a loaded one, evoking the suspicion of oppressed individuals' inauthentic appropriation of privileged or majority identities, it also contains associations that disturb assumptions of authentic, irrevocable, and unexchangeable identity. Stein's phenomenological account of empathy, in her 1916 dissertation on the topic, offers a model of "passing" between self and other that is prerequisite to the experience of the self.[10] In manifold ways, the figure of Edith Stein seems to pass among categories assumed to be hostile to one another, so that her appropriation within scholarly feminist, German-Jewish, philosophical, and theological canons is necessarily fraught. I am interested in the degree to which this troubled status prefigured the agendas of late twentieth-century canonizers—secular and clerical—and belonged to an unruly self-representation of Stein's own making.

To identify the structure of this self-fashioning and its implications for the positioning of subjects within contexts, it is necessary to focus on the very tensions that most contemporary writing on Stein has felt obliged to resolve. Stein's self-portraits brush against the grain of familiar models of identity and representation, just as she seems to offer intimate histories that, in contrast to the rhetorical strategy of most memoir writing, resist being understood as personal narratives representing grand narratives in microcosm. Thus, I want to explore how the intimate history, in its rejection of consonance with forceful master narratives, is not a subgenus of history as much as it is a challenge to it. In this sense it is similar to the "literary self-portrait" that, according to Michel Beaujour, operates on a different level from the autobiography or memoir: "It is no longer a question of standardizing the individual's memory to fit a cultural model but, on the contrary, of working with fragments that do not conform to the stereotype and out of which the subject can fashion an idiosyncratic ensemble of metaphors where he will find himself (again) or get lost."[11] In Stein's case, it is valuable to trace how this self-fashioning takes form and to keep in mind the contexts, or big pictures, it reconfigures in the process. These include the narratives supporting a German academic context that systematically marginalized a promising philosopher on the basis of gender, a religious Christian theological context that identified Judaism either as completely alien or else as a necessary precursor to be overcome, and most saliently, the rise of the racial state. Both instances and instruments of these subversions can be identified in Stein's rather idiosyncratic formulations of phenomenological empathy at one end (her 1916 dissertation under Husserl) and in the equally original theological and mystical writings from the end of her life at the other. Centrally, I refer to the rich and underread text from late in Stein's life, her draft memoir later published as *Aus dem Leben einer jüdischen Familie (Life in a Jewish Family)*.[12] This text, more than any other, has informed my notion of intimate history.

Family Portraits

Born in Breslau on Yom Kippur in 1891, Stein was raised in a ritually observant family of seven children. Her father died before she was two years old. As a young teenager, Stein lost her faith in Jewish religion and was absorbed by intellectual pursuits. Following her early ambition to study women's law, she became interested in philosophy and took up study with Husserl in Freiburg, completing her doctorate in 1916 and becoming his assistant—the first woman *Assistentin* in philosophy in Germany—in 1917. This promising academic position soon yielded disappointment: she felt neglected by Husserl, who knew of her limited academic prospects as a woman, and so she voluntarily dropped the assistantship early the next year. Between 1920 and 1932 she made four attempts to continue to the advanced degree required for professorship, without success.[13] It may be salutary not to succumb too quickly to the temptation to read Stein's turn to Catholic religion—and eventually the cloth—in terms of this academic and intellectual marginalization. Yet the forms taken in her thought from this point on cannot be seen apart from this experience of exclusion, particularly those relating to the external world of society and of history and their complex relation to spiritual life. In any event, an interest in Christian thought and mysticism inspired by religious friends was set aflame one night in 1921, according to her own much-repeated account, as she read straight through the autobiography of Teresa of Ávila, and her decision to convert to Catholicism was sealed. Then followed a brief career in Catholic education in Speyer and Munster, until this option was barred by the Nazi racial laws of 1933. In response to this situation, she was finally accepted into the Cologne Carmel, which she had tried to enter some years before. She remained in Carmel the rest of her life and was transferred to another convent in Echt, the Netherlands, in 1939, in light of increased persecution of ethnic Jews in Germany. As the war went on, her efforts to transfer to a Swiss Carmel failed. In August of 1942, a missive of the Dutch bishops protesting the Nazi deportation of Dutch Jews was answered by the detention of Jewish converts at Westerbork and their ensuing deportation to the east. The train from Westerbork to Auschwitz—the same one in the likely apocryphal story with which I began—is believed to have traveled over the stations of Stein's life: from Holland to Cologne, over Speyer and Breslau.

In turning to Stein's memoir *Life in a Jewish Family*, we turn to the twin concepts empathic portraiture and intimate history. Central to these is the sublation of several sets of oppositions: self and other (through empathy, the subject of Stein's dissertation), private experience and official narratives or histories (through intimate accounts such as *Life in a Jewish Family*), and synchronic image and diachronic narrative (portraits and histories). Indeed, the stated intention of Stein's memoir, written chiefly in the first year after the Nazi seizure of power, is to provide an alternative history of German-Judaism, a counternarrative to the National Socialist vision of Jews in German history.[14] But Stein's narrative is also generically informed by an early modern central European tradition of writing on Jewish life and Judaism by apostates; the rhetorical force of knowing the Jewish world from within and then coming out of it into the light was an important strategy of Judaism's Christian opponents.[15] In her foreword, Stein subtly articulates this dual source of her book: a priest's suggestion that Stein commit to writing her "insider's" knowledge of Judaism is first taken up years later, when an unbearable Nazi image of Jews dominates the scene and calls for repudiation.[16] Indeed the book's title, *Aus dem Leben einer jüdischen Familie*, syntactically contains this double movement, claiming authenticity—*aus* points in this sense to an originary source—while also suggesting that the author has emerged from that world, come out of it. Of course one can take the expression *aus dem Leben* (from the life of) in a more pedestrian sense, and yet the memoir constantly returns to this structure of passing between intimate, immediate experience and the perceptual experience of the oppositional outsider. Attention is called to the binary of internality and externality, in and out, a structure of identity and alienation that is dissipated within this intimate history so that it seems as if the goal of intimate history itself were to do away with these dichotomies, or to render senseless the segregation of the most private experience from public narratives of peoples and politics.

Aus dem Leben is a kind of autobiography, but its impetus and its first chapter is the story of another life, that of Edith's mother, Auguste Courant Stein. The powerful identification between mother and daughter is unmistakable in the text. On the other hand, this most important relationship in Edith Stein's life is also identified as conflicted and adversarial: it is the single obstacle to her surrender to Christian faith. Fearing her mother's reaction, she keeps her Catholic enlightenment a secret at first; then she conceals her desire to become a nun and her sister's subsequent conversion. The narrative construction of this mother as an external obstacle to Christian faith while also a model very clearly prefiguring it is a symptomatic gesture of Stein's memoir text, and one that is worth tracing more closely.

This brings us to the shift alluded to above between histories (or narratives) and images (or portraits). Stein claimed her first idea for the memoir was to tell her mother's story, to reproduce her inexhaustible storytelling. But the "stream of memories" could not be domesticated in a narrative that would offer "order and clarity" to the reader standing outside Jewish life; tangible and reliable facts proved impossible to verify.[17] This apologia serves to prepare the reader for a narrative that will not only treat foreign and unfamiliar experience but call for an innovation of form. In place of the expected narrative, Stein offers short sketches of her mother's reminiscences, out of which should emerge a "life image" of her mother.[18] This transition from narrative to image conforms to what a French critical tradition has identified as a subversive move (sometimes unconscious) in certain literary self-portrayals, in which fragmented analogic correspondences, cross-references, superimpositions, and collage disrupt the logical sequence of autobiography or historical narrative.[19] This move is not incidentally related to the structure of epiphany, in which mechanically sequenced logic is displaced by more synchronic revelation.[20]

Thus, Stein foregrounds the element of intimacy in her own text and, with the pretext of apologizing for it, breaks down the boundary between rational narrative and impressionistic image making. In fact the Nazi story this narrative is intended to repudiate is also principally a series of images. The speeches and programmatic writings of the bearers of power had constructed an unbearable portrait of the Jew: "From these sources, as though from a concave mirror [*Hohlspiegel*], a horrendous caricature [*Zerrbild*] looked out at us."[21] The distorted image, or horrendous caricature (*Zerrbild*), the image from a distorting mirror (*Zerrspiegel*), is intended to be shattered by the detailed picture of life in a Jewish family that follows the preface. The text is clearly written with a Christian German public in mind, although these references may also imply the text's utility as a mirror for Jews, like the texts called "mirrors" for Renaissance princes—a model, a strategy, and a warning on how to behave. Already on this first page, Stein admits a certain antisemitism or Jewish self-hatred into her text that continues throughout: the caricatures were "possibly copied from living models," the manifest examples of "powerful [Jewish] capitalists, insolent [Jewish] literati, or restless [Jewish revolutionaries]."[22] She objects principally to the thesis that the exaggerated image applies to all Jews as an inevitable consequence of Jewish blood. But more is at stake in both Stein's conjuring of antisemitic images and her dissimulation of them than an answer to National Socialist propaganda. Built into the claim of painting a portrait from the inside out is the possibility of constructing an alternative Jewish image and self-image, reconcilable with German Christianity, indeed a Jewishness that passes into figures German and Christian and that allows these to pass in turn into itself.

Empathy, in Passing

Stein's portrait of a Jewish family is carefully engineered to be an intensely empathic text, and for this reason I return to the complex dynamics of empathy outlined in Stein's dissertation, *On the Problem of Empathy*. For now it is worth noting that the phenomenological term "empathy" (*Einfühlen*) is conceptually and philologically linked and simultaneously contrasted to the related term "sympathy" (*Mitfühlen*). The terms share the root "feeling" and differ in the prepositional prefixes of *ein* (in, or into) and *mit* (with). "Sympathy"—"feeling-with," or "fellow feeling"—may have noble origins and charitable outcomes, but it also guarantees the discreteness of self and other: one does not feel or move or act "with" oneself, of course, but with another.[23] Empathy ("feeling-into") on the other hand is an experience of being led by the foreign experience, of identifying *as* another.[24] In empathy Stein finds a moment of fusion of perception and sensation, a "double mode of experiencing" that overcomes dichotomies of inside and outside, native and foreign. Thus, these Jewish portraits are not designed as sympathetic depictions of a fellow community on German soil but seduce the reader into seeing herself in portraits that nonetheless retain the mark of an exoticized other. The figure of the Jew in this text thus passes into figures of Christian faith, of German patriotism, or of German bourgeois values at respective moments; similar moves in Stein's feminist texts, as we will see, perform provocative passing gestures in the field of gender. Thus, empathy informs a narrative pattern in Stein's texts in relation to the triptych of spiritual, national, and gender identities, each troubled within by empathic alternations with their others, and stressed from without by hostile Weimar and Nazi contexts.

The first section of the memoir, the one focusing on the memories of Auguste Courant, stresses images of piety, respectability, and German loyalty. In the earliest description of Stein's great-grandfather's home, she focuses on his strictness as father and teacher, the patriarchal order of the home, and the prayer room in the family house where sons-in-law and patriarch congregated for intimate worship. The great-grandmother, too, is described as a "truly pious woman" whose religiosity is closely associated with her intense suffering; she concludes each prayer with the plea, "Lord, send us only as much as we can bear." If these romantic constructions of Jewish piety contain more than a touch of orientalism, which Stein continues in her descriptions of Jewish religion throughout the memoir, they resist antisemitic and older anti-Jewish stereotypes of Judaic religion as mechanical, legalistic, and empty ritual. The reader senses a touching authenticity of faith, even if it seems a naive and somehow unresolved faith. It is a primordial Christianity, a Judaism to remind the reader of Christian faith's Jewish roots. Hence, in her lengthy description of the Passover observance she points out to "unaware" Christians that the feast "continues to be celebrated today in the identical manner in which it was celebrated by our Lord with his disciples when he instituted the Blessed Sacrament and took leave of his followers."[25] This fact colors the exoticizing description of the Passover rituals, which suddenly seem more immediate to the life of Christ than they are alien to modern Christians. The theme of secularization is at work in the three-page description of holiday practices, as Stein confesses relief at having others perform religious duties after her "enlightenment," which she put in skeptical quotation marks, and the passing of her father leaves the duty of prayer recitation in the unreliable and disrespectful hands of assimilated brothers.

So in this sense, the modern Christian's remoteness from the mystical moment of the Sacrament or Passover ritual is mimetically reproduced in the assimilated Jewish environment. In spite of the visceral response of many Jewish observers to the figure of the Jewish nun, Stein's turn to Christianity was never described by herself in terms of disavowal; to the contrary, she insisted there was close kinship between her Catholic spirituality and her Jewishness—but as in other close kinships, the relationship was complicated.[26]

In the same passage of the text, for instance, two references to Jewish ritual serve as vessels for figures that are not supposed to share a single space: the Jew and the Christ. The first of these is the paschal lamb, the sacrificial creature so symbolically significant for both ancient Judaism and early Christianity. To some degree, it could be argued, even this strange overlaying of symbols proceeds from a convention in the anti-Jewish theological literature, granting a primordial authenticity to the ancient Jewish tradition whose manifest legitimate heir is the Christian one. Even stranger is the reference in Stein's description of Yom Kippur to the "'scapegoat' [*Sündenbock*] upon whose head, symbolically, the sins of all the people had been laid [and which was] driven out into the desert." Stein resists sanitizing Jewish ritual as kindred religious celebration and locates it instead as a site of authentic and originary Christian experience, even as Christ's own experience. Just as the Carmelite nun knew that the task of the Christian life was to enter the life of Jesus himself, her Christian readers were positioned to see Jewish religion as a key to revelation rather than as alien to Christian faith. The word "scapegoat" conjures the figure of a vessel for the sins of others that is ritually expunged or sacrificed, and it is a vessel that in this textual setting contains several objects corresponding to parallel historical moments: the original creature sacrificed by the ancient Jewish community, the Christ (whether as scapegoat of the Jews or as the lamb who dies for the sins of humanity), and now the Jews, victims of a contemporary cleansing ritual uncannily identical to the one they created. Stein's own birth on the Day of Atonement is given some gravity in this passage and not only allows her own prophetic identification with the *Sündenbock* but also is the key to her special intimacy with her mother. The complexity of this mother-daughter relation rests on this tension between identification and opposition. Stein's piety is her mother's, but the latter's more instinctive and unprocessed faith is transformed (or converted) in the daughter into a Catholicism run through with phenomenological philosophy, with thinking.

As striking as the ellipsis from Jewish to Christian identity is in this portrait, the Jewish family's intimate bond with Germanness is no less impressive, similarly containing the radical ambivalences of double gestures that subvert no more than they collude. In particular, we continually encounter a representation of a fervent and threatened German patriotism. The most familiar moments of this representation include listing relatives who sacrificed their lives in World War I and the tale of the Jewish hero uncle who slipped through enemy lines in disguise to save important papers and enlist in the army.[27] Descriptions such as these were common in the efforts of Jews to contradict the *völkisch* challenge to their Germanness in the Weimar Republic and the Third Reich. But this sympathetic model of Jewish Germanness (or the me-too structure of such descriptions) is different in kind from the patriotism of Edith's mother and of herself: a veteran defending his country is somehow standing apart from it. "I can be in love with Germany," Edith wrote to Roman Ingarden in 1917, "so little as I can be in love with myself, for I am indeed [Germany] itself."[28] Thus, from the sympathetic assertion of fellow-German patriotism, Stein passes, or claims to pass, into Germanness, to elide herself and her country; in doing so, she escapes the possibility of "loving" her country in the way that she might love someone else's. As with Jewish religion, a powerful identification is constructed in the text as inherited from her mother yet refracted in a complicated way through the empathic dynamic. Her mother is the most zealous of German nationalists, setting her wedding song to the tune of "The Watch on the Rhine," and "she finds it incomprehensible that anyone should dare to dispute her German identity."[29]

Stein recounts the story of the loss of the homeland after World War I, when a plebiscite turned the Courant hometown of Lublinitz over to Poland.[30] The family's patriotic struggle to keep the German homeland, and the impossibility of their staying once it was no longer German, operate in this text in the same way the figure of the *Auslandsdeutsche* and *Volksdeutsche* (ethnic German communities outside the Reich) operated within Nazi propaganda leading up to 1939. That is, the issue of ethnic Germans facing the loss of their German homeland or the integrity of their German identities to Poles, Czechs, and Russians played an important role in the inscription of German national identity in the heartland, and thus those ethnic Germans played a role quite out of proportion to their numbers. A certain priority was given those Germans whose nationality was under fire and who could not take their national identities for granted or who had to fight for it. In Stein's text, the Polish threat to the German Courants is set against a second and present challenge to the Courants' German legacy represented by those racialists who "should dare to dispute her German identity." It is not that Auguste Courant was more German than the Germans; but by empathizing with the figure of Auguste Courant, a German identity under siege, the reader is invited to come to a more active realization of his or her Germanness—empathically to experience the terrible possibility of its slipping away even as one, as German Christian outsider, sees why it is slipping away from these Jews. This empathic portrait is structured to allow an experience of identification with the plight of the othered figure at the same moment that its otherness is brought into relief.

Empathy, as a section title of Stein's dissertation asserts, is the condition of possibility of constituting the individual self (*das Ich*).[31] In making this point, Stein defines the dual nature of the body with twin terms: the *Leib*, or living body, which is the subject of immediate or "primordial" experience, and the *Körper*, or physical body, such as those bodies one perceives around oneself. But the experience of the living body is not purely primordial, it is itself subject to the empathic relation. The experience of touching involves both the sensation of the living body—internal sensation—and the perception of my hand touching an object that I know from seeing other bodies touching other objects—an act that I can therefore identify as "touching." This dual nature of corporeal experience is called "reiterated empathy" and "is at the same time the condition making possible that mirror-image-like givenness of myself" that belongs to a host of primordial experiences, such as memory, fantasy, expectation, and so forth. All are "primordial as present experience though non-primordial in content."[32] The double mode of experiencing is crucial to the possibility of emergence of "the pure self" or "the pure 'I,'" which, without the empathic relation to other selves, cannot be given to itself—its "selfness" first appears through the empathic encounter with "the otherness of the other."[33]

It is obviously my concern not to locate the innovation of Stein's analysis of empathy within the field of phenomenology but rather to bring Stein's discussion of empathy to bear on a reading of her life and work. Yet because of the issue of history at stake in Stein's intimate and empathic turn, it is worthwhile to take a moment to look at one of her precursors and her reaction to him: the philosopher of the human sciences Wilhelm Dilthey. Dilthey is addressed in force, and for the first time in her dissertation, in its final chapter, "Empathy as the Understanding of Spiritual Persons." Stein identifies Dilthey's lifework as a search for the ontological foundation of the human sciences (*Geisteswissenschaften*; the German term foregrounds its relation to Stein's subject, the spirituality of persons). Stein's interest in Dilthey makes sense, given his connection of historical knowledge to the notion of subjective experience and empathy.[34] In Dilthey she finds a philosopher who is working through an empirical system that will yield natural laws of culture or of spirit.[35] This approach to history, which she defines as "empathic comprehension," is taken further in the 1916 dissertation and used as the way to steer her text away from its systematic review of the relationship of subjectivity and the apperception of others, toward an unresolved conclusion on religious consciousness and revelation. ("Non liquet," she interpolates in the argument; "it is not clear.")[36] The intimate histories she would spin out after her conversion go a step further, moving from Dilthey's empirical empathic comprehension toward mystical experience that defies observation, for it is hidden from view.

Redressing Subjectivity: Jewishness as a Masquerade

If the pedestrian association of empathy with the feminine was already close to the surface of the text even as it was being written, its connection to Jewish identity and, further, to Jewish history is exposed in the Jewish memoir. Yet neither of these identifications is constructed in ways that simply appropriate a discrete space of canonical philosophy for these marginalized elements—each contains the complex and sometimes unsettling double movement I have been describing, in which innovative cross-identifications and appropriations reiterate and reinforce the rules of the game. For instance, to refer briefly to Stein's writings on the nature of woman, while empathy is delineated within the feminine province, the philosophical career would seem, according to her apparently strictly essentialist essay "The Calling of Man and Woman According to the Orders of Nature and Grace" to be practically reserved for men: "overwhelmingly abstract reasoning ability" being, along with physical strength, the most exclusively masculine quality.[37] In a manner that rather remarkably parallels her moves between Jewishness and Christianity (and that evokes similarly visceral reactions in contemporary readers), Stein's inscriptions of a space for women in spheres from which they have been excluded are continually accompanied by the reinscription of the boundaries that have excluded them. These newly inscribed boundaries, however, are passable: in her reading of masculine and feminine essences, she also incorporates the notion of the influential misogynist philosopher-psychologist Otto Weininger that all beings are located on a spectrum between male and female ideal poles. Via this fairly orthodox adoption of his system, Stein opens a passage between incontrovertibly male and female spheres and passes. That is, in the same essay on the vocation of the genders, she stresses that the professions should *not* be reserved for men or for women in light of (and here she practically quotes Weininger) the "strong individual differences" that make some women "closely approach the masculine type" (*Typus*) and some men the feminine. Weininger's ideal types are placed in service of the delegitimation of assumptions of gendered ability, as they take on quotation marks in Stein's text: "Hence every 'masculine' profession may also be very satisfactorily filled by certain women, and every 'feminine' one by certain men."[38] The proximity of this passage to the characterization of the philosophical profession as masculine, coming as it does in a woman philosopher's essay, marks the whole as another self-portrait that constitutes a gesture of passing, or identifying across gender lines.[39]

This gesture is usefully set against the figure of masquerade that has informed gender studies. A text that is contemporary with Stein's that has been discussed in that literature is a psychoanalytic essay of 1929 by Joan Riviere, "Womanliness as a Masquerade."[40] Riviere also works from a spectrum model of gender and sexuality partially founded by Weininger, according to which "we all" figure to some degree as "bisexual" or "intermediate" figures along the line between oppositional poles of the ideal masculine and ideal feminine.[41] The case study Riviere presents in her essay is meant to represent one particular type of homosexual woman, the intellectual who fulfills classic feminine roles but who excels in masculine arenas. In Riviere's essay, the masquerade is constituted by an enacted, exaggerated femininity to mask the possession of the masculine object (in psychoanalytic discourse this is obviously the phallus, the possession of which implies the castration of the father).[42] This thinking could take the phenomenon of Stein's textual passing in several directions. It turns out that the least convincing model is that represented by the most immediate association of the figure of passing: the anxiety about passing expressed by hegemonic subjects, the response to a woman (Jew, black) inauthentically clothing herself as a privileged subject. The Riviere text, written just as Stein was working on issues of gender and vocation, posits an antithetical relation between exterior identity and interior (psychic) life; the feminine mask is a symptom of the possession of the phallus. Is Stein positing her role of philosopher, then, as a masculine essence in feminine guise (the objectionable implication of the essay on the vocation of the genders)? Or do we have to look further to get at the prickly question of selves and identities, of truth and disguise?

The special status of the photograph, Roland Barthes famously asserted, is that it appears to be a message without a code, the perfect *analogon*.[43] The well-known power of photographic images to deceive rests on this assumption of the special status of the medium. In three photograph portraits taken of Stein (figures 1–3), we see the subject looking at the camera and spectator, with her head tilted at the same angle downward and to the left, her dark eyes aimed in a pensive glance up and to the right, at the viewer, with an arguably inscrutable expression. The first is Edith the seated student, with short hair and some work in her lap, her head resting thoughtfully on her hand. One is reminded of a style of female intellectual we think of in relation to her contemporary, Hannah Arendt—a self-presentation that leans toward the androgynous. A second portrait hails from two years after writing the essay on woman, at her clothing day of entry into the Carmelite order in the spring of 1934. The same face in angle and expression glances out from a traditional bridal gown, and she holds in her hand a white scepter, signifiers of her weddedness to Christ until her death. The last is the best-known image of Stein, clothed in her Carmelite habit; it is the passport photograph taken in 1938 before her transfer to the Echt convent. On the one hand, these three images together could be read as gestures of passing, in their surrender to clearly cited conventions. Or as Linda Haverty Rugg has suggested in her book on photography and autobiography, such a series could be said to "supply a visual metaphor for the divided and multiple ('decentered') self."[44] And yet if Stein could have had control over these images and the way they work against one another, they might have looked like this: as though a powerful, if somewhat inscrutable, self survived throughout these transformations, a hidden life independent of exterior identity.[45] The clothing ceremony itself is interesting because of its self-conscious surrender of a certain kind of subjectivity (while simultaneously claiming the priority of an essential, inner, and hidden subjectivity). The novice surrenders her name—and to the last, Stein would prefer her works to appear under the name she chose for her life in Carmel, Sister Teresa Benedicta of the Cross.[46]

The surrender of the name and the re-dressing of the subject are consistent with Stein's increasing devaluation of external identities and given narratives, just as they resonate with contemporary discussions of gendered subjectivity. These have circulated in large part around Judith Butler's work on gender performance, which again emphasizes the contingency of a central category of identity. Butler herself points out that the performativity of these identities is less controversial than what lies, or does not lie, behind them, or what the masquerade masks.[47] In a contribution to these discussions, Slavoj Žižek has referred to Hegel's notion that subjectivity itself is something *angezogen*—dressed up, donned, or worn—and hence the association of femininity with masquerade privileges rather than denies female subjectivity.[48] What I have been tracing in Stein's writing can be seen as a re-dressing of identities through an empathic move that requires something Stein might call a "giving itself away."[49] The re-dressing (and a degree of surrender) of the subject takes place chiefly through Stein's textual device of empathic portraiture. In fact, as Stein promised in her introductory reference to "sketches," *Life in a Jewish Family* is full of portraits, chiefly of women in her family. Some such sketches are taken from portraits and photographs from the family home: Stein describes the portrait of her grandmother that hung there, her "fine, delicate features" reflecting a profound "nobility of spirit." Another portrait, a photograph of her aunt Mika, demonstrates a "wonderful graciousness, her maidenly purity and her deep seriousness."[50] Thus, these portraits serve as counterimages to antisemitic stereotypes, just as these two women are strongly associated in the text with preservation of Jewish identity and reinforcement of a Jewish foundation to family life. This piety, too, takes forms familiar to Christian German readers: reading psalms in German, a family life based on principles of simplicity and thrift. The dominance of empathic portraits of women in the family is particularly notable in light of the relative dearth of such portraits of men. The father, who died suddenly in 1893 when Edith was still a small child, is described hardly at all or else appears as a sort of phantom. Her brother Arno's paternalistic posing is mocked as form without content, as the family (and Stein, throughout the memoir) refers to him as "der 'Chef'" (the "boss"), framed by ironic scare quotes. The matriarchal order of the household is naturalized in the memoir, even as it remains disguised, for this is a household that seems to match every model of stereotypical German bourgeois (i.e., patriarchal) life.

Stein's intense identification with her mother in the portrait (the whole first part of the memoir) renders it a strange sort of self-portrait; strange because the young Edith herself appears in the text as the other and yet occasionally also as the eyes through which the life of the mother is seen. Central here is the image of Auguste as matriarch and patriarch of the family after the early death of the paterfamilias—her powerful role driving the successful family lumber business, culminating in the chapter's final note on an overheard comment in a Breslau streetcar: "Do you know who is the most capable merchant [in German the term is more clearly gendered as masculine: *der tüchtigste Kaufmann*] in the whole trade in the city? Frau Stein! [*Das ist* die *Frau Stein!*]"[51]

This passing between gender roles, mentioned above in the context of Stein in the masculine role of philosopher, is interestingly set against a family photograph portrait of 1895 (see figure 4). On the surface, this seems to be a typical, traditional family portrait, with the seven children around the paterfamilias, the tall sons framing the back row, the young girls in front, and the dutiful mother seated deferentially by her husband's side. But Herr Stein had died, we know, two years earlier. Upon the sudden death of Auguste's husband, or rather upon reflection at least a year after his death, the absence of an image of the family with the father at the center was felt (presumably by Auguste).[52] The mother and children positioned themselves around an unoccupied space in the center of the composition, into which a passport photograph of him was superimposed. The photograph effected a powerful illusion of the patriarchal order of the family that was eerily at odds with what no one could doubt: the center of this family circle was occupied by the figure Edith Stein identifies with in her own text, Auguste Courant Stein.

Empathic portraiture brings us around again to the figure of passing in a provocative way. If this text is, as the preface confesses, meant to be in dialogue with an "unsympathetic" image of the Jew promulgated by the Nazis, the question of passing takes on sinister implications. A central didactic goal of Nazi antisemitic propaganda was of course to redraw boundaries of difference between Jew and German that had become invisible in the postemancipation period: recall, for instance, the scene from Fritz Hippler's *The Eternal Jew* discussed in chapter 2, in which eastern European Hasidic Jews, presented as radically and unappealingly foreign, are groomed as if to pass in German society, followed by the successive dissolve to a bourgeois cocktail party of Berlin Jews. Even this specifically racialist valence of passing is touched on in the memoir. Stein recalls her large family as a series of pairs, negative doubles. Her own negative double is the sister Erna (see figure 5), darkly complected, overanimated in her gestures, and garrulous in contrast with the young Edith, described as blonde, deep thinking, and reserved. The apparently unironic description of Edith as an Aryan double of a Jewish Erna is startling in the same way as other moments in Stein's texts, appearing to shore up the contemporary antisemitic contexts the memoir was intended to attack. But this apparent discursive complicity is not easy to sort out. What could it mean to figure her relationship with her closest sister in terms of racial opposition, to paint Aryan portraits of herself and other women in her family? Does it subvert the foundation of the notion of race (blood is character) through an acceptance of the normative values of contemporary racism? Does it represent a crossing, or passing gesture, that fortifies or that attacks notions of authentic identity and difference? Is it an example of the famous copy that authorizes the original?[53] Or perhaps the question is whether we can be satisfied with the uneasy way these meanings are overlaid and confounded *as an integral component of their construction*, so that a radically malleable vision of identity is—and unmistakably, irredeemably—fused with a conviction in an irreducible, certainly essential, if hidden, truth.

Hidden Histories

Between the portrait of life in a Jewish family written chiefly in the Cologne Carmel and the image of the nun in the freight train bound for Auschwitz, Stein left a series of additional portraits: the hagiographic pieces written in the Echt Carmel.[54] Collected in a slim volume under the title *The Hidden Life* (*Verborgenes Leben*, the word for "hidden" being connected with the notion of a diversion into the invisible, or to a safe haven) in the year of her beatification, these sketches of the holy lives focus mainly on women: Saint Elizabeth of Thuringia, Saint Teresa Margaret of the Sacred Heart, Sister Marie-Aimée de Jésus, and Stein's inspiration to convert to Catholicism, Saint Teresa of Jesus (Teresa of Ávila).[55] Neither the predominance of sketches of women nor their status as empathic portraits, or even thinly veiled self-portraits, was lost on the German and Dutch editors of the original volume. In their preface and introduction, they note that in these portraits "she frequently finds a mirror image of herself": her encounter in the image of Marie-Aimée of "her own self," the focus in the sketch of Saint Teresa Margaret on "the saint's spontaneous empathic ability," which was Stein's own strength, and the possibility of reading "between the lines" how the lives of Edith Stein and her Catholic namesake Saint Teresa of Ávila "have all along been parallel."[56] Thus, these sketches, they contend, are more autobiographical than her memoir and the correspondence they published under the title *Self-Portrait in Letters*.[57]

The value of these insights lies in their recognition of the rhetorical construct seen in Stein's writings all along: a dialectic between interiority—the hidden, true spiritual life of the subject—and the often deceptive apprehension of exterior life, social and political contexts, or history. Conceiving what seem to be problematic narrative strategies in this way permits a reassessment of the troubling double movement in Stein's texts, in which exclusionary narratives on race, gender, and religion are buttressed at the same moment as they are undermined. If the rethinking of contextuality that Stein's work engenders indeed entails a dialectic of selves and contexts, we can begin to make sense of simultaneously linked and antithetical poles such as spiritual subjectivity and the world of politico-historical objects, interior selves and exterior identities, or the hidden and the represented.

It is not surprising that a sketch of Teresa of Ávila should be found among these empathic (self-)portraits. As I have mentioned, Stein's construction of her own epiphany turns around the image of a furtive reading of the saint's famous autobiography, and this experience led her not only to Christian faith but of course to Carmel, where she would take the name Teresa. Yet the editors' description of these sketches as "mirror images" of the author reminds us, as Stein did herself in her reflection on images of Jews, that the mirror reflects at the same time that it reverses; some mirrors distort, whereas others invert. What is the nature of the parallel lives of the two Teresas? The sketch reflects on the way the moment in which it is being written (February 1934) mirrors the moment of Carmelite reform:

> While outside in carnival's frantic tumult people get drunk and delirious, while political battles separate them, and great need depresses them so much that many forget to look to heaven, at such still places of prayer hearts are opened to the Lord. . . . The desire for new foundations is surfacing in the most varied places. One almost feels transported into the time when our Holy Mother Teresa, the foundress of the reformed Carmel, traveled all over Spain from north to south and from west to east to plant new vineyards of the Lord. One would like to bring into our times also something of the spirit of this great woman who built amazingly during a century of battles and disturbances.[58]

While this opening explicitly suggests a parallel between these periods and between these women's lives, this model of allegory proves somewhat deceptive. Both Teresas live in embattled times and battle for the spirit, both ceaselessly seek the truth and know that the journey is a spiritual one. Just as Edith is put on the path to truth in her reading of Teresa's autobiography, in that same autobiography we learn of the young future saint's identification with the subjects of the classic hagiographies she reads (the *Lives of the Saints*). With the knowledge that the easiest path to God is martyrdom, the young Teresa runs away from home with the wish to perish for her faith among the Moors.

The portrait of Teresa is set against the backdrop of sixteenth-century Spain. The walled city of Ávila is a fortress of Christianity, the heart of the castle or fortress of Christendom that is Castile. The Castilian knights were a crusading army of faith—from "such a race of heroes" came Teresa, the "bold warrior for God."[59] It is difficult to disregard Stein's uncolloquial description of Teresa's wandering "from west to east" to crusade for her faith or, furthermore, to read this mirrored—or reversed—image of Stein's voyage as a parallel. Unless the author's clear identification with the centered figure of Teresa is a signal that in a world turned on its head we need to look for centers in the most unlikely of places: from the heart of Castile to Breslau the borderland, from a fervent Catholic to a pious Jewish upbringing.

The central inversion in the piece has to do with history. The identification of Teresa's turbulent century with the 1930s seems sensible in the opening quoted above, but this correspondence is, again, vexed. Teresa's embattled time is identified with the proximity of her birth to the expulsion. The "disturbance" of her century is not named as the battle of Reformists and Catholics, for instance, but is associated with the struggle against the Moors (and with them, of course, the Jews), as though the Catholic Reformation were a continuation of the ongoing battle with the infidel. To comprehend the strangeness of this move in Stein's text we need to recall that, in 1934, a comparison to the same historical period—the Inquisition—would be the commonest rhetorical move by a critic of the new German regime. But here Stein presents an unequivocally affirmative image of that battle against Europe's and Christianity's others, and she openly identifies with the Castilian crusader. The hidden, spiritual truth (all Stein's words, frequently repeated in the Carmel writings) of this figure is a life independent of, even in opposition to, the apparent history surrounding it. Intimacy again appears as a counterfigure of history in a time demanding such a move. To illuminate this operation of the hidden life I turn finally to the brief mystical writing with that title, a 1940 meditation on darkness and light, concealment and revelation, titled "The Hidden Life and the Epiphany."

In this piece written for the Feast of Kings in the dark months of winter, Stein begins with the image of the Advent candles providing a feeble but unceasing consolation and illumination of an increasingly dark and fallen world. The origin of this light, like the dark history it challenges, is not paradise but the expulsion from it. In the following account Stein carefully maintains the opposition of this inner light to external history, even as she charts the equally hidden relation between the two:

> A ray of this light fell into the hearts of our original parents even during the judgment . . . an illuminating ray that awakened in them the knowledge of their guilt. . . . Hidden from the whole world, it illuminated and irradiated them. . . . Seen by no human eye, this is how living building blocks were and are formed and brought together into a church first of all invisible . . . it finally comes down to inner life; formation moves from inner to the outer. The deeper a soul is bound to God, the more completely surrendered to grace, the stronger will be its influence on the form of the church. Conversely, the more an era is engulfed in the night of sin and estrangement from God the more it needs souls united to God. And God does not permit a deficiency. The greatest

> figures of prophecy and sanctity step forth out of the darkest night. But for the most part the formative stream of the mystical life remains invisible. Certainly the decisive turning points in world history are substantially co-determined by souls whom no history book ever mentions. And we will only find out about those souls to whom we owe the decisive turning points in our personal lives on the day when all that is hidden is revealed.[60]

Oddly, this oblique and unsystematic piece posits explicitly what earlier texts at best implied. For the unseen and unseeable subject here is not merely prior to the visible one, authentic in contrast to the latter, if not verifiable; these two (inner and outer life, as well as the most covert spirituality of the individual and the broadest outlines of human history) are powerfully united. Since external form never reflects this inner reality but more often opposes it, the relationship between the two is almost always illegible. The darkest historical moment, Stein writes in 1940, masks the most brilliant spiritual light; the decisive souls of such periods, saints of the present, remain unrecognized in the exterior world. These are the paradoxes represented by the figures of (inner, spiritual) light and (external, historical) darkness above. The true life is spiritual, hidden, and virtually inaccessible—as often obscured as it is exposed by exterior living. It reveals itself even to the subject only through the empathic relation, through the encounter with a simultaneously discrete and identical other. As was already recognized before her conversion, in the dissertation on empathy written by an agnostic Stein, this single path to the self is simultaneously the unique way of encountering God.

Stein's mystical turn, her faith in a hidden and immutable truth, and the encounter with God may seem irreconcilable with contemporary critical approaches to modern philosophy, German-Jewish identity construction, and feminist writing. But this is only so if we forget the way the true subject actually emerges in Stein's work: it is utterly invisible, an inversion or else an utter reconfiguration of the way subjects appear within their historical and social surroundings. It emerges out of a network of contradictory relations, patterned by negative doubles and unidentical selves, compelling an inescapable intimacy with the other and a link between dissimulation and authenticity that brushed perhaps no more against the grain of Stein's historical moment than it does our own. This is a subjectivity that confects itself in ways that protect it from and allow it to defend itself against hostile contexts. The controversies associated with Edith Stein's afterlife in public historical consciousness—her contextualization within competing histories of the Holocaust, canonical appropriations of her work and herself as a figure—seem overdetermined in light of these self-constructions. That is why focusing on issues such as identity and essentialism, both of which appear particularly relevant to the Edith Stein case at first glance, may lead readers astray. Stein's work may be better served by the notion of "contextuality" or by a rethinking of contextuality that takes seriously not only historico-political influences but also contexts of reception, including those anticipated by subjects: by attending to the ongoing project in which many figures engage—if not all as relentlessly and creatively as Stein—to create contexts for themselves.

Notes

For our good discussions about this topic I thank Lauren Berlant, Crisca Bierwert, Todd Endelman, Sander Gilman, Barbara Hahn, Julie Skurski, Jackie Stevens, and Michael Steinberg, as well as the editors and reviewers for *New German Critique*, where this chapter originally appeared and which has graciously permitted this reprint. See Scott Spector, "Edith Stein's Passing Gestures: Intimate Histories, Empathic Portraits," *New German Critique*, no. 75 (1998): 28–56. It has also been published as Scott Spector, "Edith Stein's Passing Gestures: Intimate Histories, Empathic Portraits," in *Contemplating Edith Stein*, ed. Joyce Avrech Berkman, 93–121 (Notre Dame, IN: University of Notre Dame Press, 2006).

1. Reports of the canonization stressed the controversy surrounding it and the "contradictions and ambiguities" associated with the new saint. See, e.g., Rachel Smolkin, "A Saintly Controversy," *Chicago Sun-Times*, October 11, 1998, p. 38; Imre Karacs, "Vatican Rushes to Canonise a Catholic Jew," *The Independent* (London), October 11, 1998, p. 23; Alessandra Stanley, "A Jew's Odyssey from Catholic Nun to Saint," *New York Times*, October 11, 1998, p. 1; "Contention Trails Nun's Elevation to Sainthood," *Associated Press*, October 11, 1998; "Jewish Groups Object to Nun's Canonization," *Chicago Tribune*, October 11, 1998, p. C9; and "Fury as Jewish Nun Who Died in Auschwitz Is Made Saint," *The Times* (London), October 12, 1998. The official approval for the canonization process came from Pope John Paul II on May 22, 1997, on the basis of the miraculous recovery of a Massachusetts two-year-old after swallowing a near-lethal dose of Tylenol a decade earlier. The child, Benedicta McCarthy, had been named for the Auschwitz martyr, and her family had prayed to Edith Stein for her recovery. News reports of the May 1997 announcement focused on the miracle rather than on the controversy over the status of Stein's martyrdom.

2. S. Heilbronner, "Canonizing of Jew Still Debated," *Religion News Service*, May 24, 1997. The *Jerusalem Post* strikes a similar chord: "The heart of the dispute over Stein is whether she should be properly remembered as a Christian martyr or as one of the countless Jewish victims of the Nazi death machine." C. Ben-David, "The Saint of Auschwitz," *Jerusalem Post*, May 2, 1997, p. 4.

3. Johannes Wieners, "Meine Begegnung mit Edith Stein," *Kölnische Rundschau*, August 9, 1982, quoted in W. Herbstrith, *Edith Stein: A Biography*, trans. B. Bonowitz (New York: Harper and Row, 1985), 111.

4. Herbstrith, *Edith Stein*, 182–183. Many such testimonies are also recorded in Teresia Renata Posselt, *Edith Stein: Eine Große Frau unseres Jahrhunderts* (Freiburg, Germany: Herder, 1963), 188–215; and Herbstrith, *Edith Stein*, 104–108.

5. The absence of the Christ figure in the peculiar representation of "a Pietà without the Christ" is worth some consideration. In the first place it seems to signal something of the paradox of the ultra-Christian figure of the saint embodied by a Jewish woman (foreshadowing the press's hyperbole that Stein is "the first Jewish-born saint . . . since the Virgin Mary"; see "Nun's Atonement for Church Stirs Sainthood Controversy," *Detroit News*, October 10, 1998, p. C3). Another provocative parallel is offered by Sigrid Weigel in her analysis of the controversial selection of an enormously enlarged reproduction of the Käthe Kollwitz sculpture *Mutter*

mit Sohn for the Berlin Neue Wache national memorial to Opfer des Krieges und der Gewaltherrschaft. In the context of a broader discussion of the symbolic place of women within Holocaust memory in Germany, Weigel argues that the Pietà figure shifts the focus of national memory from the victims (the "silent ashes" in the quotation from Auschwitz survivor Cornelia Edvardson's memoir opening Weigel's article) to the perpetrators as victims. This particular use of gendered symbols pertains to a "universeller Opferkonzept" (universal victim concept) or "überhistorischer 'Existenzmetapher'" (superhistorical existence metaphor), eclipsing a perpetrator identification unavoidable in thematizations of father figures. See S. Weigel, "Der Ort von Frauen im Gedächtnis des Holocaust: Symbolisierung, Zeugenschaft und kollektive Identität," *Sprache im technischen Zeitalter* 135 (September 1995): 260–268.

6. Either two miracles or such a martyrdom are required for beatification. Once beatified, a miracle is prerequisite to canonization.

7. See, e.g., Abraham Foxman and Leon Klenicki, "An Unnecessary Saint," *Jerusalem Post*, October 20, 1998, p. 10; Deena Metzger, "Pilgrimage to Auschwitz," *Los Angeles Times*, August 19, 1989, p. 8; Edgar M. Bronfman, "Once Again, the Pope Has Disappointed Jews," *New York Times*, September 26, 1987, sec. 1, p. 27; Lea Levavi, "Church Putting Christian Stamp on the Holocaust," *Jerusalem Post*, June 13, 1989, p. 7; and David E. Anderson, "A Papal Act Ruffles Jewish Community," *UPI*, May 15, 1987, http://www.upi.com/Archives/1987/05/15/Religion-in-AmericaNEWLNA-papal-act-ruffles-Jewish-community/4093548049600.

8. The issue of Stein's essentialism is discussed below. The tensions between her feminist interpretation and conventional Catholic doctrine become apparent in several editorial correctives to texts collected in a 1956 edition of selected writings in English translation, culminating in this symptomatic note: "Here the author's feminist tendencies have evidently carried her too far in her criticism of the Apostle and allowed her to forget that his words are inspired." See E. Stein, *Writings of Edith Stein*, ed. and trans. Hilda Graef (London: Peter Owen, 1956), 111. Indeed, a *Toronto Sun* article, "Let's Claim Edith Stein for Women Everywhere," was accompanied by her photograph with the caption "EDITH STEIN ... A feminist saint," but the suggestion is made chiefly tongue-in-cheek, and the article in fact focuses on the difficulty of appropriations of Stein. See Liz Braun, "Let's Claim Edith Stein for Women Everywhere," *Toronto Sun*, October 18, 1998, p. C13.

9. One of the flagrant tensions informing this controversy takes form in the contrast between Stein's last recorded words, to her sister as they were being deported to the camp, "Come, Rosa, we are going on behalf of our people," and the reference in her Carmelite spiritual last will and testament to her penance "for the sins of the unbelieving people." See, e.g., "Jewish Groups Object to Nun's Canonization," *Chicago Tribune*, October 11, 1998, p. C6.

10. Edith Stein, *On the Problem of Empathy: The Collected Works of Edith Stein*, trans. Waltraut Stein, 3rd ed. (Washington, DC: ICS, 1989).

11. See Michel Beaujour, *Poetics of the Literary Self-Portrait*, trans. Yara Milos (New York: New York University Press, 1991), 197.

12. Edith Stein, *Edith Steins Werke*, vol. 7, *Aus dem Leben einer jüdischen Familie: Das Leben Edith Steins; Kindheit und Jugend*, ed. L. Gelber (Leuven, Belgium: E. Nauwelaerts, 1965); Edith Stein, *The Collected Works of Edith Stein, Sister Teresa Benedicta of the Cross, Discalced Carmelite*, vol. 1, *Life In a Jewish Family: Her Unfinished Autobiographical Account*, ed. Lucy Gelber, trans. Josephine Koeppel (Washington, DC: ICS, 1986).

13. See Hanna-Barbara Gerl, "Edith Stein (1891–1942): Eros der Erkenntnis, Eros des Glaubens," in *Frauen in den Kulturwissenschaften: Von Lou Andreas-Salomé bis Hannah Arendt*, ed. Barbara Hahn (Munich: C. H. Beck, 1994), 235.

14. Any relation of this antisemitic account to the theologically based anti-Jewish accounts of early modern Christian thought is eclipsed in Stein's narrative by another discourse on the

relation of Jewish to Christian religion: that Judaism is the necessary forerunner of Christian faith, an authentic, primordial form of faith that needed and needs to be overcome but that cannot have been done without. I discuss below how Stein's assertion of this more complex relation disables the simple adversarial relation of Jew against Christian (or German).

15. See Sander L. Gilman, *Jewish Self-Hatred: Anti-Semitism and the Hidden Language of the Jews* (Baltimore: Johns Hopkins University Press, 1986), 22–67. In fact, one of the concerns surrounding the canonization expressed by the Baltimore cardinal William Keeler was that the church might be seen to be glorifying "a public apostate" from Judaism; see John Dart, "Sainthood for Jewish Convert Stirs Debate," *Los Angeles Times*, October 10, 1998, p. B4.

16. Stein, *Aus dem Leben*, 3.

17. The original passage reads, "Ich mußte bestimmte Fragen stellen, um in den Strom der Erinnerungen so viel Ordnung und Klarheit zu bringen, wie für einen fremden Leser zum Verständnis unerläßlich war, und oft war es nicht möglich, greifbare und zuverlässige Tatsachen festzustellen. Ich stelle im Folgenden die kurzen Aufzeichnungen im Anschluß an die Gespräche mit meiner Mutter voran. Darauf soll ein Lebensbild meiner Mutter folgen, wie ich es selbst zu geben vermag." Ibid., 4. Translations are adapted from Stein, *Life in a Jewish Family*.

18. Ibid.

19. See the excellent discussion in Beaujour, *Poetics of the Literary Self-Portrait*, 1–21. In *L'Autobiographie en France*, Philippe Lejeune writes that in Michel de Montaigne "there is no continuous narrative nor any systematic history of the personality. Self-portrait rather than autobiography." Quoted in Beaujour, *Poetics of the Literary Self-Portrait*, 2. Michel Riffaterre writes of André Malraux's *Anti-Memoirs* that the memoir follows a "chronology" or "logic of events" ("then they are narrative"), whereas the *Anti-Memoirs* "rest on analogy" and Malraux's "superimposition method," "therefore they are poetry." Quoted in Beaujour, *Poetics of the Literary Self-Portrait*, 3.

20. An incidence of this is offered in an obituary of the historian Donald Nicholl, which stresses the deceased's shifting concern with spiritual rather than material truth, as he increasingly came to identify thinking with the Fall and to replace it with "gazing" at a portrait of Edith Stein, among other exemplars. See "Obituary," *Daily Telegraph*, May 20, 1997, p. 23.

21. Stein, *Aus dem Leben*, 3.

22. Stein, *Life in a Jewish Family*, 23.

23. The description of sympathy to work with in this case is that explicated at length by Max Scheler. Another Jewish convert to Catholicism who had also (for quite different reasons) been marginalized in the academy, Scheler was the most prestigious figure in the circle around Husserl in Freiburg in the period of Stein's dissertation. See Max Scheler, *The Nature of Sympathy*, trans. Peter Heath (London: Routledge and Kegan Paul, 1954); also see Stein, *Empathy*, 27–34.

24. Stein, *Empathy*, 16–18; see also xviii.

25. Stein, *Aus dem Leben*, 38; Stein, *Life in a Jewish Family*, 69. In a later text, Stein writes at greater length on the space shared by the Seder and the Last Supper, or the old and new covenants. See Edith Stein, "The Prayer of the Church," in *The Collected Works of Edith Stein, Sister Teresa Benedicta of the Cross, Discalced Carmelite*, vol. 4, *The Hidden Life*, trans. Waltraut Stein (Washington, DC: ICS, 1992), 7–8.

26. Part of the problem of appropriating Stein into a contemporary Jewish studies canon must be attributed to this somewhat unreflected and visceral response, demonstrated in an exemplary way by a highly charged exchange in the spring of 1996 on a Jewish studies internet discussion list over the appropriateness of discussing her in that setting. Stein's most striking contrast to the provocatively comparable figure of Simone Weil, for instance, must be the former's continued identification with Judaism. See Erich S. J. Przywara, "Edith Stein et Simone

Weil: Essentialism et existentialisme," trans. Henri Leroux, *Cahiers Simone Weil* 6, no. 3 (1983): 249–258.

27. Stein, *Aus dem Leben*, 6.

28. Letter from Edith Stein to Roman Ingarden, February 20, 1917, in Edith Stein, *Edith Steins Werke*, vol. 8, *Selbstbildnis in Briefen, Erster Teil: 1916–1934*, ed. L. Gelber and P. Fr. Romaeus Leuven (Druten, Netherlands: De Maas and Waler, 1976), 18.

29. Stein, *Life in a Jewish Family*, 47.

30. Stein, *Aus dem Leben*, 11.

31. Stein, *Empathy*, 63.

32. Ibid.

33. Ibid., 38.

34. Dilthey's concept of the historian's relationship to the past as a "re-experiencing" (*Nacherleben*), for instance, contains both empathic and experiential qualities that seem to inform Stein's encounter with history. See, e.g., W. Dilthey, "Das Verstehen anderer Personen und ihrer Lebensäußerungen," in *Gesammelte Schriften* (Stuttgart, Germany: Teubner, 1961), 7:205–220.

35. See Dilthey, *Einleitung in die Gesiteswissenschaften*, in *Gesammelte Schriften*, 1:3–120.

36. Stein, *Empathy*, 107.

37. See Edith Stein, "Beruf des Mannes und der Frau nach Natur und Gnadenordnung," in *Edith Steins Werke*, vol. 5, *Die Frau: Ihre Aufgabe nach Natur und Gnade*, ed. Lucy Gelber and Romaeus Leuven (Leuven, Belgium: Nauwelaerts and Herder, 1959), 40–41. My translation is adapted from Edith Stein, *Writings of Edith Stein*, ed. and trans. Hilda Graef (London: Peter Owen, 1956), 101.

38. The original passage reads, "Mit Rücksicht auf die starken individuellen Differenzen, die manch Frauen stark dem männlichen Typus und manche Männer stark dem weiblichen Typus annähern und es mit sich bringen, daß jeder 'männliche' Beruf auch von gewissen Frauen, jeder 'weibliche' auch von gewissen Männern durchaus sachgemäß ausgeübt werden kann." Stein, "Beruf des Mannes," 40. My translation is adapted from Stein, *Writings of Edith Stein*, 122. While this argumentation and rhetoric is, as I have stressed, a rather orthodox embodiment of the principles outlined in Otto Weininger, *Geschlecht und Charakter: Eine prinzipielle Untersuchung* (Vienna: W. Braumüller, 1903), the Weininger text itself oscillates between an insistence on mutability and the fluidity of the scale from the ideal points M and W and the reification of these ideal types with the actual genders. Thus his conviction that, despite the potential masculinity of an individual woman, no woman can be far enough from the W pole to produce true art, for instance. Stein is, from a certain perspective, more strictly Weiningerian than Weininger himself.

39. In considering what today's readers readily identify as Stein's essentialism, the constantly reinscribed figures of passability and passing would seem to be a crucial issue and yet one that has not been considered in the literature on Stein's feminism. For more on the question of essentialism and Stein's feminist writing, see Linda Lopez McAlister, "Edith Stein: Essential Differences," *Philosophy Today* 37 (Spring 1993): 70–77; and Przywara, "Edith Stein et Simone Weil."

40. J. Riviere, "Womanliness as a Masquerade," reprinted in *Formations of Fantasy*, ed. V. Burgin, J. Donald, and C. Kaplan (London: Methuen, 1986), 35–44; see also Stephen Heath, "Joan Riviere and the Masquerade," in Burgin, Donald, and Kaplan, *Formations of Fantasy*, 45–61; Mary Ann Doane, "Masquerade Reconsidered: Further Thoughts on the Female Spectator," *Discourse: Journal for Theoretical Studies in Media and Culture* 11, no. 1 (1988–1989): 42–54; and Judith Butler, *Gender Trouble: Feminism and the Subversion of Identity* (New York:

Routledge, 1990): 43–57. Stein's "Beruf des Mannes" has been dated 1931; see Stein, *Edith Steins Werke* 5:xxv.

41. Riviere's spectral model cites not Weininger but Ernest Jones, whose typology of female sexuality has the same structure as Weininger's, even appropriating the term "intermediate types," but gives much more attention to the specificity of the female subject.

42. While Butler provides a nuanced reading of this essay, it is most useful to the general work of her book (with its subtitle "Feminism and the Subversion of Identity") and to Stephen Heath in its refusal to posit "a femininity that is prior to mimicry," since, at the end of Riviere's text, she confesses that the homosexual woman's compulsive masquerade is "the same thing" as "genuine womanliness." See Butler, *Gender Trouble*, 53; Heath, "Joan Riviere and the Masquerade"; and Riviere, "Womanliness as a Masquerade," 3.

43. Roland Barthes, "The Photographic Message," in *Image, Music, Text*, ed. and trans. Stephen Heath (New York: Hill and Wang, 1977), 17–18.

44. Linda Haverty Rugg, *Picturing Ourselves: Photography and Autobiography* (Chicago: University of Chicago Press, 1997), 1.

45. Rugg bases her study on precisely this tension within both photography and autobiographical portraiture: the "double consciousness" of the self as "decentered, multiple, fragmented, and divided against itself in the act of observing and being," on the one hand, and "the simultaneous insistence on the presence of an integrated, authorial self, located in a body, a place, and a time," on the other. Rugg, *Picturing*, 2; see also 19. Self-imaging plays on the border between these competing claims of artifice and authenticity, as between public (identities) and private (selves): "Images can represent the most *intimate* expressions of ourselves . . . and images allow the escape of our private or guarded sphere into the unguarded public." Rugg, *Picturing*, 4 (emphasis added).

46. This choice of name could be discussed at length. In short, one notes figures that are central in Stein's subject construction: Teresa of Ávila, the reformer of Carmel, whom I discuss below; her follower John of the Cross, another saint and the first male Discalced Carmelite; and finally the figure of the cross itself. Stein's most sustained mystical work was the *Kreuzeswissenschaft* (*Science of the Cross*), on Saint John, a very interesting text that has been discussed by Hanna-Barbara Gerl-Falkovitz. See Hanna-Barbara Gerl-Falkovitz, "Im Dunkel wohl geborgen: Edith Steins Theorie der 'Kreuzeswissenschaft' (1942)," *Communio* 36 (2007): 463–477. The combination of male and female figures in this chosen name is worth noting, particularly since the masculine figure is himself associated with a certain gender crossing. The image of the cross is pervasive in the late writings; a fascinating valence it has (for our purposes) is its coupling with Jewish suffering under the Nazis, implying the very gesture (conflation of the Jewish Kiddush Hashem with a martyrdom of Christian faith) that informs this chapter: "I said to the Lord that it was His Cross that was now laid on the Jewish people. Most of my people did not understand that, but those who did had to bear it willingly in the name of all the others. I wanted to do that. . . . But I did not know in what way my bearing of the Cross would happen." Edith Stein, quoted in Philip J. Scharper, "Edith Stein," in *Saints Are Now: Eight Portraits of Modern Sanctity*, ed. John J. Delaney (Garden City, NY: Doubleday, 1981), 128.

47. Butler, *Gender Trouble*, 47–48. The Lacanian answer seems to be that the mask disguises a lack; there is nothing behind the mask, or "the secret is there is no secret."

48. See S. Žižek, *Metastases of Enjoyment: Six Essays on Woman and Causality* (London: Verso, 1994). I am more convinced by and more comfortable with Butler's account, but Žižek's particular description of the nature of subjectivity is most relevant here. Cf. J. Butler, "Critically Queer," *GLQ: A Journal of Lesbian and Gay Studies* 1, no. 1 (1993): 17–32; and J. Butler,

"Lana's 'Imitation': Melodramatic Repetition and the Gender Performative," *Genders* 9 (Fall 1990): 1–18.

49. I take the phrase from Stein: "God is love, and love is goodness giving itself away." Stein, *Hidden Life*, 38.

50. Stein, *Life in a Jewish Family*, 26, 31, 34.

51. Stein, *Aus dem Leben*, 32.

52. The photograph appears in an English edition of Stein's works with the date 1893, indicating it was taken just before the death of the father (July 1893). The later date is confirmed by close examination of the photograph, in which the montage is apparent, and because the young Edith (seated in foreground) cannot be twenty months old. In a letter to me, archivist Sister Maria Amata Neyer, OCD, reports on the account of Edith's sister Erna, confirming that the photomontage was constructed using a passport photograph of the father when, after his death, members of the family regretted the lack of a family portrait.

53. To learn more of these crosscurrents of masquerade and gender performativity one needs to read Butler's *Gender Trouble*, and especially the spate of articles citing it, alongside J. Butler, "Critically Queer," esp. 21–24; see also J. Butler, "Imitation and Gender Insubordination," in *Inside/Out: Lesbian Theories, Gay Theories*, ed. Diana Fuss (London: Routledge, 1991), 13–31. This literature suggests the danger of celebrating Stein's passing gestures, or performativity, as unqualified subversion of identities at the cost of glossing over the complicity of these moves with their ultranationalist, sexist, and racist discursive contexts.

54. Until now, of all the contexts and canons into which Stein might be subsumed, the theological is the only one in which a very serious attempt has been made to resolve contradictions and inconsistencies (and indeed literally to canonize Stein). If a single justification is to be found for this, it must be found in chronology: for Christian canonizers, the move from secular literary and philosophical to theological and hagiographic writing follows the pattern of revelation, whereas modern literary canons are founded on the assumption of a reverse chronology of a corpus of secular texts emerging from the Renaissance onward. A productive antidote to this literary-canonical version of the secularization thesis is in Julia Lupton's analysis of a dialectic of secularization and Christianization, or modern literature and hagiography, in *Afterlives of the Saints: Hagiography, Typology, and Renaissance Literature* (Stanford, CA: Stanford University Press, 1996).

55. Edith Stein, *Edith Steins Werke*, vol. 11, *Verborgenes Leben: Hagiographische Essays, Meditationen, Geistliche Texte*, ed. L. Gelber and Michael Linssen (Freiburg, Germany: Herder, 1987). Translations are taken from Stein, *Hidden Life*.

56. Lucy Gelber and Michael Linnsen, introduction to Stein, *Hidden Life*, xi–xv.

57. Michael Linssen, preface to Stein, *Hidden Life*, ix.

58. Stein, "Love for Love: The Life and Works of St. Teresa of Jesus," in Stein, *Hidden Life*, 29.

59. Ibid., 30. Another provocative parallel is suggested by the probable Jewish origins of Teresa of Ávila's family, but it cannot be established that Stein had any inkling of these origins.

60. Stein, "The Hidden Life and the Epiphany," in Stein, *Hidden Life*, 109–110.

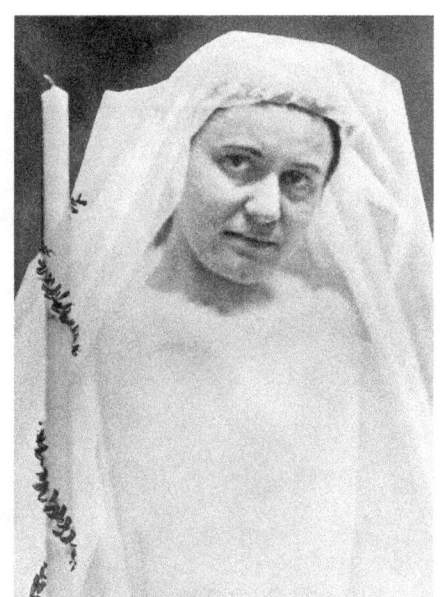

Figures 1–3. *Top left:* Stein as a student; *top right:* Stein on her Clothing Day, 1934; *bottom:* passport photo before her transfer to Echt, 1938. Photographs courtesy of Archivum Carmelitanum Edith Stein, Cologne, Germany; published with permission of ICS Publications, Washington, D.C.

Figure 4. Stein family, 1895 (father superimposed). Photograph courtesy of Archivum Carmelitanum Edith Stein, Cologne, Germany; published with permission of ICS Publications, Washington, D.C.

Figure 5. Edith Stein (*right*) with sister Erna. Photograph courtesy of Archivum Carmelitanum Edith Stein, Cologne, Germany; published with permission of ICS Publications, Washington, D.C.

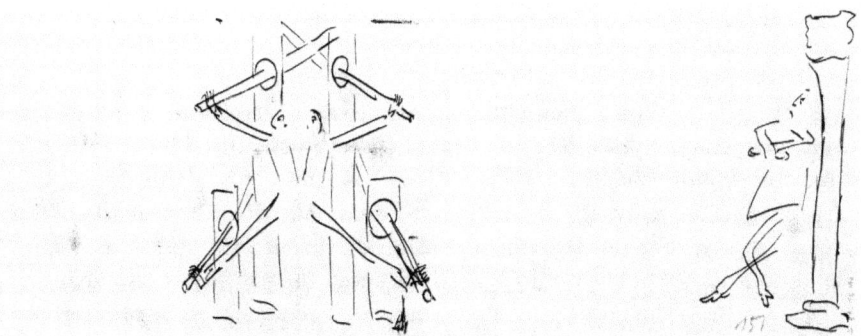

Figure 6. Kafka's drawing in a letter to Jesenská, September 1920. Reproduction courtesy of the Deutsches Literaturarchiv Marbach, Germany.

5 Two Vultures

Freud between "Jewish Science" and Humanism

Psychoanalysis, the Artful Science

The historical work on Sigmund Freud and psychoanalysis makes abundantly clear the centrality of Freud's identity as a scientist to his self-perception. The much broader sense of the German words *wissenschaft* and *wissenschaftlich* to our English translations "science" and "scientific" notwithstanding, Freud's biographers have been right to stress his career-long preoccupation with the scholarly recognition of himself and of psychoanalysis in terms of *scientific* legitimacy.[1] But did this insistence on assigning the contribution to the province of science equate to a resistance to thinking of it as a cultural or humanist contribution? My too highly subjective, unscientific, and unsystematic response to this question is that if *I* wanted to avoid an association with the humanities at all costs, I would not name my complexes after Greek mythological heroes, I would not punctuate my scientific texts with classical, historical, and literary references, and I would not write books on Moses and Michelangelo and Leonardo da Vinci. Freud's self-professed "partiality for the prehistoric" manifested itself, as is well known, in his collection of Greek, Egyptian, and Roman antiquities and an ample library on archaeology and ancient history.[2]

In the afterlife of Freud's contribution, we are faced with two apparently irreconcilable positions, equally staunchly held: first, the historical appearance of the psychoanalytic mode of inquiry and concomitant epistemology had an immeasurably consequential effect on nearly all registers of culture, and second, psychoanalytic theory and practice have little or no empirical, scientific validity. This chapter finds itself between these two hostile and absolute propositions. Since Freud's death, ample accusations have been made that the science of psychoanalysis is not one at all or that it fully merits the epithet pseudoscience.[3] Whatever our convictions about the validity of psychoanalytic theory, resort to the talking cure has certainly been eclipsed by medical practices deemed more expedient. The claim that the practice of psychoanalysis (if not therapeutic practice altogether) has been superseded by pharmacological medicine would be of somewhat less concern were it not to appear to have been supported by Freud himself. In *Outline of Psycho-Analysis*, composed in 1938, he predicted,

> The future may teach us to exercise a direct influence, by means of particular chemical substances, on the amounts of energy and their distribution in the mental apparatus. It may be that there are other still undreamt-of possibilities of therapy. But for the moment we have nothing better at our disposal than the technique of psychoanalysis, and for that reason, in spite of its limitations, it should not be despised.[4]

If "despised" (*verachtet*) seems a strong and emotionally charged word in this context (psychoanalysis might sooner be disregarded or discredited), it may bluntly hit on some critiques of Freud's contribution, no less today than in his own time. The immediate context of its use by Freud here, however, is his London exile, beginning in 1938. *Verachtet*—despised, or held in contempt—is always a heavily charged term, and in this context it was charged in a particular way. *Verachtung*, "contempt," I am suggesting, signals a displacement of sorts, with psychoanalysis standing in for the Jew. But one does not have to take such an analytic or interpretive risk; it can be demonstrated through a series of texts from Freud's very first forays into psychoanalysis that his anxieties about the acceptance of the science, about his own academic success, and about the status of Jews in central European society were of a piece.

Historicizing Contempt

To point out the elision of categories of Jewishness and pseudoscience, quack science, or literature in perceptions of psychoanalysis is not to say anything new. This point in particular is standard fare in the North American historical reception of Freud, in spite of other disagreements, by Carl Schorske, Peter Gay, or Sander Gilman. In fact, the impetus for including this chapter in *Modernism without Jews?* was that the contemporary humanistic treatment of Freud—particularly the discussions of Freud and psychoanalysis in cultural history—cannot resist the gravitational pull toward German-Jewish studies. Carl Schorske wished to place Freud (rightly) in the context of fin-de-siècle Viennese modernist innovation and offered as his particular context the struggle for legitimacy in an antisemitic central European scientific milieu. Ironically, in doing so, he needed to characterize the discovery of the unconscious as itself a kind of defense mechanism, specifically a "repression" of Freud's hostile context.[5] As I have stated elsewhere, this description of psychoanalytic theory as aestheticism, as a "retreat into the psyche," in Schorske's famous phrase, completely belies its actual operations.[6] Gilman aptly reproduces the antisemitic (and misogynist and homophobic) discourses of Freud's world and shows their echoes in Freud's own mind—this strategy echoes such discourses more than anywhere else in the historiographical work.[7] Peter Gay, for his part, comes to Freud's defense by wishing away the fin-de-siècle Vienna context—Freud's world was the international arena of science and decidedly not the particularity of Vienna, to which he belonged only casually (Gay is resisting not only Schorske here but Allan Janik and Stephen Toulmin's *Wittgenstein's Vienna* and what he accurately saw as a rising star of the new historiographical image of Vienna 1900).[8] Freud himself saw the focus on the uniquely Viennese context of psychoanalysis as code for its Jewishness and regarded early permutations of the Vienna 1900 thesis as "quite exceptionally senseless, so senseless, in fact, that I have sometimes been inclined to suppose that the reproach of being a citizen of Vienna is only a euphemistic substitute for another reproach which no one would care to put forward openly."[9]

Hence the tensions and associations among figures of science, pseudoscience, literature or humanities, Vienna, and centrally, Jewishness were as active between 1895 and the world wars as they are in the foreign historiography from the 1970s onward. Between these eras, in the postwar period, these associations took particularly crude form in books such as David Bakan's scandalously titled *Sigmund Freud and the Jewish Mystical Tradition*.[10] Marthe Robert, with characteristic eloquence, dismisses these crude accounts to suggest a subtler if no less insistent thesis about the fusion of German and Jewish currents in Freud's thought (reminiscent of Rosenzweig's notion of a German-Jewish *Zweistromland*, or land of two streams).[11] This she signals with the term "two cultures."

From Culture to Vulture

In 1959, C. P. Snow coined the term "two cultures" to describe a rift in educated society between those who identified themselves as intellectuals, but whom Snow insisted on calling literary intellectuals or "modernists," and those speaking the language of science (most exemplarily, physical science).[12] The rift Snow decried was not just one of language and mutual incomprehensibility; it was ideological: while those he called the modernists—humanist intellectuals basking in existentialism—were pessimistic, the scientists in contrast were bubbling enthusiasts, imagining themselves to be the bards of a new Elizabethan age. This particular rhetorical configuration is clearly a product of a cold-war context disconnected in some ways from Freud's period as well as the post-1968 Freud reception in the United States (it was a polemic on education, among other things). But the term "two cultures" adroitly characterizes what must be described as a fierce competition between kinds of knowledge in the nineteenth century, as we will see.

Snow's context of discussion was hence in some ways removed from this chapter's; I focus on the late- and post-cold-war reception of psychoanalysis in the humanities and sciences as they relate to the fin-de-siècle to mid-twentieth-century contexts of the origins of psychoanalysis. In the previous chapters and this one we observe not only reflection, reiteration, and repetition of discourse clusters but also a suggestion that reading these moments against one another is potentially fruitful. In particular, the two regimes of knowledge, science and humanism, can sooner be seen as "two vultures" in these contexts: instead of mutual incomprehensibility, one can describe a fierce competition of the sort that does not so much disregard as defiantly insist on the irrelevance, inertness, lifelessness of the other. Each declares the other dead and at the same time consumes and incorporates its material.

Of all the most schematic ways psychoanalysis has been pegged and put away by grand intellectual histories (from secularization theses to repressive hypotheses), a moderately compelling one can be discerned through the well-known work of Jürgen Habermas.[13] The emergence of a modern, formally autonomous notion of aesthetics is linked in this conception to the idea of a disaggregation from the spheres of morality and science or knowledge.[14] In fact, various nineteenth-century ideologies reached toward formally synthesizing an integral substantive reason that had been torn asunder by the fall of a metaphysical holism. Modernism in this sense represented the fracturing of reason into three moments, aesthetic, ethical, and scientific, each with its own specific criteria (beauty, justice, and truth, respectively). Extrapolating from these terms, new intellectual systems of modernity can appear as colonizing projects emerging from one or the other of these realms to consume the others: in Marxism, normative rightness, justice, and morality should come to govern the boundaries of truth and beauty; Nietzsche represents the primacy of the aesthetic over politics and knowledge; and so on. If psychoanalysis is another such grand intellectual project, making claims to comprehend these discrete spheres of knowledge, it clearly does so from the perspective of *science*.

To Freud's scientific critics, this very move from the psyche to culture is proof of the inauthenticity of psychoanalysis as science, rather than, say, literature (meant as disparagingly as possible). Even the revolutionary Richard von Krafft-Ebing, whose scientific studies of sexual pathology were themselves perennially suspect by the medico-scientific establishment, declared Freud's account of hysteria to "sound like a scientific fairy-tale."[15] The passage from the scientific to the literary can even be fairly precisely located in Freud's biography as being the abandonment around 1895 of a reliance on an organic model of neurology to interpret hysteria.[16] This key moment in the history of psychoanalysis—the move away from the idea that hysteria and other psychic disorders were symptoms of an undiscovered anomaly or lesion in the brain and toward an exploration of the subject's past experience—may signal a move toward or away from scientism, depending on one's perspective. It speaks for psychoanalysis's grounding in hard science that the discipline emerged out of biology and physiology rather than psychology (and Freud's devotion to Jean-Martin Charcot would never wane, in spite of this arguably radical break).[17] Of course, it is easy to anticipate the logic of another spectator, who might identify the shift from an anatomical and physiological focus to the talking cure as a hard shift from science to literature. It is worth remembering, however, that the neurological interpretation of hysteria from which Freud seceded was dominated by the contemporary view that hysterical symptoms were manifestations of the broad processes widely understood under the rubric of degeneration. This must seem ironic today. The literature on degeneration—densely metaphorical, penetrating a broad spectrum of cultural phenomena in the latter nineteenth and early twentieth centuries but providing no scientific or medical models usable for contemporary science—is the province of the "other" culture, literary and cultural studies.[18] What those studies constantly remind us is that the figure of degeneration, as a sign of the generalized discomfort with modernity around 1900, was also, and in different ways, identified with Jewishness.[19] The move away from a degeneration model of hysteria toward a psychoanalytic one of neurosis was in this sense a flight from an essentialism that also essentialized the Jew.

A Family Affair

Still, the science that psychoanalysis would become was, as everybody knows, vulnerable to the epithet of Jewish science.[20] It is not just that everybody knows about this vulnerability. It continues to make sense to them. When teaching on the ideology and politics of National Socialism I can make great use of the tale of the German physicists' attack on Einstein and relativity as "Jewish physics," an epithet that strikes students as an absurd and transparently ideological contradiction of terms. I cannot do the same with the accusation of psychoanalysis as Jewish science. It is not that students would think such a thing themselves; it is simply thinkable—it makes sense in a way that Jewish physics cannot, and this difference is clearly linked in part to the questionable scientific status of psychoanalysis.

The association of Jewishness and psychoanalysis was of course not lost on the latter's earliest practitioners, most of whom were Jewish. C. G. Jung was of course the most notable exception, and the well-known story of his centrality to, and then break from, the core psychoanalytic circle is relevant here. A key document in this regard is the letter Freud wrote to Karl Abraham in 1908, in which the founder of the discipline somewhat patronizingly asks his Berlin deputy Abraham to tolerate Jung's theoretical deviations from certain foundations of psychoanalytic theory, in the spirit of keeping Jung in the circle. He writes,

> Be tolerant, and do not forget that really it is easier for you to follow my thoughts than it is for Jung, since . . . you are closer to my intellectual constitution through racial kinship, while he as a Christian and a pastor's son finds

his way to me only against great inner resistances. His association with us is therefore all the more valuable. I was almost going to say that it was only by his emergence on the scene that psychoanalysis was removed from the danger of becoming a Jewish national affair.[21]

The climax of the letter in the last line of this quotation may be seen as *sort of* an inverted family romance, in which the father fantasizes for himself a different and inauthentic legacy. It differs from Freud's notion of the family romance in that, rather than an unconscious stratagem screening the inadequacies of the true parents, Freud's is a conscious strategy to win legitimacy by moving out of the Jewish circle of his most loyal and dogmatic followers. This complicated moment in the history of psychoanalysis is relevant to our exploration here in a particular and ironic way: Abraham's objections to Jung were based on the latter's deviations from the rational mechanics of the psychoanalytic process (psychosexual stages and so forth) toward the mystical. Freud counseled Abraham to understand that, as Jews, it was "easier" for "us." Clearly, in this case, and enduringly, mysticism stands in not only for rationalism's other but for the other of *science*; the threat or promise that one might consume the other compels it to the constellation of figures I am bringing into relief. Of course, the gesture identifying Jewishness with hyperrationality and dogmatic attention to laws and Christianity with mysticism and spirituality was one that belonged to an established tradition of antisemitism.

The quarrel between humanistic and natural scientific discourse in nineteenth-century central Europe was far from innocent of these associations. The end of the nineteenth century was marked by a wide-ranging cultural conflict that is lost to the historiography to a large degree, in part because its consequences were subtle and its boundaries vague. Humanism in this context was buttressed by historicism: deep knowledge of one's cultural traditions as well as the cultural traditions of the ancients and, to some degree, of other peoples; erudition; and rhetorical power. This humanism, a tradition of classical education, cultivation, and historicism, had come to be seen as potentially reactionary by a generation of positivistically oriented or objectivist thinkers, for whom mathematics and natural science were the methodologically model disciplines. An apt central European example is the young Tomáš Garrigue Masaryk, by discipline a philosopher, in the 1890s a young professor (six years Freud's elder). In his defense of the challenge to the authenticity of Czech national treasures that turned out to be forgeries, as well as in his fierce defense of the Jew Leopold Hilsner, who was convicted and imprisoned on charges of Jewish ritual murder, Masaryk was not acting as a less than nationalist philosemite. In fact he confessed a personal and visceral antisemitism that he felt he must govern with his own rationality.[22] These politically risky stances were principled not on behalf of German nationalists or Jewish victims but on behalf of this new scientific culture. While the history of ideas takes more twists and turns and contains more contradictions than its textbooks imagine, one can hear in this conflict the echo of the struggle between the defenders of the French Revolution—those believers in universal and natural laws—and those who held more faith in the organic traditions of deep-rooted culture (say, Mary Wollstonecraft vs. Edmund Burke).

But such an excursion to the aftermath of the Enlightenment raises another crucial context implicating Jewish identity in the schematic conflict between science and humanism. The Jew was a privileged figure in the exercise of European thought meant to place the relationship of the particular to the universal—universality being the essence of natural law, particularity embodied by the Jewish other within European civilization. Emmanuel Lévinas would later do much to complicate these relations, but it is within these categories that he works.

Another Vulture

Freud's *Leonardo da Vinci and a Memory of His Childhood* of 1910 is particularly illuminating as a text that on several levels reproduces the conflicted dialogue between scientism and humanism.[23] The focus on Leonardo himself, a central figure of humanism, is too tempting to resist—and the place of Italy, the voyage to Italy, and the Italian Renaissance in the German imaginary has been the subject of quite a bit of study. But this troubled dialogue between scientistic and humanistic thinking is also interesting in part because this is an interior dialogue: first, an interior struggle of Leonardo's; second, one with which Freud can be said to identify. The text itself, furthermore, was Freud's most literary piece to date—a psychoanalytic novel. He considered it his most beautiful piece of writing up to that time ("the only beautiful thing I have ever written," he wrote to Lou Andreas-Salomé in 1919).[24] So here we have the most literary, humanist exercises of analysis in the mode of psychoanalytic biography.

In outline, Freud recounts and analyzes a childhood memory of Leonardo's in which a bird alights on the child's crib and places its tail in his mouth. The bird, as good fortune would have it, or at least as Freud would have it, is a vulture (*nibbio* in Leonardo's text and translated into German as *Geier* in the texts Freud was working with).[25] Freud quotes Leonardo: "It seems that I was always destined to be so deeply concerned with vultures; for I recall as one of my very earliest memories that while I was in my cradle a vulture came down to me, and opened my mouth with its tail, and struck me many times with its tail against [later: inside] my lips."[26] It is this vulture that bears particular weight in Freud's psychosexual reading of the dream, a tour de force that leads to a masterful investigation into Egyptian myth and the Egyptian vulture-headed goddess Mut, whose name suggests a connection to *Mutter* and, through a set of associations, of this god to the phallic mother. In its delicate braiding of the mechanics of psychosexual processes and the humanistic moment of culture, the book is a brilliantly consummate work. It encroaches even on art history, in Freud's analysis of Leonardo's painting of Saint Anne—beyond the analysis of the presence of two mothers, Anne and Mary, in relation to Leonardo's own biography, Freud discerned a vulture pictorially encoded in the drawing in the folds of Mary's shawl. This connection of mother and vulture is the occasion in Leonardo's text for a foray into Egyptian myth and the avian goddess Mut, both mother and vulture, finding its way into Leonardo's consciousness. Although the Egyptian goddess was unknown to Renaissance Italy, Freud postulates the routes through which this fragmentary, subterranean knowledge might have traveled, spilling out into archetypal motherhood.

The problem came later, when it became apparent that "vulture" was actually a mistranslation of the Italian *nibbio*, which is not a vulture at all, but another bird altogether, a kite, or sort of raptor. Descending on Freud's text as if vultures or raptors, many of psychoanalysis's staunchly scientific critics argued as though here was purest evidence of the fraudulence of the technique. So here we have, at odds with one another, a high point of the literary-humanist Freud, producing a text that is still seen as a landmark of a certain kind, and the assumption that the same text completely discredits any scientific merit of the venture.

After a first reading of *Leonardo*, the argument of which he had known from Freud directly as the text was being written, Sándor Ferenczi was deeply impressed and enthusiastic. He agreed that the public would find the text shocking: "shocking this time not so much in a moral as in a *logical* sense. People don't suspect that in mental life other than logical rules exist, and they will again make you out to be a dreamer and draw the most unfavorable conclusions about your other works."[27] Quite apart from the question, not yet revealed, of the mistranslation, this closest of allies corroborates Freud's anticipation of being misunderstood and rejected; not for any offense on *morality* inherent in his interpretation but for what will be understood as its defiance of *logic*. The interpreter of dreams must himself be not a thinker but a dreamer. We may link this to the binary of science and humanities, perhaps, but the two analysts are not speaking of those categories or audiences. At issue is the foundation of logic itself and whether it is the appropriate mode of inquiry for a realm not governed by its rules.

Two decades after the "psychoanalytic novel" that violated the rule of logic, Freud writes, "We approach the id with analogies: we call it chaos, the cauldron full of seething excitation.... The logical laws of thought do not apply in the id."[28] Note that this is not an assertion that logic is not at work in the realm of the id but that we, the external observers, approach it with other tools: with analogy, with metaphor—with the tools of literature and rhetoric, not science and philosophy.

Love

We are beginning to see how, for Freud himself, the psychoanalytic enterprise could be the supreme product of Enlightenment reason—the pinnacle of the maxim "The proper study of mankind is man"—and at the same time the embodiment of the Romantic challenge to the Enlightenment faith in reason and objectivity. Even in its process, in its method, psychoanalysis altered the relationship of scientific observer to the analysand—rather than a subject-object relation, the psychoanalytic relationship is intersubjective. Freud put it more provocatively to Jung at the end of 1906: "Essentially, one might say, the cure is effected by love."[29] This extraordinary claim was repeated a month later at the 1907 meeting of the Vienna Psychoanalytic Society, where Freud ventured that "our cures are cures of love."[30]

The dichotomy of science on the one hand and humanism or literature on the other, like all such binaries, suggested gendered difference: the power of objectivity, hard science against the pliable sensitivity of what Freud here calls love. The notable absence of gender in our analysis of this Freudian complex up until now should be addressed, but so should be a different kind of historical reception: popular consciousness. Attempting to fill out both lacunae, I briefly turn to what may seem at first to be an unlikely source: Alfred Hitchcock's 1945 film *Spellbound*. This adaptation of a 1927 novel was not the first example of a popular representation of psychoanalysis, but it was an early and significant one. It represents the absorption into popular culture of a crude understanding of the psychoanalytic account of the self and also of a critique of that account. Even in establishing these two sides of the debate over psychoanalysis, the film (and Hitchcock himself) demonstrated resistances to its own insights, in certain ways.

The center of the film and the key to its representation of psychoanalysis is the initially cold and relentlessly professional Dr. Constance Petersen (played brilliantly by Ingrid Bergman). One could say that the master narrative of the movie concerns this character's self-discovery as a woman and as an analyst: this is set up at first (mainly by her jocularly if aggressively sexually harassing colleagues) as a scientific hyperefficiency screening a feminine incompleteness. By falling in love, she becomes not only a real woman but a complete analyst. For one thing, science alone, cold and detached, is not enough to make an effective psychoanalyst (and we are introduced to some difficulties in her psychoanalytic practice early on). But love is also the key to her ability to solve both the mystery and cure the patient. The melodrama literalizes transference, and especially countertransference, and Freud's provocative remark that psychoanalytic treatment is effectively a love cure.

None of this makes it easy for contemporary viewers to regard the film as feminist or as a sophisticated treatment of psychoanalysis. Indeed, the film is left out of the canon of Hitchcock classics by many fans precisely for what seems to be a hokey treatment of both gender dynamics and, especially, psychoanalysis—although this judgment, it seems to me, dramatically misreads the film. It is worth mentioning that the lone, heroic female analyst in a field of men had a referent outside the frame, the Russian-Jewish émigré May Romm, who served (to Hitchcock's chagrin) as psychiatric advisor for the film and who had treated producer David O. Selznick.[31]

Gregory Peck appears in the film first as Anthony Edwardes, a prestigious psychiatrist who has arrived at Green Manors to replace the outgoing director Murchison. His attention to the hyperprofessional Petersen is not lost on the other physicians in the institution, and in the first romantic scene between them, Petersen seems receptive—even as she voices her skepticism about love:

> CONSTANCE PETERSEN: I think the greatest harm done the human race has been done by the poets.
>
> ANTHONY EDWARDES: Oh, poets are dull boys, most of them, but not especially fiendish.
>
> CONSTANCE PETERSEN: They keep filling people's heads with delusions about love . . . writing about it as if it were a symphony orchestra or a flight of angels.
>
> ANTHONY EDWARDES: Which it isn't, eh?
>
> CONSTANCE PETERSEN: Of course not. People fall in love, as they put it, because they respond to a certain hair coloring or vocal tones or mannerisms that remind them of their parents.
>
> ANTHONY EDWARDES: Or . . . or . . . sometimes for no reason at all.
>
> CONSTANCE PETERSEN: That's not the point. The point is that people read about love as one thing and experience it as another. Well, they expect kisses to be like lyrical poems and embraces to be like Shakespearean dramas.
>
> ANTHONY EDWARDES: And when they find out differently, then they get sick and have to be analyzed, eh?
>
> CONSTANCE PETERSEN: Yes, very often.
>
> ANTHONY EDWARDES: Professor, you're suffering from "mogo on the gogo"!
>
> CONSTANCE PETERSEN: I beg your pardon!

After this exchange, her male colleagues at Green Manors note a change in her. Interestingly, her receptivity makes her vulnerable to the gazes of the male doctors, and Dr. Fleureau, who had waggishly attempted to seduce her earlier in the film, becomes her interrogator-doctor, diagnosing her as lovestruck.

Soon after Petersen falls in love with Edwardes, it becomes clear that Peck's character is not Dr. Edwardes at all but an imposter and a psychiatric case himself, an amnesiac with what Petersen hopes is a delusion that he is a murderer. But with the real Dr. Edwardes unaccounted for, a warrant is put out for the imposter's arrest, and Petersen says to him, "[I will] take care of you, cure you, and remain with you till that happens." Doctor and lover, the two are on the lam.

While scientism, humanism, and love map easily onto this popular representation as discussed so far, the central component of Jewishness seems thus far to have been sanitized from the film. In fact, in the first half of the movie, psychoanalysis has been displaced not only from its German-Jewish origins but then also from its Manhattan home, to the white-Christmas set of what was then the WASPiest of venues: the institution Green Manors was in the Green Mountains of Vermont. But the couple's escape route leads them to what we might call the return of psychoanalysis's repressed Jewishness, Petersen's mentor Dr. Brulov. But this association is itself arguably ambiguous and complicated. Half-Jewish actor Mikhail Chekhov did "mark" Brulov as Jewish, through Yiddish inflection and via the clear portrayal of the doctor as a double of Freud (who is referred to in the film; Brulov is not supposed to *be* Freud but is a father figure and mentor of that most un-Jewish of supposed crypto-Jews, the figure a production assistant called "our Christmas tree"—Ingrid Bergman).

A central scene animates the dialogue between scientific objectivity and humanist subjectivity, or love—the *mind* and the *heart*. The setup is that Petersen has brought her fugitive amnesiac—identity still unknown—to Brulov's house without revealing the situation to the latter, telling him she has come to introduce him to her fiancé. In the night, Peck's character (we later learn his name is Ballantyne) has a psychotic break and, razor in hand, wanders about the house. He finds Brulov awake, who drugs him. This is Petersen's conversation with Brulov in the morning:

> PETERSEN: You don't know this man; you know only science. You know his mind, but you don't know his heart.
>
> BRULOV: We are speaking of a schizophrenic and not a valentine.
>
> PETERSEN: We are speaking of a man. . . . You know only science, but you don't know his heart. . . . The mind isn't everything; the heart can see things at some times.
>
> BRULOV: This is the way science goes backward. . . . Who told you this, Freud? Or a crystal ball?

Brulov also remarks, "We both know that the mind of a woman in love is operating on the lowest level of intellect."

One could argue (shallowly, I think) that this is a kind of rejection of psychoanalysis as too mechanical, a rejection of expert knowledge, and so forth. But we have seen that in spite of this portrayal of Brulov's one-sided embrace of scientism and disdain for feminine empathy, it is Petersen who becomes the true—and successful—analyst. She resolves the patient-lover's identity puzzle only to see him tried and convicted of murder, and it is only through her love that she is able to persist in the investigation and solve the crime. An actual critique of psychoanalysis as an unscientific, literary fiction is reserved in the film for one skeptical remark from an unreliable amnesiac:

> BALLANTYNE: I don't believe in that dream stuff. All that Freud stuff is a lot of hooey.
>
> BRULOV: You are a piece of work. You have amnesia and a guilt complex, you don't even know if you're coming or going, but Freud is lot of hooey; this you know.
>
> BALLANTYNE: You don't like me, papa.

Tellingly, this comical skepticism is embedded in something like a rudimentary understanding of psychoanalytic relations, even as it reflected Hitchcock's own skepticism: to May Romm's insistent interventions to make the portrayal of analysis more accurate, Hitchcock is said to have interjected, "But, my dear, it's only a movie." He regarded the psychoanalytic superstructure as an alibi for an ordinary whodunit plot structure. As little as any sort of endorsement or indictment of psychoanalytic science must have meant to him, it is all the more notable how he directed the tension so centrally throughout *Spellbound*.

It is somewhat free associative to cast out a set of binary figures as though they map onto one another neatly when they do not: science and humanities, universal and particular, European and Jew, Germany and Italy, philosophy and rhetoric, disciplining and love. These figures are variously at play in much of the discourse surrounding psychoanalysis's emergence and in the historical reception of its emergence, not within a systematic grid on the analytic surface, but overlying one another in paper-thin layers, bleeding into one another through suggestion, being linked by virtue of their association. Psychoanalysis is at home in the humanities not because it has strayed from its scientific origins. From the start, it was deeply humanistic and scientific at once. This is not surprising for a mode of scientific analysis that was defined as interpretation and, at that, an interpretation of dreams.

Notes

1. This was already clearly established in the three-volume "official" biography by Ernest Jones, *The Life and Work of Sigmund Freud* (New York: Basic Books, 1953), but is equally clear in classic biographies, such as Peter Gay, *Freud: A Life for Our Time* (New York: W. W. Norton, 1988); and Sander L. Gilman, *The Case of Sigmund Freud: Medicine and Identity at the Fin de Siècle* (Baltimore: Johns Hopkins University Press, 1993).

2. Peter Gay, *Freud, Jews, and Other Germans: Masters and Victims in German Culture* (Chicago: University of Chicago Press, 1978), esp. 39–41.

3. Well before the attacks of the 1990s focusing on the disingenuousness of Freud in particular, manipulation of data, and so on, articulate critics had decried the scientific method apparent in the case histories. The philosopher Frank Cioffi's career of Freud critique was an exemplary case, focusing on the question of pseudoscience. While Cioffi (like so many other critics) is completely tone deaf to the broad and fundamental insights of psychoanalysis that have changed human self-understanding, he is scrupulous (if sometimes mistaken) in his analysis of the relationship of theoretical hypothesis to the emergence of evidence in the therapeutic process. See Frank Cioffi, *Freud and the Question of Pseudoscience* (Peru, IL: Carus, 1998). Cioffi's original intervention was published as early as 1970; see Frank Cioffi, "Freud and the Idea of Pseudoscience," in *Explanation in the Behavioral Sciences: Confrontations*, ed. R. Borger and F. Cioffi (Cambridge: Cambridge University Press, 1970), 471–516. The term "pseudoscience" itself has no clear parameters but suggests a false discipline or system of scientific thought, along the lines of alchemy or astrology. Cioffi focused on the relationship of the universal theorem or hypothesis to the particular case study. See also Adolf Grünbaum, *The Foundations of Psychoanalysis: A Philosophical Critique* (Berkeley: University of California Press, 1984).

4. Sigmund Freud, *An Outline of Psycho-analysis*, in *The Standard Edition of the Complete Psychological Works of Sigmund Freud*, ed. James Strachey, vol. 23, *1937–1939: "Moses and Monotheism," "An Outline of Psycho-analysis" and Other Works* (London: Hogarth Press, 1964), 182. *Abriss der Psycho-Analyse* was first published in 1940 in *Internationale Zeitschrift für Psychoanalyse und Imago* 25, no. 1 (1940): 7–67.

5. Carl Schorske, "Politics and Patricide in Freud's *Interpretation of Dreams*," in *Fin-de-Siècle Vienna: Politics and Culture* (New York: Knopf, 1980), 181–207.

6. Scott Spector, "Marginalizations: Politics and Culture beyond Fin-de-Siècle Vienna," in *Rethinking Vienna 1900*, ed. Steven Beller (New York: Oxford University Press, 2001), esp. 143–144; Scott Spector, "Beyond the Aesthetic Garden: Politics and Culture on the Margins of *Fin-de-Siècle Vienna*," *Journal of the History of Ideas* 59, no. 4 (1998): 701–702.

7. The best example is Sander L. Gilman, *Freud, Race, and Gender* (Princeton, NJ: Princeton University Press, 1993).

8. See Gay, *Freud, Jews, and Other Germans*, 31–33; Gay, *A Life for Our Time*, 748, 777–778; and Allan Janik and Stephen Toulmin, *Wittgenstein's Vienna* (New York: Simon and Schuster, 1973). For an explicit thesis about the relationship of Freud's secular Judaism to his work, see Peter Gay, *A Godless Jew: Freud, Atheism, and the Making of Psychoanalysis* (New Haven, CT: Yale University Press, 1987).

9. Sigmund Freud, *On the History of the Psycho-analytic Movement*, in *The Standard Edition of the Complete Psychological Works of Sigmund Freud*, ed. James Strachey, vol. 14, *1914–1916: "On the History of the Psycho-analytic Movement," Papers on Metapsychology and Other Works* (London: Hogarth Press, 1957), 39–40. Freud's reference was responding to a critique of Pierre Janet. See also Yosef Hayim Yerushalmi, *Freud's Moses: Judaism Terminable and Interminable* (New Haven, CT: Yale University Press, 1991), 125n20.

10. David Bakan, *Sigmund Freud and the Jewish Mystical Tradition* (Princeton, NJ: D. Van Nostrand, 1958). The book has been reprinted several times, including in Boston by Beacon Press in 1975 and in London by Free Association Books in 1990.

11. Marthe Robert, *From Oedipus to Moses: Freud's Jewish Identity* (Garden City, NY: Anchor, 1976), 13–59.

12. C. P. Snow, *The Two Cultures and the Scientific Revolution* (London: Cambridge University Press, 1959). The piece was originally delivered as the annual Sir Robert Rede's Lecture at Cambridge University in 1959.

13. A starting point is Jürgen Habermas, "Modernity: An Unfinished Project," in *Habermas and the Unfinished Project of Modernity*, ed. M. P. d'Entréves and S. Benhabib (Boston: MIT Press, 1997), 38–55. The piece, originally a lecture delivered in September 1980 upon Habermas's receipt of the Theodor W. Adorno prize bestowed by the city of Frankfurt am Main, also appeared as Jürgen Habermas, "Modernity versus Postmodernity," special issue, *New German Critique*, no. 22 (1981): 3–14.

14. The neo-Kantian conception of the emergence of three separate spheres of reason described more fully below is outlined in Jürgen Habermas, *The Theory of Communicative Action*, trans. Thomas McCarthy, vol. 1, *Reason and the Rationalization of Society* (Boston: Beacon, 1984).

15. The source for Krafft-Ebing's much-cited remark in response to Freud's lecture on the etiology of hysteria in the Psychiatrischer Verein is Freud himself, in a letter: Sigmund Freud, *Briefe, 1873–1939*, ed. Ernst L. Freud (Frankfurt am Main, Germany: Fischer, 1960), 193; see also Max Schur, *Sigmund Freud: Leben und Sterben* (Frankfurt am Main, Germany: Suhrkamp, 1973), 131. The anxiety about psychoanalysis's status as an independent scientific discipline is apparent from its earliest history. See, e.g., the letters to Wilhelm Fliess and other materials in Sigmund Freud, *Aus den Anfängen der Psychoanalyse: Briefe an Wilhelm Fliess, Abhandlungen und Notizen aus den Jahren, 1887–1902* (Frankfurt am Main, Germany: S. Fischer, 1962), 38–60.

16. Many sources confirm this approximate date for the break with Jean-Martin Charcot's organic model. A succinct one is Edward Erwin, *The Freud Encyclopedia: Theory, Therapy, and Culture* (New York: Routledge, 2002), s.v. "Psychoanalysis, Origin and History of," esp. 439–440.

17. See the obituary he wrote for Charcot and other relevant materials in *The Freud Reader*, ed. Peter Gay (New York: Norton, 1989), 45–55. I thank my friend and colleague John Carson for the insight that this bifurcation of science and art is complicated by the tradition that places medicine in particular between these two realms, in spite of the explicit competition of scientific and humanistic thinking burgeoning in the late nineteenth century.

18. See, e.g., Daniel Pick, *Faces of Degeneration: A European Disorder, c. 1848–1918* (Cambridge: Cambridge University Press, 1989); and J. Edward Chamberlin and Sander L. Gilman, eds., *Degeneration: The Dark Side of Progress* (New York: Columbia University Press, 1985).

19. This association was made even by the Jews themselves; see Stefan Vogt, "Between Decay and Doom: Zionist Discourses of 'Untergang' in Germany, 1890–1933," in *The German-Jewish Experience Revisited*, ed. Steven E. Aschheim and Vivian Liska (Berlin: De Gruyter, 2015), esp. 80–86.

20. See Morris Vollmann, "'Jüdische Wissenschaft'—Sigmund Freuds Psychoanalyse im Fokus von Fremdzuschreibung und Entstehungskontext," in *Deutsch-jüdische Wissenschaftsschicksale: Studien über Identitätskonstruktionen in der Sozialwissenschaft*, ed. Amalia Borboza and Christoph Henning (Bielefeld, Germany: Transcript, 2006), 101–134.

21. Letter from Sigmund Freud to Karl Abraham, May 3, 1908, letter 28F in *The Complete Correspondence of Sigmund Freud and Karl Abraham, 1907–1925*, ed. Ernst Falzeder (London: Karnac, 2002), 38.

22. See Roman Szporluk, *The Political Thought of Tomáš Garrigue Masaryk* (Boulder, CO: East European Monographs, 1981), 61.

23. Sigmund Freud, "Eine Kindheitserinnerung des Leonardo da Vinci (1910)," in *Studienausgabe*, ed. A. Mitscherlich (Frankfurt am Main, Germany: S. Fischer, 1969), 10:87–160. The English title *Leonardo da Vinci and a Memory of His Childhood* has stuck since the original English edition by Strachey.

24. Ernst Pfeiffer, ed., *Sigmund Freud–Lou Andreas-Salomé: Briefwechsel* (Frankfurt am Main, Germany: S. Fischer, 1966), 100.

25. Sander Gilman, "Preface," in *Reading Freud's Reading* (New York: New York University Press, 1994), xiv. Gilman provides an enlightening bibliographic genealogy of the misreading.

26. Sigmund Freud, "Leonardo da Vinci and a Memory of His Childhood," in *The Standard Edition of the Complete Psychological Works of Sigmund Freud*, ed. James Strachey, vol. 11, *1910: "Five Lectures on Psycho-analysis," "Leonardo da Vinci" and Other Works* (London: Hogarth Press, 1957), 82.

27. Letter from Sándor Ferenczi to Sigmund Freud, June 5, 1910, letter 139, in *The Correspondence of Sigmund Freud and Sándor Ferenczi*, ed. Eva Brabant, Ernst Falzeder, and Patrizia Giampieri-Deutsch (Cambridge, MA: Belknap Press of Harvard University Press, 1993), 178 (emphasis in original).

28. Sigmund Freud, *New Introductory Lectures on Psycho-analysis*, in *The Standard Edition of the Complete Psychological Works of Sigmund Freud*, ed. James Strachey, vol. 22, *"New Introductory Lectures of Psycho-analysis" and Other Works* (London: Hogarth Press, 1964), 73.

29. Letter from Sigmund Freud to C. G. Jung, December 6, 1906, letter 8F in *The Freud/Jung Letters*, ed. William McGuire (Princeton, NJ: Princeton University Press, 1974), 10.

30. Herman Nunberg and Ernst Federn, *Minutes of the Vienna Psychoanalytic Society*, trans. M. Nunberg (New York: International Universities Press, 1962), 101.

31. Useful information on this dynamic is provided by Leonard J. Leff, *Hitchcock and Selznick: The Rich and Strange Collaboration of Alfred Hitchcock and David O. Selznick in Hollywood* (Berkeley: University of California Press, 1987), 115–173.

6 Elsewhere in Austria

Jewish Writing between Habsburg Myth and Central Europe Effect

Writing Elsewhere

For a long time, cultural histories of Habsburg modernism focused on fin-de-siècle Vienna, which seemed an ample enough stage to accommodate the literary modernity of a Hugo von Hofmannsthal, a Young Vienna movement, and an Arthur Schnitzler; the musical novelty of a Gustav Mahler and an Arnold Schoenberg; new intellectual currents from Freud to Ludwig Wittgenstein; in art, a Gustav Klimt and his student Egon Schiele, an Oskar Kokoschka; in design and architecture, a Wiener-Werkstätte, a Secession, an Adolf Loos, and an Otto Wagner; and much more.[1] Many of these producers or their patrons were Jewish, and that was noted often if unevenly in the historiography, which still nonetheless focused on Vienna Jews.[2] The fin-de-siècle Vienna thesis divorced these innovators and their work from the German cultural realm, but it also seemed to cut them off from their imperial context, even if many of these creators had roots elsewhere in Austria-Hungary. More strikingly, this approach neglected the connections of these innovations to modernist developments in Prague, Budapest, Ljubljana, and other imperial centers.[3]

In this chapter I argue that some peculiar features of Habsburg modernism—even modern Habsburg German literature—can be discerned most clearly by shifting focus to cities away from the imperial center, where the majority language was not German and Jews were the authors of so much German-language culture. This is the first and most literal sense in which the "elsewhere" of this chapter title is meant. But a hint of what is denoted by it can be detected even in authors of the Viennese center—and even in such central works of the Vienna scene as Stefan Zweig's much-read memoir, *The World of Yesterday*.[4] The work is not a modernist masterpiece, to be sure, and not perhaps even entirely honest—at least, in a certain reading, the most quotable and quoted parts of the opening chapter on the "world of security" may seem a dissimulation, more than merely romantic ideation. Zweig's image of the pervasive sense of stability and certainty about the future rings hollow in relation to the world in which Zweig was reared: in the years of disgracefully trumpeted ritual-murder accusations in

Bohemia and in eastern Hungary, during the rise of populist antisemitic politics at both local and imperial levels, and as the definition of national belonging became increasingly race based. Yet *The World of Yesterday* may be seen to stand for a certain symptomatic self-positioning of Habsburg literature: it sets particular coordinates of nostalgia. We have a hint, here, of a centripetal compulsion in the imaginary of Habsburg-oriented Austrian culture. While we can think of Austrian modernism in terms of specific locations or centers—institutes and academies, Café Griensteidl, or the Secession building—even in this most Viennese of popular writers, the world of which he speaks ("of yesterday") is not of a fixed point where one is, with others, but somewhere else.[5] And while the memoir, like all memoirs, is meant to rescue a universal story out of the particulars of a most idiosyncratic life—"memories of a European," as the German subtitle has it— Europe is the epicenter of "unceasing volcanic eruptions," and Zweig's particular qualification for presenting his as an exemplary life is the *singular* one, which is actually a plural one: that "as an Austrian, a Jew, an author, a humanist, and a pacifist, I have always stood at the *exact point* where these earthquakes were the most violent."[6]

This is the 1940s, this is exile literature, and Zweig in his time had been the most successful Viennese popular writer—and yet in these temporal displacements and losses of footing, Zweig's letters begin to resemble the Austrian modernist literature that is the focus of this chapter: Jewish writing in German from elsewhere, from parts of the Habsburg monarchy that were not majority German speaking.

Beyond Vienna and Beyond German

My inquiry, like many a curiosity that may come to border on an obsession, began as the result of assignments and commissions. First, I was invited to contribute one of the major articles on literature, "German Literature," to *The YIVO Encyclopedia of Jews in Eastern Europe*.[7] At first, I confess, that seemed perilously big. But upon consulting the boundaries and definitions set by the encyclopedia's editors, the still intimidating difficulty of the assignment altered. What were the bounds of eastern Europe, according to our editors? It was defined as the territory east of German-speaking lands. This proved the most explicit paradox of the assignment—German language beyond the terrain of German language—but it was not the only problem: the definitions of "Jewish" and "German" could be as porous. What was German—did it include Judeo-German? Was it a matter of what language the authors thought they were using or how it was received by its audience? As for the problem of defining Jewish writing, we have this in the German-Jewish field more generally and certainly in the western Habsburg scene—as discussed in previous chapters, how are we to consider, for example, a Hofmannsthal, a

Wittgenstein, a Blumenberg, or an Adorno a Jewish author? So the piece turned out to be an extended discussion of these problems of definition and of placement.

The second of these commissions was for a project at the Simon Dubnow Institute for Jewish History and Culture in Leipzig on "German as Jewish language of scholarship" (which later became the somewhat different "German in the Jewish culture of knowledge").[8] The impetus was explicitly that German was frequently the language chosen by Jewish authors from eastern Europe, including those parts of the Habsburg Empire where it was not the majority language. This held true in the nineteenth century up until the end of the monarchy and even after, in high literature and in many branches of scholarship. The readily available explanation for this phenomenon—and the one the project in its outlines already implied—is that German was the lingua franca that connected these writers to others in the Habsburg and German Empires and beyond. In this view, German was the entry ticket, or *entrée billet*, to the terra firma of Western civilization (not to be unfair to Heinrich Heine, who said conversion played this role). Yet this observation is at odds with an element of displacement that seems to characterize much of this writing and that also pervades its historiography. The "elsewhere" in the chapter title refers not only to the use of German beyond the bounds of the German-speaking majority populations of Vienna and Upper and Lower Austria but also to the element of dislocation that seems to threaten to undermine an easy understanding of German as a common language for Habsburg Jewry.

There is another point to put up front. The character of dislocation or displacement that I describe as a hallmark of this literature is not lost on the critical reception of Habsburg literature but is, rather, embraced. It entails what I have to call a mystique of central European displacement, marginality or liminality. It is that mystique to which I hope to call attention. I begin with an example from a series of paradigmatic Habsburg literary figures. Part of the appeal of this mystique lies in the fantasy of something being salvaged in an idiosyncratic environment, an element or a nuance that has been lost to more grounded national territories, cultures, and literatures. In the period in which it was not only claimed but increasingly accepted that there should be a direct correspondence of language, ethnicity, territory, and national culture, that Austria was out of sync with this normative state was linked to its special access to the modern. Its pathology was its magic.

From Asylum to *Radetzky March*

Consider the case of the insane locksmith Karl Piehowicz, interned in the Czernowitz nerve clinic, whose brilliance as a poet is discovered by Alfred Margul-Sperber (1898–1967), who in turn publishes the inmate's poems in a German-language newspaper in interwar Czernowitz (then Romania). In 1928 the poet is lauded by Karl Kraus in *Die Fackel* in these emphatic terms: "The greatest poet working in German today, perhaps the only great one, and one of the greatest who have ever lived, is a locksmith living in the insane asylum at Czernowitz."[9] The end of this story is as important to tell as this crescendo moment: the monomaniac locksmith was actually simply repeating on an endless loop a great number of poems he had memorized as a way of whiling away the time in the Foreign Legion in Morocco. Of course, the last thing one wants to imply is that there is something inherently fraudulent about central European modernism and, inseparably, the Jewish contribution to it. It is simply that its greatness has always been wrapped up in a complex of assumptions about the origin of central European creativity and that these sometimes unspoken assumptions are perpetuated in historiographical discourse. Kraus himself appeared less contrite about the revelation than buttressed in his claim that this man was a genius of German poetic language (who seems to have been unable to speak fluent German when he was not reciting poems). "No matter what the results of the investigation into the authorship, and even if it turns out that admirers of spiritual values have found and memorized a poet who has gone unknown for centuries—it cannot produce a greater miracle than the work itself, and editors around the world will remain shamed by the fact that the asylum is, if not the source, then the refuge and sanctuary of this creation."[10] It bears noting that the circuit of this mystique surrounding lost poetic purity runs not only from insane Piehowicz over the Bukovinian publicist Margul-Sperber to the legendary acerbic Viennese critic Karl Kraus but emerges again in full in the retelling of this true fiction in the inventive novel *An Ermine in Czernopol* (*Ein Hermelin in Tschernopol*, first published in 1958) by Gregor von Rezzori.[11] This latter-day self-fashioned Habsburg author (and figure) par excellence could not but land on this incident as a symptom of a shared condition of Czernowitz (Czernopol), and its province Bukovina (Teskovina), in an empire best dismembered and re-membered.

Ermine's absurd Hungarian hussar and nostalgically Habsburg loyalist hero Tildy must on some level recall Baron von Trotta in Joseph Roth's *Radetzkymarsch*.[12] The questions of the national, the modern, and the central European converge on literature poignantly in this epic, written after the dismemberment of the empire, by a Jew from Galicia for whom German was something other than a mother language and taking off from a work by the very differently Austrian Franz Grillparzer a century earlier. Roth's example is hence a peculiar and nonetheless excellent center for an inquiry into modernist central European literature and culture, although he cannot be called representative—his position is in fact too complex to represent anything fixed. Roth's homage to the Slovene field marshal does not so much ground a place for a supranational Habsburg identity (as has often been claimed) as it articulates Roth's own *dis*placement—the Galician Jew writing in German language from the tiny rump remaining of the Habsburg

Empire after its dissolution—to Berlin. Whether this literary moment is considered in terms of time or space, language, or history or politics, Roth seems free-floating, unanchored, always elsewhere.

German-language Jewish culture in the Habsburg and post-Habsburg realms sheds a different light on broad questions of central European historiography, as I have been arguing, because the very displacement Roth represents, this eternal elsewhere, is intimately connected to the Habsburg mystique at the heart of the representation and self-understanding of central European culture. This mystique is as much at the core of Kraus and Margul-Sperber's romanticization of a lunatic poet as it is at the heart of Rezzori's Tildy and Roth's von Trotta; it is present both in the historiographical clichés about Habsburg central Europe and in the articulations of some of its famous subjects. Roth's Radetzky occupies this function differently from Grillparzer's, from Johann Strauss's, and from the Bohemian-born noble who was to become the historical field marshal.

The Displaced Modern

Radetzkymarsch also occupies modernism differently than other masterpieces of the modern novel. While it clearly displays modernist elements such as shifting narrative perspective, it does so without the formal innovations of classic literary modernism. I speculate below about whether these sorts of differences are what keep Roth (perhaps also Robert Musil) out of the inner circle of canonical European modernists or if this is connected to a specifically central European character.

What is the connection of the central European to the national and to the modern? How are we to place it spatially and temporally? Even asking this question raises specters of the Habsburg imperial problematic that haunt the literatures that emerged in late nineteenth- and early-twentieth-century central Europe as well as the histories of them that are written. As a state of multiple nations in an age of nation-states, the empire was living on borrowed time (so the argument goes). An old-fashioned continental empire neurotically burdening itself with the unbearable baggage of its own history, the Danube Monarchy could not move forward with modernity, as had the lithe and nimble German or western European capitalist empires. If we define central Europe as it has traditionally been defined in historiography—that is, as the region claimed by the Habsburg Empire and its successor states—then central, in the case of Europe, is peripheral.

On the other hand, we have the facts of the contributions to the cultures of modernism that emerged from this realm, from the literary modernism of, say, a Kafka or a Musil to modernism as a critical category in Hermann Bahr, to its particular brands of *Jugendstil*, to music, to psychoanalysis. This sounds enough like a citation of Carl Schorske to point to another truism of studies of central European culture: the anachronism of Habsburg politics must have been specifically, if inversely, linked to the innovations of central European culture. (Hence, the peripheral becomes central to the modernist project.)[13]

The Myth of Central Europe

Writing from post-Habsburg Trieste, Claudio Magris read Roth as a paradigmatic voice, to be sure, but he did not take that voice at its word. He instead identified it as embodying what he consequentially named the "Habsburg Myth."[14] According to this interpretation, Roth's forever-tenuous position was a concentrated exemplar of the overall displacement of central European identity, and his fantasy production of a grounded central European identity and patriotism was a kind of defense mechanism (in psychoanalytic terms, a reaction-formation). Further—and here Magris's interpretation is particularly compelling—the nostalgia for a place that had never existed represented by this Austrian interwar literature harkened back to a powerful nineteenth-century myth of Habsburg dynastic history, which had been produced to resist the centripetal force of national movements after 1848. This is why Roth's *Radetzky March* embodies the myth so well, so literally. What Magris's contribution does so brilliantly is to allow us to think of German-language central European literature (central Europe in this, the classic, definition, excluding the lands that would be joined in the German *Kaiserreich*) in terms other than but comparable to discussions of national cultures proper. The Habsburg myth thesis allows us to see a unity in central European literature from 1806 on, not through the ascription of a reductive thesis of national essence but rather through ideological necessity.

A different and arguably simpler solution to the problem of placing central European culture is Maria Todorova's.[15] She has steadfastly asserted that there never was any central Europe in a culture-historical sense and that this term emerged as an ideological instrument only relatively recently and, further, that it should be rapidly and unapologetically purged from the historiography. This line of argument may be seductive as an antidote to idyllic constructions of central Europe such as, most famously or notoriously, Milan Kundera's in the often-republished essay "The Tragedy of Central Europe," but on the other hand "central Europe" as a term or as a problem is not simply of cold-war vintage.[16] Todorova is right in reminding us that the placement of central European culture is, and has perhaps consistently been, a problem of ideology, both while it was engaged by subjects at the time and in our own critical and historical literatures. Rather than discarding that complex, it is I think worth trying to capture, and to do so we must take the construct of central Europe seriously on some level.

One thing I am not trying to capture, at any rate, is a unitary central European experience or, in this chapter's particular case, a unitary experience of Habsburg Jewry. The actual sociocultural experience of Jews in the monarchy—their everyday lives, their social interactions, the bodies of knowledge they commanded or had access to, what they read and could read, the languages they spoke and understood, the foods they ate—varied as widely within the empire as it was in various cases apparently identical to lives of Jews in other nations and empires. These differences were not occluded in the period but, rather, often discussed. Most evidently, while Jews in Vienna, Czernowitz, Prague, Lvov, and Trieste might have identified as Habsburg Jews or even as Austrians, they retained a critical distinction of eastern and western Europe and were aware that their empire embraced Jews of both of these not only distinct but perhaps even oppositional realms. None of this belies the reality of a cultural entity, or even an imaginary, that could be called central Europe. To the contrary, the displacement I am describing—the lack of a clear territorial, sociocultural integrity (or again, the fantasy of one) is precisely what defined this central European culture for many of its inhabitants. This sense of displacement—territorial as well as temporal—lent central Europe its peculiar mystique. A crucial element Magris missed is the way that the cultural historiography of Habsburg modernism, including his own, takes on this myth in its own way. The ungrounded, illusionary, and displaced position of the Habsburg cultural producer puts her in a privileged position vis-à-vis the modern. Modernism is itself a notoriously slippery category, but whether critics decide to define it by its pervasive sense of self-reflection and self-consciousness, its self-irony and ironic stance toward the outside world, its moods of alienation or neurosis or paranoia, or its play with the very category of language, central Europe is suddenly "central" once again. That is, the creative minds of the Habsburg Empire would seem to have had privileged access to the hallmarks of modernism, not as a result of their position so much as by virtue of the story they told themselves about the place of central Europe in the modern world. This historiographical circle is not broken, if you thought it might be, by the much-heralded passage from the modern to the so-called postmodern. Witness Stefan Jonnson's insightful book on Robert Musil, *Subject without Nation*, in which the conventional (even old-fashioned) historiography on the Habsburg nationality conflict merges seamlessly with antifoundationalist philosophy's critique of the existence of a modern self.[17]

Where, then, is central Europe; where is the "there, there"? Where, if its spokespersons and its histories are merely echoes of nonexistent imaginaries, themselves echoing fantasy histories, always displaced, forever elsewhere? Is it not possible that this system of echo chambers is the phantom country we call central Europe? It is for this reason only that I would even consider burdening an already overburdened terminological historiography with another category, or rather metacategory, and it is what I call the Central Europe Effect. For some time now structuralist (and, in their wake, poststructuralist) thinkers have identified author-functions, author-effects, subject-effects, and so on, where authors used to be, replacing models of intention, message-coding, and reception with complex, controlled but not controllable operations of meaning.[18] A starting point of these theoretical investigations has often been that objects that had been taken for granted as essential, immutable, natural, and so forth (author, subject, self, what have you), have particular and sometimes quite short histories. The same must be held of the category of central Europe, of course, and this model of metacriticism may be useful to bring into the discussion of culture from this diverse region, not to expose any general category of central European culture as a sham but to give us insight into how all such discussions are structured to operate. Another parallel is the observer effect—the scientific problem shared by physicists, psychologists, ethnologists, and computer programmers of gauging and accounting for the effect of the presence of an observer on the processes or subjects being observed. I am hence proposing the Central Europe Effect as a category to contextualize this discussion historically, critically, and conceptually.

In every instance of this effect—wherever a location of central Europe has been identified in its dislocation, an idea of Austria in the need to define an "idea of Austria," and so on—the Jews seem to have played a paradigmatic function.[19] In its most literal form this appears as the assertion that the Jews, in their nationlessness and their status as minority par excellence, in their motility and their adaptivity, in their negative doubling as elastically assimilatory and rigidly inassimilable, were the monarchy's most loyal subjects or only true patriots. This truism was indigenous to the period as well as a commonplace of the historiography. Beyond the question of allegiance to the monarchy, what the assertions equating the Jews with the Habsburg monarchy do is reflect the twin symbolic function not of Jewish communities or individuals and Habsburg state actions or positions but of the Jews and central Europe as figures.

This figurative similarity, as you will guess from my argumentation so far, was not lost on subjects in the period. One example of this analogic correspondence is found in the Prague Zionist weekly *Selbstwehr*, in which an editorialist does the good etymological work of relating the practices of translation or cultural mediation and the geographical centrality of central Europe: he describes a Habsburg future in which the Jews flourish in the empire's mosaic of nations, a confederation of peoples stretching from Hamburg to the Persian Gulf. To reach this progressive and attractive end, the empire will depend on the Jews, their key to *Mitteleuropa*, the means (*Mittel* or *Mittler*) to unite east and west, their mediators (*Vermittler*): "For this reason the maxim on which the future of Austria *and the Jewish Volk* depend must be: Eastward and Forward!"[20]

In the historiographical imagination, the special function of central Europe and that of the Jews is conflated, particularly as these converge on the modern. We do not have to go to Steven Beller's 1989 standard work of cultural history, *Vienna and the Jews*, to find the thesis that the Vienna modern and Jewry coincide and coincide with modernism *tout court*. Vienna Jewish contemporaries like Stefan Zweig and George Steiner in more immediate retrospect made similar gestures in the most extreme terms, as we recall from chapter 2. Readers need no reminder that the metonymic correspondence of central European Jews and modernism came in handy, and was indeed indispensable, to the *völkisch* antisemitic and then the Nazi critiques of both.

Hybridity and the Habsburg Jews

Let us move on to a term more recent than the Habsburg myth, and widely influential. "Cultural hybridity" is a term that has been deployed by theorists of colonialism to describe the ambivalent effects of the identities produced by the colonial processes. While the stage for these investigations has typically been the developing world, it is ironic that the model Homi Bhabha and others have used has been that of the central European Jew between the Enlightenment and the Holocaust.[21] This complex ambivalence is spelled out in Bhabha's essays in *The Location of Culture*, and it is fair to say that the intervention has been misappropriated by those who understand it as an acceptance of a genus or category of the hybrid that is then celebrated for subverting the original, pure, colonizing species. In an analysis informed by psychoanalytic sources, Bhabha usually avoids denoting a type (the hybrid) who acts in certain ways under colonial conditions but instead refers to hybridity as either a process or a sign of processes of domination and resistance.[22] It is specifically not "a third term that resolves the tension between two cultures," a description in which we more than faintly recognize the image many have painted of certain groups of Habsburg Jews in the period of nationalist conflict, such as the German-speaking Jews of eastern central Europe. Central Europe, and paradigmatically, its Jewry, is hence seen not as a sign of a (post)colonial hybrid representing a process of hegemony, but as an actual cross of two or more worlds, capable of mediating among them. Even more interesting than this widespread historiographical misreading is the discovery of its presence among the historical subjects themselves; at least in many very different cases, the historian of Habsburg Jews may unearth a self-recognition of an inheritance, the positioning within East and West, past and future, Europe and its Other, and on and on. A captivating example of this self-referential claim of hybridity is Franz Kafka's fragment "A Hybrid" ("Eine Kreuzung"), written in 1917 and included in the posthumous collection *Beim Bau der Chinesischen Mauer*. Readers who know the piece will remember that it is the uncanny description of an unusual pet, half kitten and half lamb (with something doggish about it), that the narrator has received as an inheritance from his father; a fascinating, loving, and also somehow pathetic creature, uncomfortable in its own skin, for whom the narrator knows the butcher's blade would perhaps be the appropriate "solution" but one that he cannot provide. I am not going to join with the many critical voices who have taken this to be Kafka's clear allegorical statement about the status of German-Jewish life in diaspora, or in central Europe in particular. Rather, that very interpretation is inscribed in the story; hybridity is in this tale what I have elsewhere called a "trap," compelling an allegorical interpretation that is itself part of the narrative.[23] Here as elsewhere, it seems to me, Kafka is appropriating his own appropriation, thematizing the hybridity of a German author born in a conflicted central Europe to Jewish parents. For what is this piece if not the purest of moments of German literary modernism? And the hybrid, the halfbreed, the cross, and the crossing of this fragment: is it Jewish or Christian (this *shohet*, this *Kreuz*), animal or human? It is arguably more than a coincidence that this figure of the crossbreed is mobilized by Kafka; this is evidence that the discourse of hybridity is more native than it would seem and that here we must have another case where Kafka adopts a problematic contemporary discourse wholesale and pushes it to an aesthetic extreme, at which point it is unusable as an instrument of hegemony but is an instrument of pure aesthetics. Kafka, so to speak, was a hitchhiker or stowaway on the Central Europe Effect.

I will leave Prague aside temporarily, in part because it is a special case of central European Habsburg Jewish identity dynamics and mainly because I cannot claim to be an impartial observer of these dynamics, but I will return to it for just this reason. First, let us look at some other historical examples of Habsburg Jews to see if this peculiar operation, rather than character, can be detected. Out of Bohemia's neighboring Moravia hailed a great many "Jewish writers of German tongue," as Max Brod referred to himself. (His essay "Der jüdische Dichter deutscher Zunge" in *Vom Judentum* is symptomatic of this alienation of the tongue from the body or from the poet himself.[24] This is another kind of deterritorialization.) An important if also idiosyncratic example is Alexander Friedrich Roda Roda (1872–1945), whose early work has been characterized as emblematic of the Habsburg spirit. He was born in Drnowitz, Moravia, in 1872, but his family soon moved to Zdenci in Slavonia, the farthest eastern province of today's Croatia. Roda Roda's central Europe ranged into German Austria and Germany itself, where he became famous as a satirist and *kabarettist* (comedy show creator), rubbing elbows with leading literati and political writers of the age. This life and career stunningly fits a certain familiar image of a central European type: peripatetic, performatively cultured, and yet distanced and sardonic, a figure that is at once perennially an insider and a hapless outsider—eternally displaced and at home in this displacement. It is Gregor von Rezzori, that latter-day, profoundly Habsburg-identified writer discussed above, who sees in Roda Roda this paradigmatically central European essence that Rezzori himself emulates.[25]

Halfway Asias and Other Romances

Galicia is another important case, idiosyncratic in its own way. Two very important examples to name are men whose background as eastern European Jews cannot be considered incidental to the content of their contributions. Martin Buber (1879–1965), born in Vienna but raised in Lemberg (Lviv), presented mediations of Hasidic tradition to a German audience that were obviously linked to this background, as was his crucial journal *Der Jude* and even his philosophical writing, or so one could argue. One could ask the provocative question: In sum, is it the historian's fantasy of the mediating, rational-spiritual central European that construes in Buber a hybrid of German Romanticism and Galician Jewish spiritualism, or was this Buber's own imaginary of himself?

Joseph Roth, discussed above, was born in eastern Galicia and became an important Austrian writer. Indeed, he is a modern author whose great significance is sometimes overlooked, as I mentioned earlier, perhaps because the great literary tradition out of which he emerged and that he paradigmatically represented—the central European—was doomed to failure. At any rate, the argument is sometimes made that the likes of Roth and Musil are robbed of the reception given to a Marcel Proust, a James Joyce, or a Virginia Woolf because of the demise of the central European idea. If instead of central Europe as idea we return to Magris's diagnosis of the Habsburg myth, Roth has a place reserved for none other—as I indicate earlier, his *Radetzky March* is the classic of a central European nostalgia for a central European nostalgia. But if we leave it at this—as though our role in this myth is nothing except for possibly as its debunkers—we miss the complicity of contemporary interpretations of central European culture. We thereby perhaps willfully forget that the histories of central Europe perpetuate a process that should be examined rather than an image that can be identified. We miss the elegantly baroque operations produced by this discourse. We miss the Central Europe Effect.

If the itinerant Galician Roth is the swansong of this Habsburg-anchored central Europe in the twentieth century, an important early exponent was another, Karl Emil Franzos (1848–1904). This novelist, essayist, and poet was a fierce German nationalist and an important contributor to the nineteenth-century German orientalist image of eastern Europe and its Jews (this last especially through several volumes of "cultural vignettes from half-Asia").[26] Franzos was one of the most popular German-Jewish writers of his generation, and the consideration of him as a prime exemplar of the phenomenon of "Jewish self-hatred" is complicated.[27] Yet I do not think it can be seen as coincidence that this particular orientalism, which would have such sway in the German perception of eastern Europe in the half century of Franzos's life and the further half century after his death (and longer), hailed from a Jewish writer from that world rather than a resident of the German Empire proper. Hybridity, it appears, does not necessarily yield sympathy. Yet in the very exoticism of Franzos's descriptions, as in the very different and yet kin ones of the fellow Galician Leopold von Sacher-Masoch, for example, is a homey familiarity. Franzos's childhood was shared by Galicia and the heavily Germanized Bukovina to its south; in his mental topography, a city like Czernowitz was clearly European, whereas all of Galicia was mired within "half-Asia."

Franzos and Roth both made their German-language literary contributions after their moves out of Galicia—after their emigration, as it were, to German-speaking lands beyond the invisible boundary of eastern Europe. This path was not unusual for a certain tier of Galician Jewish society, who took German to be the language of higher culture and education and had their children schooled in it, even if as a second, third, or fourth language (after Yiddish, Polish, scholarly Hebrew, and sometimes Ukrainian). Such was the path of writers Manès Sperber (1905–1984), Soma Morgenstern (1890–1976), Salamon Dembitzer (1888–1964), W. H. Katz, the scholar Nahum Glatzer (1903–1990), and psychoanalytic writers such as Sigmund Biran. Most made their path over Vienna; many studied or worked in Germany.

This relationship of Jewish residents to German-language culture was historically quite different from the neighboring Cisleithanian province of the Bukovina.[28] Bukovina was the northeastern corner of what was considered Romania and was the part of Romania under Austrian control. Jews were present in substantial numbers in Romanian lands ruled by the Hungarian half of the Habsburg monarchy but did not tend to identify with German speakers. Transylvanian Jews acculturated to the politico-culturally dominant Hungarian population rather than its Romanian and German cohabitants, and other Romanian Jews identified strongly with the Romanian majority. Bukovina, in contrast, had a long history of mixed populations and had been under the sovereignty of various kingdoms, principalities, and empires in every direction (including the Ottoman Empire, the Kingdom of Hungary, Rus, Moldau, the Habsburg monarchy, and then Romania). Hence, Bukovina had been considered by the German leaders of the Habsburg Empire to be a key strategic site for Germanization since the reign of Joseph II, whose campaign included the settlement of many Germans from the west as well as the active Germanization of some local populations, including especially Bukovina's Jews. German-language education was formally required of them in various ways (as prerequisites of Talmudic study or marriage, for instance), and by the nineteenth century the Jews of its many country towns and especially its capital, Czernowitz, were largely German-speaking and strong supporters of the monarchy. The region continued to attract Yiddish-speaking Jewish immigrants from surrounding areas, however. In the early twentieth century, Jews made up nearly half of the population of Czernowitz and well over a tenth of the population of nearly one million where no ethnic group commanded a majority. In the twentieth century the German poetry of this region blossomed because of the extraordinary creativity of Bukovina's Jews.

The most important of the German poetry written by Jews in Bukovina was created in the twentieth century, especially after World War I and the succession of the region to Romania. Here the most apt comparison may be made to the German literature produced by Jews in Prague earlier in the century. The disproportionate contribution can be thought of in the context of minority cultures, in which the hegemonic status of the German language had already been superseded by other national claims so that the previously privileged language of culture was now a minority culture maintained and promulgated largely by German-acculturated Jews. Contemporaries and scholars have argued that the disproportionate literary talent in Bukovina and Bohemia might be linked to the isolation of these language islands and perpetuation of a high-cultural tradition from centuries past. But these sites were hardly considered language islands before the onset of the national movements that would create them as such, and the assumption that isolation from working-class elements or dialects is salutary seems transparently ideological. It is true that the Jews of Bukovina cherished a high-cultural European heritage that seemed old-fashioned to many residents of the surrounding Slavic and Romanian populations and those of most of German-speaking Europe as well. Another important influence is the so-called Ethical Seminar at the University of Czernowitz, where some Jewish students, notably Rose Ausländer (1901–1988), were steeped in a German neoidealist philosophical tradition. The poetry of German-Jewish Bukovina is perhaps best known as Holocaust literature, although the greatest contributions clearly begin in the interwar period. Many and perhaps even most of the writers emigrated to or spent substantial time in Germany, Austria, France, England, the United States, or Israel. Some of the most important, in addition to Ausländer and Paul Celan, include Margul-Sperber, Klara Blum (1904–1971), Alfred Kittner (1906–1991), Alfred Gong (Alfred M. Liquornik, 1920–1981), Selma Meerbaum-Eisinger (1924–1942), Moses Rosenkranz (1904–2003), and Immanuel Weissglas (1920–1979), to name only the best known of many authors.

Bukovina and Czernowitz in particular are certainly privileged sites for the phenomenon framing my discussion of Habsburg Jews: the power of a mystique of displacement, of uprootedness or of lack of synchronicity, of dual or multiple or elastic identities, or of untimeliness.

The case of the region's most extraordinary poet, Paul Celan, was symptomatic, if also unique. Born with the name Paul Antschel in the city of Cernăuți

(Czernowitz in its Romanian iteration) shortly after World War I and the dissolution of the empire, he experienced and survived the Holocaust, then became active as a poet and translator in Romania, the Soviet Union, Vienna, and finally and for the longest period, in Paris. His poetry—the most powerful and canonical of which reflected obliquely on the Shoah—has all the marks of high modernist lyric. In his work he mines gems of forgotten German language in a way that makes his work sometimes difficult to decipher, producing at the same time marvelously otherworldly effects within German writing. Obscurity and difficulty are hallmarks of modern lyric, at least according to a canonical definition of poetic modernism, which holds that the effects of language seem in such poetry to be liberated from a rigid mooring to worldly referents.[29] Celan was aware of this famous definition, for he rebutted it in his now famous acceptance lecture upon receiving the coveted Georg Büchner Prize in 1960. In the talk, published under the title "Meridian," he argued that modern poetry may seem obscure but that its obscurity is not a turn from referentiality at all; rather, it is the only access to an obscure contemporary world.[30] The obscurity of great modern German poetry emanates from the "thousand darknesses of death-bringing speech" of recent central European history.[31] The tragedy of Celan—his ever-alienated state, the antisemitic accusations by Claire Goll (attacking him as a plagiarist of her deceased husband Yvan), his depression and eventual suicide—this outsider fate of his fits poignantly within the frame explored here. A latecomer to the Central Europe Effect, to be sure, but Celan was ever painfully if often beautifully elsewhere.

Prague and the Central Europe Effect

With respect to Prague writers and in particular the Czech-to-German translators, I have argued that, rather than hybrids, these particular central European Jews could be conceived as a middle nation (again, from *Mitteleuropa*): their poetry was a new sort of national literature, grounding an alternative to nations in the ordinary sense of the word. To the degree this can be said to be true it is important to recall that such a literature was not a Jewish literature and that such a nation—middle nation—was not Zion. It functioned, I argue, as an alternative—and, yes, a subversive one—to the ideological complex binding essential peoples to eternal literatures and sovereign territories.[32]

I confess here—and it is emphatically not a disavowal of that thesis—that the sketch I draw of the ideological dilemma of German-speaking Jews in Prague was a subspecies of the more general genus I am calling the Central Europe Effect. A special attention to all moments of displacement—spatial, temporal, and ideological—and the extraordinary outcomes of this sense of displacement establishes the overall architecture of *Prague Territories*. Think of the voyages to eastern Galicia of Jiří Langer and of Hugo Bergman, among others; the fantasy

Hebraism melded with socialism in the untimely Rudolf Fuchs (central treatment given to his poem "Unzeit"); his work and the other Czech-to-German translators, and on and on.[33] What is more, observers at the time, and the Praguers themselves, shared in these self-descriptions. There is no doubt that some sort of conditions helped bring forth what must be considered an extraordinary literary contribution from a very small demographic group, but part of the cultural phenomenon of Prague German writing was the excitement generated in Germany about this language island, this eccentric and displaced corner of central Europe. The very particular circumstances surrounding the Prague Circle cannot be generalized throughout central Europe at all—the particularity and exceptionality of the case was a principal point of the book. It is, however, in another way a special case of a central European literary topography that I outline; one that is generously proportioned to accommodate so many different spirits, including Habsburg Jewish writers of both eastern and western Europe and above all those hard to fit within these increasingly hardening categories. I have left out of the discussion the tremendous and important literary production of those Habsburg Jews who wrote in other languages than German, notably Yiddish and Hebrew. Their writings arguably inscribe another and different kind of territory. Among non-Jewish-identified German-speakers and those writing in Slavic languages, Hungarian, or Romanian there may be many other examples that fit this model, but it was not my intention to produce an alternative catalogue to that provided by Magris or Kundera. Those visions, along with those of modernist canonists, belong, as I argue, to the same world. They do not so much describe or analyze as they *perform* the place, if it is one, called central Europe.

Notes

1. The origin of what I call the fin-de-siècle thesis is often and rightly identified in Carl Schorske, *Fin-de-Siècle Vienna: Politics and Culture* (New York: Knopf, 1980).

2. This is done most prominently and classically in Steven Beller, *Vienna and the Jews, 1867–1938: A Cultural History* (Cambridge: Cambridge University Press, 1989).

3. A group of scholars began to address this in a special issue on "the 'Other' modernisms"; see Scott Spector, "Introduction: Uneven Cultural Development? Modernism and Modernity in the 'Other' Central Europe," *Austrian History Yearbook* 33 (2002): 141–147. Works on Czech, Polish, Romanian, Slovene, Hungarian, and many other modernisms have positioned themselves as revisions of the fin-de-siècle Vienna thesis. A prominent example is Péter Hanák, *The Garden and the Workshop: Essays on the Cultural History of Vienna and Budapest* (Princeton, NJ: Princeton University Press, 1998), and there are many others.

4. Stefan Zweig, *Die Welt von Gestern: Erinnerungen eines Europäers* (Berlin: G. B. Fischer, 1968); Stefan Zweig, *The World of Yesterday: An Autobiography by Stefan Zweig* (New York: Viking, 1943).

5. See Svetlana Boym, *The Future of Nostalgia* (New York: Basic Books, 2001), 3–56.

6. Zweig, *The World of Yesterday*, v. The original reads, "Ich weiß mir . . . keinen anderen Vorrang zuzusprechen als den einen: als Österreicher, als Jude, als Schriftsteller, als Humanist und Pazifist jeweils just dort gestanden zu sein, wo diese Erdstöße am heftigsten sich auswirkten." Zweig, *Die Welt von Gestern*, 7. Here he ends dramatically with the oath to fulfill the "chief conditions of any fair portrayal of an era; namely, honesty and impartiality," a promise he does not, in my judgment, make good on in the following chapter.

7. *The YIVO Encyclopedia of Jews in Eastern Europe*, ed. Gershon D. Hundert, vol. 1 (New Haven, CT: Yale University Press / YIVO Institute for Jewish Research, 2008), s.v. "German Literature," 584–587.

8. Arndt Engelhardt and Susanne Zepp, eds., *Sprache, Erkenntnis und Bedeutung— Deutsch in der jüdischen Wissenskultur* (Leipzig: Leipziger Universitätsverlag, 2015).

9. The original reads, "Der größte heute in deutscher Sprache denkende, vielleicht der einzige große Dichter, und einer der größten, die je gelebt haben, ist ein Schlosser, der in der Irrenanstalt von Czernowitz lebt." Karl Kraus, *Die Fackel*, nos. 781–786 (1928): 91 (my translation).

10. This postscript of Kraus's, like the original adulation, is reproduced in Rezzori's *An Ermine in Czernopol*, trans. Philip Boehm (New York: New York Review of Books, 2011), 248.

11. Gregor von Rezzori, *Ein Hermelin in Tschernopol: Ein maghrebinischer Roman*, ed. Gerhard Köpf, Heinz Schumacher, and Tilman Spengler (Berlin: Berliner Taschenbuch, 2004).

12. Joseph Roth, *Radetzkymarsch: Ein Roman* (Berlin: Gustav Kiepeneuer, 1932).

13. This was the core argument of Schorske's *Fin-de-Siècle Vienna: Politics and Culture*. The thesis of fin-de-siècle modernism's function as cultural surrogate of a politically disempowered (Viennese) liberal bourgeoisie is genuinely famous and, as are all such successful theses, widely discredited in the professional historiography. Some of the most pointed detractions have been Michael S. Roth, "Performing History: Modernist Contextualism in Carl E. Schorske's *Fin-de-Siècle Vienna*," in *The Ironist's Cage: Memory, Trauma, and the Construction of History* (New York: Columbia University Press, 1995), 47–70; Michael P. Steinberg, "Fin-de-siècle Vienna Ten Years Later: *Viel Traum, Wenig Wirklichkeit*," *Austrian History Yearbook* 22 (1991): 151–162; and Deborah R. Coen, *Vienna in the Age of Uncertainty: Science, Liberalism, and Private Life* (Chicago: University of Chicago Press, 2007). In disclosure of my own positions on this, I cite Scott Spector, "Beyond the Aesthetic Garden: Politics and Culture on the Margins of *Fin-de-Siècle Vienna*," *Journal of the History of Ideas* 59, no. 4 (1998): 691–710.

14. Claudio Magris, *Il mito absburgico nella letteratura austriaca moderna* (Turin, Italy: G. Einaudi, 1963).

15. See Maria Todorova, "Between Classification and Politics: The Balkans and the Myth of Central Europe," in *Imagining the Balkans* (London: Oxford University Press, 1997), 140–160.

16. Milan Kundera, "The Tragedy of Central Europe," trans. Edmund White, *New York Review of Books* 31, no. 7 (1984): 33–38.

17. Stefan Jonnson, *Subject without Nation: Robert Musil and the History of Modern Identity* (Durham, NC: Duke University Press, 2000).

18. Seminal texts in this regard have been Michel Foucault, "What Is an Author?," in *Language, Counter-Memory, Practice*, ed. Donald F. Bouchard, trans. Donald F. Bouchard and Sherry Simon (Ithaca, NY: Cornell University Press, 1977), 124–127; and Roland Barthes, "Death of the Author," in *Image, Music, Text*, ed. and trans. Stephen Heath (New York: Hill and Wang, 1977), 142–148.

19. The locus classicus of the "idea of Austria" as problem is Robert Musil's unfinished masterpiece *The Man without Qualities*. Robert Musil, *Der Mann ohne Eigenschaften* (Reinbek, Germany: Rowohlt, 1930–1943).

20. Quoted in Scott Spector, *Prague Territories: National Conflict and Cultural Innovation in Franz Kafka's Fin de Siècle* (Berkeley: University of California Press, 2000), 167 (emphasis in original).
21. Homi K. Bhabha, *The Location of Culture* (London: Routledge, 1994). See also Aamir Mufti, "Jewishness as Minority," in *Enlightenment in the Colony* (Princeton, NJ: Princeton University Press, 2007), 37–90.
22. Bhabha, *Location of Culture*, esp. 112–115.
23. See Scott Spector, "From Big Daddy to Small Literature: On Taking Kafka at His Word," in *Evolving Jewish Identities in German Culture: Borders and Crossings*, ed. Linda E. Feldman and Diana Orendi (Westport, CT: Praeger, 2000), 79–93.
24. Max Brod, "Der jüdische Dichter deutscher Zunge," in *Vom Judentum: Ein Sammelbuch*, ed. Verein jüdischer Hochschüler Bar Kochba in Prag (Leipzig: Kurt Wolff, 1913), 261–263. See my discussion in chapter 7.
25. See Alexander von Roda Roda, *Roda Roda's Geschichten*, ed. Gregor von Rezzori (Hamburg, Germany: Rowohlt, 1956).
26. Karl Emil Franzos, *Aus Halb-Asien: Kulturbilder aus Galizien, der Bukovina, Südrußland und Rumänien* (Leipzig: Dunder and Humblot, 1876); Karl Emil Franzos, *Vom Don zur Donau: Neue Kulturbilder aus Halb-Asien* (Stuttgart: Dunder and Humblot, 1877); Karl Emil Franzos, *Aus der großen Ebene: Neue Kulturbilder aus Halb-Asien* (Stuttgart: Bonz und Comp, 1888).
27. See, e.g., Sander Gilman, *Jewish Self-Hatred: Anti-Semitism and the Hidden Language of the Jews* (Baltimore: Johns Hopkins University, 1986); and Paul Reitter, *On the Origins of Jewish Self-Hatred* (Princeton, NJ: Princeton University Press, 2012).
28. See Amy Colin and Alfred Kittner, eds., *Versunkene Dichtung der Bukowina* (Munich: Wilhelm Fink, 1994); and Cécile Cordon and Helmut Kusdat, eds., *An der Zeiten Ränder: Czernowitz und die Bukowina; Geschichte, Literature, Verfolgung, Exil* (Vienna: Theodor Kramer Gesellschaft, 2002).
29. See Paul de Man, "Lyric and Modernity," in *Blindness and Insight: Essays in the Rhetoric of Contemporary Criticism* (Minneapolis: University of Minnesota Press, 1983), 166–228. De Man makes use of the classic definition found in Hugo Friedrich, *The Structure of Modern Poetry: From the Mid-nineteenth to the Mid-twentieth Century*, trans. J. Neugroschel (Evanston, IL: Northwestern University Press, 1974).
30. Paul Celan, "Der Meridian: Rede anläßlich der Verleihung des Georg-Büchner Preises," in *Selected Poems and Prose of Paul Celan*, trans. John Felstiner (New York: W. W. Norton, 2001), 401–413.
31. Ulrich Baer, "Modernism and Trauma," in *Modernism*, ed. A. Eysteinsson and V. Liska (Amsterdam: John Benjamins, 2007), 1:312.
32. See Spector, *Prague Territories*, 195–233.
33. Ibid., 168–172, 207–210.

Part III

"No Fixed Abode": The Place
of Kafka, Friends, and Modernism

7 Max Brod's Homelands, Kafka's Patrimony

Baggage Claims

Max Brod took homeland seriously. He can be said to have had several homelands in the course of his lifetime, and this chapter explores what some of these might have been. This is not meant to delegitimate his loyalty to the State of Israel, his home at the time of his death late in 1968. Among his many and possibly contradictory declarations of homeland allegiance, we must include the reported statement that he felt fulfilled upon arriving on Palestinian soil in 1939: "For I finally stood there, where I should always have stood."[1] More important, though, than this instant of arrival was the urgent departure that preceded it: the moment in 1939, on the eve of the German invasion of his hometown of Prague, when Brod packed many of his own and his deceased friend Franz Kafka's unpublished writings into two midsized leather suitcases and fled.

Nearly three-quarters of a century after this escape, some of the contents of these suitcases, still in private hands, came into very public dispute. Upon the death of Max Brod's former secretary and heir Ilse Esther (Ester) Hoffe, a cache of manuscripts, including literary manuscripts of Kafka's in his own hand, were to be passed to Hoffe's daughters, who expressed an intent to sell them to the German Literature Archive in Marbach-am-Neckar, Germany.[2] The unfortunate contest over the proper archival home of these materials revisits the vexed questions of home and belonging as they were experienced by this generation of German-speaking Jewish writers. While the court case determining the proper repository for these materials did not formally or even implicitly rest on these questions, the heated debate surrounding it was saturated with the discourses of national cultural property, the true culture and legitimate homeland of authors Kafka and Brod, and the proper recipient of their respective or collective legacies. Haggai Ben-Shammai, the academic director of the National Library of Israel, the institution that would eventually be awarded the archival materials, put it this way: "When [Max] Brod's life and Kafka's heritage that he was protecting were endangered, he chose to come to the Land of Israel."[3] Not perfect English, but crystal clear in its linkage of authentic homeland on the one side and heritage, as he calls it here, or what in this chapter title is called patrimony, on the other. Ben-Shammai made this comment to buttress the claims of the Jerusalem library on the literary remains or estate of Max Brod, which included some documents in the hand of his friend Franz Kafka, and to do so indexes the key moment in the historical trajectory of this legacy that I have already described: that moment in March 1939, on the eve of the German invasion of Prague, when Brod fled in the direction of Hungary, carrying many of his and Kafka's unpublished writings.

Ben-Shammai said more, adding that "from a young age [Brod] described himself as a Zionist and was active in the Zionist movement and in furthering Jewish culture in Prague," further linking this right of legacy not only to Brod's immigration to British Mandate Palestine and later Israeli citizenship and residence, but explicitly to his youth in Prague. This and other remarks surrounding the proper home of the contents of Brod's two suitcases is central to the analysis in this chapter, as is the apparently irresistible draw of the figures of homeland and legacy in those discussions, but it is also important to give some attention to the place of these figures in the early work of Brod and Kafka. Homeland and patrimony, in other words, function centrally in the discourses of both these historical subjects at various points and in their historical reception.

But let us return to the pivotal image of Brod, a suitcase in either hand, hurriedly departing Prague by train on the eve of the German invasion. For this image is central to the ideas of both homeland and patrimony. It links the question of where Brod belonged to the legacy or cultural heritage of his and Kafka's literary pasts, contained in material remnants packed in the suitcases. Some of the contents of that luggage are precisely the items that have been in dispute (finding their way to a safe deposit box in Switzerland). These are some of the conditions that have led those vying for the material as well as onlookers repeatedly to link the question of the legal and proper place of Brod's literary remains to that of authentic homeland.

Brod's commitment first to Jewish nationalism and thereafter explicitly to Zionism, at a relatively young age, can be verified; much more ambivalent was Franz Kafka's relationship to Palestine, the Hebrew language, and Zionism. Not surprisingly, perhaps, much of the commentary on the case has circulated not around Brod's proper homeland but Kafka's, on the assumption that the items of greatest interest are those manuscripts in Kafka's hand that remain in Brod's papers. (That is probably not the case, by the way.) But let us leave the suitcases on the shelf, at the moment, and ask how Franz Kafka and his friend Max Brod viewed the question of "homeland."

Prague Circles

Kafka and Brod were born in 1883 and 1884, respectively, in Prague when it was a regional capital within the Austro-Hungarian Empire ruled by the Habsburg monarchy. That these young men grew up as part of both the Jewish and

German-speaking minorities of Prague did not equate to not belonging or to feeling like outsiders. German-speaking Jews had not only had a place in Prague; they had an important place—even if it was a place that was rapidly shifting in their lifetimes. Above all, there was a strong consciousness among Brod and Kafka's generation of Jews of the relative openness of their identity positions and of this place they held being in motion. At the time of Brod's and Kafka's youth, Jews made up half, or probably slightly more than half, the German minority in Prague—Prague's population was roughly 10 percent German speaking at the century's turn, and that 10 percent was both relatively affluent and culturally predominant in many ways. So people in Brod's and Kafka's position in some ways were part of a privileged minority and in other ways being increasingly marginalized, a complex phenomenon trapping them both inside and outside the power structure and yielding complex effects. It is useful to return to the Prague of the early 1900s, when these two were budding writers, college students meeting in the literary section of the Reading and Lecture Club of German Students in Prague (Lese und Redehalle der Deutschen Studenten in Prag, or simply the Halle). Kafka and Brod were just two of the young writers from this really very small demographic group who would become famous in the world of German letters—expressionist poet and novelist Franz Werfel, the so-called roving reporter Egon Erwin Kisch, Zionists Felix Weltsch and Hugo Bergman, dramatist Paul Kornfeld, and others like blind writer Oskar Baum and the brothers Franz and Hans Janowitz. This was the basis for what would later be called the Prague Circle, after a memoir written by Max Brod with this title.[4] Here and elsewhere, Brod described a situation in which creative young minds were pushed into the literary section, as it were, by the rising tide of antisemitic German nationalism, which already commanded student life through the fraternity system and now came to take over the leadership of the Halle: "We created from within the modest membership of the Halle a center of opposition . . . the 'Section for Literature and Art.' . . . We thirsted for cultural achievement, we wanted to invite the great poets of Germany to lecture."[5] In this image and many others, the turn toward culture was a retreat from the nationalist politics that threatened these young German-speaking Jews. German culture was ironically an island of protection from an encroaching German nationalism.

Brod and Kafka shared an intense preoccupation with literature—but this preoccupation seems to have operated differently in them. Max Brod's polymath engagement with culture was, for lack of a better metaphor, centrifugal: his broad and deep interests in culture drove him to look ever outside himself to the worlds of culture, not just literature but music and theater, very importantly, and the visual arts; he sought to connect with the many circles of artists and writers; and he was a tireless advocate for artists whose work he found compelling. He is rightly known as the discoverer and promoter not only of Kafka but also the great poet and then novelist Franz Werfel and the great Moravian composer Leoš Janáček, already in advanced age and relatively unknown even in his own country when Brod's review of his opera (*Její pastorkyňa*, which only after Brod's own translation into German would come to be known to the world as *Jenufa*). Indeed, the entire notion of the Prague Circle comes from Brod's own hand. As many have since argued, there really was no formal literary circle but only a fantasy of Brod's—to be more precise, one's membership in the circle depended on a connection to Brod, who was the common element holding them all together (the center of the ring). Anyone researching the literary life of Prague, and not only Prague, in that period will encounter literally hundreds of letters by Max Brod in every spot she looks. When I was doing that very research I wondered how he could possibly have the time to produce so much literary correspondence and once asked about it in the very archive in Jerusalem that has now come to win rights to hold his papers. The archivist recalled how Brod, when he came to work in the archive or library, would order a book or archival holding and then rush to a desk and feverishly write out missive after missive as he waited.[6] It could not be otherwise, so wide is the net cast by his literary correspondence.

Brod's life was culture—like Kafka, he took a degree in law and worked a steady job (Kafka at an insurance company, Brod in the post office)—but his "real" life was the life of letters. But Kafka never conceptualized his relationship to literature in terms of literary networks, movements, connections, or circles. While he produced a correspondence prodigious in its own right, it is impressive in an entirely different way: his letters to his fiancée Felice Bauer, his lover Milena Jesenská, his friends, and his family have all been mined by critics as works of literature as complex and rich as his fictional writing.[7] The metaphors he used when he described his writing in these letters and in his diaries were always those of solitude and isolation, imprisonment, punishment, pain, and torture. He describes in letters to Felice the fantasy of locking himself in a dungeon to write, a fantasy she could only misunderstand, because it excluded even the possibility of a happy life with herself; and in this same correspondence he endeavored in vain to explain to her that he did not have literary interests but was made of literature.[8] The very different relationships of these two writers to writing itself, to literature and to culture, are linked to their ultimately very different potential relations to the concept of homeland or, for that matter, legacy and patrimony.

The two writers' relationship to Prague is a case in point. Everyone in this group of German-speaking Jewish writers identified their Prague homeland as where they deeply belonged, at some point, but differently. Egon Erwin Kisch thought all his work could be summarized as memories of Prague, for instance. Kafka, as a young man, speculated to his friend Oskar Pollak that they would never get away: "Prague doesn't let go. . . . This little mother [a reference to the Czech nickname of the city as Matička Praha] has claws."[9] On the other hand, as

Barbora Srámková has noted, Brod expressed his attachment to the Bohemian homeland with a specificity and precision of place, whereas such markers are absent in Kafka's prose, abstracted. In both cases, expressed positively or negatively, and in others of their generation, the attachment to Prague was salient. As late as 1930, Brod confessed that "for my part, I must say that I do not consider my relationship to Prague as happenstance or casual. I am at home in Prague, and I have no other real homeland."[10] Of course, things were to work out differently. And long before 1930, Brod had already explored other homelands, in various ways.

The Literary Homeland

The young Max Brod was a searcher. Disabled as a result of an illness at a young age, the world of books and culture had long been important to him, and at university this interest came to full blossom. The term "searcher" even implies wandering, and that is apt in Brod's case. His cosmopolitan impulse to connect to the strongest cultural currents forced him from the first to look abroad for kin of the soul. (The literary section of the Reading and Lecture Club, it is true, enlisted the participation of the most recognized literary figures of their own country—Hugo Salus and Friedrich Adler, of German Prague's literary organ *Concordia*—but the style of these writers was decidedly not local.) His strongest literary influences at this time were French—he was enamored of the work of Gustave Flaubert and especially the symbolist poet Jules Laforgue. These and other French models represented a kind of aestheticism—art for art's sake—that pulled away from the alternatively neoclassical and new Romantic models of the *Concordia* giants. Philosophically, he was steeped in the tradition of Arthur Schopenhauer (but so too had been these late nineteenth-century aestheticist poets).

So the young Brod—the first literary Brod, if you will, these years corresponding to his earliest success as a writer—strayed from the literary homeland of official German-language culture embodied in the *Concordia* and looked to late nineteenth-century France. But the homeland he thus embraced was not a French one but an aestheticist one: it was art itself, *l'art pour l'art*; it was beauty presumed to be detached from national affiliation, ideology, or any other factor extrinsic to the work of art itself. His variation of this movement (embodied in his first successful novel, *Nornepygge Castle*, and in the short pieces with the modernist revolutionary title *Death to the Dead!*) he called indifferentism.[11] Indifferentism was a life philosophy that was really a self-conscious attempt to short-circuit or leap over the heavily contested differences on the ground of his contemporary Prague—namely, those sharpened by the contest between Czech and German nationalists for political and social power. Indifferentism was an aestheticism, therefore, that grew very much out of the soil of Bohemia and specifically of Prague. That was its homeland.

Kafka would generally not be identified under the labels of aestheticism, decadence, art for art's sake, and so on, yet one could argue that his attitude toward writing was an extension and intensification of aestheticist positions. Certainly, life and art may seem for Kafka to have been opposing realms at times, as asserted by Max Brod himself as the earliest in what would become an astonishingly long line of Kafka scholars.[12] On the other hand, Kafka's more consistently held position was not the segregation of art and life, but rather a view of art that was deeply connected to living or that promised or threatened to consume it: "Writing as a form of prayer" is one oft-cited example of such an expression.[13] But what does this fragment—it is not even a full sentence, appearing in his notebooks—mean? Does it point to a sacralization of writing or a secularization of prayer? In one of the letters to Felice he makes the well-known claim that "I have no literary interests, but rather I am made of literature, I am nothing else and can be nothing else."[14] As extravagant as these claims may seem to be, they belong to Kafka and Brod's time and place.[15] The very local context of a group of Jews forced to take the island of culture seriously as the territory of their very existence coincided in the first decade of the twentieth century with a central European fascination with the promise of the abolition of the hard line demarcating art from life.

After aestheticism came Germany. In the frenzied atmosphere of artistic innovation leading up to World War I, the gravitational pull for German-language literati in Prague drifted from Vienna, the imperial capital that might have been its natural direction, to Berlin and even other cities in the German Empire to its north. I recall finding a postcard Brod wrote to another writer who was in the German capital, confirming this secession with the note "How's Berlin? I hate Vienna!" Although he would later criticize the expressionist craze ("the less talented [one is], the more expressionist"), he played an important role in the movement, as previously mentioned.[16] More than one critic identified Franz Werfel's reading of "The World Friend"—an appointment Brod had arranged—as the literary movement's founding moment.[17] But above all, it was the presses of the *Kaiserreich*—first Axel Junker, then Kurt Wolff—who picked up on the diverse if offbeat writing of the likes of Brod, Werfel, and Kafka and marketed them as the new literary wave out of Prague. Prague German literature was in, and it was not Vienna but the German Empire to the north that made it so.

Owning Kafka

These very brief comments on the literary scene in imperial Germany and in Berlin in particular constituting a chosen homeland for Brod do not amount to a claim, similar to that of certain representatives of the German Literature Archive, of a worthiness for that institution as repository for German-language culture. Brod himself never lived in Germany, and Kafka's relatively brief residence in Berlin-Steglitz hardly constituted a choice of homeland. In all events, the German republic in which Kafka took up residence would outlive him by less than a decade. It is, on the other hand, erroneous to assume, as so many critics of the court decision and of the Tel Aviv case against the Hoffe daughters have done, that the grounds for any claim of cultural heritage must be Zionist or based on the acceptance of the thesis that all writing by Jews is Jewish and hence Israeli national property. That was not the claim, in spite of the words of the National Library of Israel's academic director Haggai Ben-Shammai, quoted above. The decision in Tel Aviv was a matter of inheritance law tried in family court and revolved around a decided ambiguity within and among several extant versions of Brod's last will and testament: we have seen that he expressly left the material to his longtime secretary and heir, Ester Hoffe, but he did so with the instruction that it be passed on to an archival collection *such as* the predecessor of the National Library of Israel *or* another collection in Israel *or* abroad. Since his death in 1968, this had not occurred, although some items had been sold at great profit, notably the manuscript of *The Trial* to the German Literature Archive in Marbach. At any rate, the national right of either the State of Israel or the Federal Republic of Germany to house these materials was not at issue in the wills or in the decision.

Nonetheless, the logic linking the rightful place of the archival material to national cultural patrimony seems to have exercised an irresistible gravitational pull on discourse surrounding the case from all quarters. One very significant example is an essay by Judith Butler in the *London Review of Books* with the provocative title "Who Owns Kafka?"[18] Butler's starting point is the very discourse I am discussing—in spite of the facts of the actual case, David Blumberg, board chairman of the National Library of Israel, had asserted that "the library does not intend to give up on cultural assets belonging to the Jewish people." Beyond this description of cultural patrimony as a literal collective asset, the Hoffe heirs' lawyers were planning to sell the remaining estate in sealed boxes, pricing the literary remains by weight.[19] One would hardly need any more evidence that Kafka has been "turned into such a commodity"—should any such evidence be needed after Brod's now deceased secretary auctioning of a manuscript of *The Trial* in 1988, receiving close to $2 million.[20] But the dual status of the Kafka corpus as spiritual treasure as well as a commodity of material worth was already in place when Brod packed his bags (as we shall see). What Butler objects to most is the attachment of this treasure, the ownership of this spiritual commodity, to "the Jewish people" and, hence, to the State of Israel.

From there Butler outlines, on the foundation of a set of Kafka's own writings on home or homelessness, belonging, his relationship to Jewishness, and so forth, the many ways his writings could be argued to challenge this relationship of self to home or author to grounded cultural identity. I could hardly disagree with these points. For they are the very ones for which I argued at length, on the basis of the very same texts and passages of texts, in *Prague Territories*.[21] But Kafka's relationship to Zionism or his thinking about cultural patrimony or grounded identity, while making for rich and interesting ironies in the context of the afterlife of his own writings and this case in particular, is not directly relevant to the case. National cultural patrimony was not the basis of the case, as I keep repeating, but it has been invoked by many advocates of keeping the material in Israel, and it was relevant to past cases against Ester Hoffe. But even the idea of national patrimony cannot be reduced to a territorial ideology that conflates nation, territory, culture, language, and personal identity, although discussions of it and of this case necessarily operate within that system. The National Library of Israel's claim to the boxes need not be based on a claim to all Jewish culture (whatever that would be). National laws against exporting cultural patrimony are not uncommon and do not pertain to objects on the basis of authorial ethnicity or racial belonging or linguistic heritage or anything of the kind. Bringing out the ironies of Kafka's homelessness and the struggle over his legacy is interesting and potentially productive, but this particular sort of critique flattens rather than brings out complications and ironies inherent in the situation.

The celebrated British author Will Self made a similar move after the decision was announced, declaring, "Brod himself was intent on canonising Kafka as a Zionist saint, and the Israeli state holding the papers ensures that this falsification will continue."[22] The metaphor of falsification itself suggests a forging of identity papers, an act of aggressive inauthenticity that is also an appropriation. Of course, Ben-Shammai's comments quoted above also belong to this register of the conversation about the proper place of belonging of Brod's papers, including those in Kafka's hand. Brod's Zionism was not technically the grounds for the judge's decision, but a less than cautious statement out of Marbach countered that Brod was "an unusual figure on the Eretz Israel landscape of the time, always dressed in suits and maintaining his European appearance."[23]

An article in *Haaretz* had a sharp retort:

> Brod was indeed an odd duck in Tel Aviv, as were many of his generation, who were uprooted from their homes, their homelands and their families and forced to build a new home in this strange, hot land across the sea. Does the German Literature Archive need to be reminded about which state was responsible for this? And, speaking of memory, would this be an appropriate place to mention the circumstances of the murder of three of Kafka's sisters in the death camps?[24]

It is, I argue, not for nothing that so many comments surrounding the case, and indeed, what seems to be the default response to the case, have come down to the question of homeland and national heritage. The poignant irony is that the high-water mark of Brod's and Kafka's work in Prague in the 1910s and the 1920s emerged from a context of entrenchment of nationalist ideologies, and in demonstrable if also very different ways the work of both resisted these ideologies. Their reactions to nationalism and to Zionism in particular were, needless to say, also different from one another. What role does Zionism have in all this?

Brod's relationship to Zionism, unlike Franz Kafka's, is uncontroversial. In Prague in the early years of the second decade of the twentieth century he was already an avowed Jewish nationalist and then, in fairly short order, he spoke of an attachment to Zionism. What did this mean? The decision to identify as Jewish national rather than German national was a political one that had specific resonance in Prague, but it did not necessarily imply the desire for a Jewish homeland in the historic Land of Israel. In identifying as a Jewish nationalist in Prague in this period, one was primarily seceding from the German-liberal camp to which so many German-speaking Jewish Praguers, along with other German speakers in the city, belonged. This was the dominant ideology of the Germans of the city, even as German liberalism—this cultural nationalism and bourgeois ideology—was elsewhere in Bohemia, as in Vienna and the German Empire, being fast overrun by an ethnic or racial German nationalism that excluded Jewish membership. The homeland of German culture that was so important to Brod and his cohort was shrinking, in other words, but it was also changing in terms of the *kind* of homeland it could be understood to be. It is true enough, as many works over the last two decades have stressed, that writers and others in Brod's generation had to choose whether to identify as German, Czech, or Jewish in the years from 1880 to 1914—but the grounds of that decision (if it even was one) were ever shifting. There was the decision of how to fill out a census form (which coyly inquired after everyday language, not ethnicity, nationality, or even mother tongue, and no particularly Jewish option was available), the decision of where to send one's children to school, and the daily plebiscite of social circles and which national theater to visit (even for instrumental music). But for the likes of Brod and Kafka, both proficient in Czech but steeped in the German literary tradition, there was a much more nebulous sense of identification and distancing involved in what Brod tried vainly to describe as a hard shift from a German to a Jewish identification.

The ideology of nationalism had not only a formidable career in Habsburg Bohemia and in its capital, Prague, but a unique formation, particularly as it impinged on the lives and consciousnesses of the city's substantial and assimilated Jewish population. It is not surprising, then, that the forms of Jewish nationalism and Zionism to emerge from this crucible were to be of a different sort from those in Vienna, in the German Empire, and in the Russian Empire. When the Bar-Kochba Association sponsored the visit of Martin Buber in 1911, he delivered three lectures that would have a seismic impact on the generation of young Jewish central European intellectuals, and the energy and excitement around the talks seems to have been the impetus for Brod's conversion to Jewish-national commitment. Before Brod, others in his closest circle—particularly Hugo Bergman and Felix Weltsch—had been won over to Zionism, but Buber's charismatic addresses opened for him and for so many others the horizon of a new homeland that was already within them; an inner community that was not rifted with unwholeness and alienation of modern European life but that was accessible to the modern European intellectual. Prague was at the epicenter of the small countermovement within Zionism that was known alternatively as spiritual or, more usually, cultural Zionism. This tendency was influenced by Zionist thinker Ahad Ha'am and was opposed to the external, statist, diplomatic thrust of Theodor Herzl's dominant political Zionism. We can see the line from this position to the sympathy for and in fact active commitment to B'rith Shalom (the Zionist faction that advocated for an Arab-Jewish state in Palestine), in spite of the irony that these central Europeans were very familiar with a binational polity that had failed.

Kafka, for his part, attended but was untouched by the Buber lectures, summarily dispatching them and his cohort's unbridled enthusiasm for them in a brief comment in his notebooks. The characteristic remark in his diary of January 18, 1914, is often quoted: "What have I in common with Jews? I have hardly anything in common with myself and should stand quietly in the corner, content that I can breathe."[25] His interest in Palestine would come a short while later, and still quite a bit later came his study of Hebrew and genuine, if ambivalent enthusiasm about Palestinian Jews (or as they were usually called then, Jews in the Yishuv, living in the historic Land of Israel). He did become extremely interested in the Yiddish theater and Yiddish language and culture generally, as is well known, but here again, a warning is in order. His fascination with Yiddish, if we take the case of the brilliant introduction he presented to an audience at the Jewish community hall in Prague before a Yiddish reading, was not a romantic identification with an integral homeland to which he might belong. The talk construes Yiddish as the opposite of a grounding for a stable national homeland or territory.

In 1913, a group of Prague German-speaking Jews published a slim volume that is paradigmatic for some of the new thinking about the relationship of assimilated central European Jewry to their Judaism; it was titled *Vom Judentum* (On Judaism) and included poetry, short fiction, and essays.[26] Brod's contribution was titled "Der jüdische Dichter deutscher Zunge" (The Jewish writer of German tongue) and is very interesting with regard to the reconceptualization of the relations I outline earlier—namely, the presumed mirrored spaces of national borders, language, personal identity, and literary culture. In it, he argues against the antisemitic claim (which by 1913 had been more widely accepted than ever, including by many Zionist adherents) that Jews, as essential aliens to the languages they spoke, had a less authentic relationship to those languages than true nationals; they lacked the deep folk grounding (and "naïve feeling") of the ordinary people and did not have access to the supreme poetic mastery of the language that its native poets had.[27] So simply racist as this position rightly appears to us here and today, it is difficult to reproduce the appeal that this image of language, poet, and national spirit had to people in this period leading up to World War I. What is remarkable about Brod's piece is that it seeks to refute the antisemitic truism not by discarding its Romantic assumptions about the mystical bonds among poet, language, and nation but by shifting its pieces in such a way that rescued both the essential and authentic bond of the German-Jewish writer to Judaism, on the one hand, and to German poetic language, on the other. In it, he argues that it is only, and first, when such an author takes the path of Jewish national identification—that is, when he or she becomes conscious of belonging to the Jewish nation and committed to this inner homeland—that access to the greatness of German poetic language is made available to that poet.

Now, thank goodness, no one believes this. But it is a nonetheless telling illustration of the complex role of homeland and cultural heritage in the thought of this particular thinker and, I argue, others coming out of his particular milieu (specifically, the German-speaking Jewish writers of Prague). After World War I and the dissolution of the Habsburg Empire, Brod remained a Jewish nationalist within a multinational state of a very different kind than the empire that had been its predecessor. Unlike Austria-Hungary, the Republic of Czechoslovakia recognized Jews as a national minority, and Brod even served as a deputy of the Jewish National Council and briefly as its vice president. In the 1920s, Brod's ideas about Jewish nationalism would evolve toward the notion that it was a love of one's own nation that could paradoxically become a universalism, or what he called "supranationalism," again, a way of understanding others.[28] All this is to say that he could be simultaneously at home in his Jewish-national skin and at home in Czechoslovakia, particularly in Prague, as the quote above implies. And then there was that line that he wrote in a letter to Alfred Weber that he was finally, after finding himself in Palestine, the happiest of men, "For I finally stood there, where I should always have stood."

But this teleology, reproduced in Brod's 1960 memoir *Streitbares Leben*, like all such teleologies, represses other stories that led or would have led to other homelands.[29] The correspondence of German émigré author Thomas Mann reveals one such alternative. We learn in it of Mann's substantial efforts to obtain for Brod a salaried position, first at the New York Public Library or another institution. In a letter dated February 27, 1939, to the director of the New York Public Library, Mann reports that Brod "is willing to give his collection of the books and manuscripts of Franz Kafka to any institution of repute which would accept it and in return offer him a position to act as assistant or curator of the collection, and so make possible his entry into this country."[30] Indeed, we have evidence that, contrary to Brod's own account in his memoir, he continued to seek a position in the United States using the Kafka manuscripts as a letter of passage even after arriving in Palestine.³¹ Knowledge of this effort does not unlock a secret inner homeland of Brod's fantasies—not a yearning for America, or a fantasy for literary exile among many great German writers, or by any means, an identification with American Reform Judaism—any more than it denies the sincerity of Brod's avowed Zionism. Anyone with any sense of the desperation of a Jew living in that historical place and moment must understand this for nothing other than what it was: an option. It was the attempt of an extraordinarily resourceful person to tap something few others could ever have recognized as a resource at all, much less one of so much potential richness and value. For Max Brod was not only the first person to recognize the critical artistic worth of Franz Kafka's imagination; he was the first to even consider the substantial—unimaginable, actually—commodity value of the contents of that suitcase. I realize that saying this seems almost to suggest that Brod was a speculator more than he was a friend of Kafka's or a lover of wealth more than literature, and nothing could be further from the truth. The sincerity of his commitment to literature and the dedication of his life to the arts are as irrefutable as his faith in the precious value of work that critics of modern literature would recognize only in his wake. But at the same time, as he hurriedly pulled together the few things he could take, he did what all refugees do: he took what was most precious or what had the most concentrated value. And because of this far-from-selfless act, we possess this great legacy or cultural inheritance: all Kafka's novels, along with many of the most important stories and fragments—by far the bulk of this great writer's production.

Two More Testaments

At this point, too, recall that Brod saved this invaluable cache of human spiritual production, this pinnacle of our culture, not once but twice. For this is not only the story of Brod's suitcases and wills but also of Franz Kafka's testament—in fact there were two—in which all these unpublished writings were entrusted to Max Brod with the instruction that they be destroyed by fire. The latter of these documents was left on the writer's desk for Brod to find:

> Here is my last will concerning everything I have written . . . the only books that can stand are . . . The Judgment, The Stoker, Metamorphosis, Penal Colony, Country Doctor. . . . I do not mean that I wish them to be . . . handed down to posterity. On the contrary, should they disappear altogether that would please me best. . . . But everything else of mine . . . without exception is to be burned, and I beg you to do this as soon as possible.³²

In more than one way it would be somewhat foolish to admonish Brod for not having carried out the last wish of the friend who entrusted it to him.³³ It is ironic (if not Kafkaesque?) that the very first of Kafka's literary remains that Brod would publish would be these two testaments: the texts are included in full in an article announcing Brod's possession of the Kafka remaining papers, along with his justification for not obeying Kafka's wishes.[34] He tells readers about the "negative posture" Kafka had to his own work, an inferiority complex that is contrasted in the piece to Brod's idolization of the great author (a reverence he describes in religious terms: "the fanatical worship that I held for his every word").[35] There is an interesting tension in the term Brod uses for the task Kafka has set out for him in the wills: he calls it "the herostratic deed."[36] It is an interesting choice. Herostratus, the chronicles tell us, destroyed the Temple of Artemis at Ephesus—one of the Seven Wonders of the Ancient World—to achieve immortal infamy, to never be forgotten. The city therefore sentenced his name to oblivion. A herostratic deed—in German and in English—ought to be a criminal act of destruction for the purpose of fame. Brod seems to misuse the term slightly, focusing on the deed as an act of destruction of a world wonder. Brod would never pass into history forever remembered as the destroyer of Kafka's papers, but he would be forever remembered as the one who spared them—twice—from the fire. Of this great contribution, he wrote, "so far as my memory, so far as my powers can reach, nothing shall be lost."[37]

To read these quasi testaments of Kafka's literally does as much violence to them as would interpreting any of his writing literally.[38] Brod was right as well in understanding that no one knew better than Kafka himself that in spite of the plea not to read they would be read, in face of the plea to burn they would be published—Brod insisted that he had told Kafka as much.[39] In a similar gesture, what we now know as the *Letter to His Father* had been placed in the hand of his mother for delivery—the one address from which the author could be sure it would be safe from ever falling into the hands of the putative addressee. Indeed, Kafka's desire to preserve rather than destroy his own legacy is apparent not only in the choice of executor but in the very texts of his testaments. The two were probably written about a year apart from one another, both addressed to Max Brod and both left behind for him in Kafka's rooms. The one quoted above demonstrably produces a canon of the Kafka corpus, even as it commands destruction of the unpublished work.[40] The shorter version of the testament does less to ensure the conveyance of the archive to fire than it does to define that archive: he provides an exhaustive index of the places his writings may be found and how he considers all of them, no matter how ephemeral, to belong to his literary papers:

> Dearest Max, my last request: that everything that is found among my papers (in the bookcase, the linen cupboard, and my desk at home as well as the one in the office, or wherever else anything at all might have ended up that meets your eye) in the way of diaries, manuscripts, letters (from others and from me), drawings, and so on be burned in its entirety and without being read, likewise all writings and sketches in your possession or in that of others; and ask those others for them on my behalf.[41]

The command to destroy the cultural legacy, in other words, is also one that provides specific instructions for defining and locating the archive—the inclusion of what we would call ephemera (letters, sketches, "everything" written or drawn), the command to get the materials possessed by others. These instructions take up most of the text of the testament, in the long space between the two parts of the compound verb "sich finden" ("everything that *is found* among my papers").

These merely apparently opposite gestures—Kafka's testaments commanding annihilation and Brod's testaments commanding preservation of the legacy and his heroic actions to preserve, to publish, to make public—are somehow coming from the same place. There is a deep kinship, if also, starkly, a fundamental rift between these two ways of looking at writing itself and its relationship to its author, where or whether that author is at home—how writing relates to place; what it can communicate about place at all; and what ground the writer, or indeed anyone, has to stand on. Withal, these twin, linked alternatives differ starkly on the very possibility of handing down and the promise of legacy.

Notes

1. The original reads, "Ich war tatsächlich hier angelangt, der glücklichste Mensch. Denn endlich stand ich da, wo ich immer hätte stehen sollen." Letter from Max Brod to Alfred Weber, August 29, 1939, quoted in Claus-Ekkehard Bärsch, *Max Brod im Kampf um das Judentum: Zum Leben und Werk eines deutsch-jüdischen Dichters aus Prag* (Vienna: Passagen, 1999), 80. See also Barbora Srámková, *Max Brod und die tschechische Kultur* (Wuppertal, Germany: Arco, 2009), 348n24.

2. Ester Hoffe had sold pieces of this inheritance in her own lifetime, including most notably the full manuscript of *The Trial*, purchased by the Marbach archive for close to $2 million, the most paid to date for any modern manuscript. See Terry Trucco, "A Kafka Manuscript Is Sold for $1.98 Million," *New York Times*, November 18, 1988, p. 1, http://www.nytimes.com/1988/11/18/books/a-kafka-manuscript-is-sold-for-1.98-million.html.

3. Ofer Aderet, "National Library: Kafka Writings Belong in Israel," *Haaretz*, December 11, 2011, http://www.haaretz.com/national-library-kafka-writings-belong-in-israel-1.400715.

4. Max Brod, *Der Prager Kreis* (Stuttgart, Germany: Kohlhammer, 1966).

5. Max Brod, *Streitbares Leben: Autobiographie* (Munich: Kindler, 1960), 228.

6. The archive was then the Jewish National and University Library, since renamed National Library of Israel, the very collection to be awarded the Brod papers in the possession of Ester Hoffe's daughters; the archivist was Reuven Klingsberg, also a refugee from Jewish Prague.

7. A great early example is Elias Canetti, *Der andere Prozeß: Kafkas Briefe an Felice* (Munich: Hanser, 1969).

8. Franz Kafka, *Briefe an Felice und andere Korrespondenz aus der Verlobungszeit*, ed. Erich Heller and Jürgen Born (Frankfurt am Main, Germany: S. Fischer, 1988), 444.

9. The original reads, "Prag lässt nicht los. Uns beide nicht. Dieses Mütterchen hat Krallen." Letter from Franz Kafka to Oskar Pollak, December 20, 1902, in *Briefe, 1902–1924*, ed. Max Brod (Frankfurt am Main, Germany: S. Fischer, 1958), 14 (translation mine).

10. Max Brod, "Praha a já," *Literární noviny*, December 10, 1930, p. 4, cited and translated into German in Barbora Srámková, *Max Brod und die tschechische Kultur* (Wuppertal, Germany: Arco, 2009), 348n23 (translation mine). Of course, in excluding all other potential homelands, Brod is also staking out a claim to Prague territory in this Czech cultural journal.

11. See Max Brod, *Tod den Toten* (Stuttgart, Germany: Axel Juncker, 1906); and Max Brod, *Schloss Nornepygge: Der Roman des Indifferenten* (Leipzig: Kurt Wolff, 1918). See also Scott Spector, *Prague Territories: National Conflict and Cultural Innovation in Franz Kafka's Fin de Siècle* (Berkeley: University of California Press, 2000), 60–66.

12. See Max Brod, *Franz Kafka: Eine Biographie; Erinnerungen und Dokumente* (Prague: H. Mercy Sohn, 1937); and Canetti, *Der andere Prozeß*.

13. Franz Kafka, *Nachgelassene Schriften und Fragmente*, ed. Jost Schillemeit (Frankfurt am Main, Germany: S. Fischer, 1992), 2:354.

14. The letter to Felice Bauer from August 14, 1913, contains this line "Ich habe kein literarisches Interesse, sondern bestehe aus Literatur, ich bin nichts anderes und kann nichts anderes sein." Kafka, *Briefe an Felice*, 444.

15. I explore this in the fin-de-siècle Prague context in *Prague Territories: National Conflict and Cultural Innovation in Franz Kafka's Fin de Siècle* (Berkeley: University of California Press, 2000) and have also identified parallels in other early twentieth-century central European texts such as those of Georg Lukács. See Scott Spector, "Beyond the Aesthetic Garden: Politics and Culture on the Margins of *Fin-de-Siècle Vienna*," *Journal of the History of Ideas* 59, no. 4 (1998): 691–710.

16. Brod, *Der Prager Kreis*, 207.

17. Spector, *Prague Territories*, 94.

18. Judith Butler, "Who Owns Kafka?" *London Review of Books* 33, no. 5 (2011): 3–8.

19. Ibid., 3.

20. Ibid.

21. Butler offers a subtle reading of several texts as articulations of a "poetics of non-arrival" that I find very interesting. Ibid.

22. Quoted in Alison Flood, "Huge Franz Kafka Archive to Be Made Public," *The Guardian*, October 15, 2012, https://www.theguardian.com/books/2012/oct/15/franz-kafka-archive-public.

23. Ofer Aderet, "German Archive, Vying for Kafka Manuscripts, Presents Odd Claims in Court," *Haaretz*, December 9, 2011, http://www.haaretz.com/german-archive-vying-for-kafka-manuscripts-presents-odd-claims-in-court-1.400426.

24. Ibid.

25. Franz Kafka, *Gesammelte Werke in der Fassung der Handschrift: Tagebücher*, vol. 2, *1912–1914*, ed. Hans-Gerd Koch, Michael Müller, and Malcolm Pasley (Frankfurt am Main, Germany: Fischer, 1994), 225.

26. Verein jüdischer Hochschüler Bar Kochba in Prag, ed., *Vom Judentum: Ein Sammelbuch* (Leipzig: Kurt Wolff, 1913).

27. Max Brod, "Der jüdische Dichter deutscher Zunge," in Verein jüdischer Hochschüler Bar Kochba in Prag, *Vom Judentum*, 261.

28. See Mark H. Gelber, "Max Brod's Zionist Writings," *Leo Baeck Institute Yearbook* 33, no. 1 (1988): 442. This thinking about the *necessarily* supranational character of Jewish nationalism seems to have emerged in Brod's thought immediately after World War I. See Max Brod, "Gegen den Nationalismus und für ihn," *Selbstwehr*, April 11, 1919, pp. 2–3.

29. Max Brod, *Streitbares Leben: Autobiographie* (Munich: Kindler, 1960).

30. The letter (composed in English) was not originally included in Thomas Mann, *Briefe, 1937–47*, ed. Erika Mann (Frankfurt am Main, Germany: Fischer, 1963), but emerged in Thomas Mann, *Letters of Thomas Mann, 1889–1955*, ed. and trans. Richard and Clara Winston (New York: Alfred A. Knopf, 1971), 296–298. See Peter F. Neumeyer, "Thomas Mann, Max Brod, and the New York Public Library," *MLN* 90, no. 3 (1975): 418–423.

31. See Gelber, "Max Brod's Zionist Writings," 437–440. These efforts yielded an expression of interest and even intent to commit by the Hebrew Union College in Cincinnati (the seat of American Reform Judaism), though in the end this did not pan out.

32. Max Brod, "Franz Kafkas Nachlaß," *Die Weltbühne* 20, no. 29 (1924): 106 (translation mine).

33. Several have done so, but a particularly detailed and instructive example is Lior Strahilevitz, "The Right to Destroy," *Yale Law Journal* 114 (2005): 781–835.

34. Brod, "Franz Kafkas Nachlaß."

35. Ibid., 106, 108 (translations mine).

36. Ibid., 107 (translation mine).

37. Ibid., 109 (translation mine).

38. In "The Right to Destroy," for instance, Strahilevitz wittily plays out the litigation of a case under contemporary American law in which Kafka, called K, is a subject forced to speak when he had the right to remain silent (832–835). That "K" in Kafka's texts stands in for "Kafka" is as naïve as the assumption that a note scribbled to Brod reflected the intention of the author to have his work annihilated. See Scott Spector, "From Big Daddy to Small Literature: On Taking Kafka at His Word," in *Evolving Jewish Identities in German Culture: Borders and Crossings*, ed. Linda E. Feldman and Diana Orendi (Westport, CT: Praeger, 2000), 79–93.

39. Max Brod, "Kafkas Nachlaß," 108.

40. Peter-André Alt has made a related observation: "The request that the manuscripts be destroyed consequentially reveals the hidden longing for a public afterlife—a desire that is not expressed directly, but rather in the form of a negative dialectic. Kafka wishes to be read without confessing this; his testament is therefore the disguised demand to rescue the papers. The logic of the text has its origin in the same world out of which his novels sprang." Peter-André Alt, *Franz Kafka: Der ewige Sohn; Eine Biographie* (Munich: C. H. Beck, 2005), 19.

41. Quoted in Brod, "Franz Kafkas Nachlaß," 107.

8 Kafka and Literary Modernism

Kafka and the Modern

Franz Kafka may be the most recognized modernist author in the German literary canon, but where does he fit within modernism? The question of Kafka's place in literary modernity is especially complicated both because of the ambiguity of the notion of the modern and because of the difficulty of interpretation of Kafka's notoriously ambiguous texts. Inseparable from the question of Kafka's relationship to the modern is that of how to place the author and his work in historical context. This is not least because literary modernism is, if anything at all, the phenomenon of a specific historical period and product of a particular context. Yet inherent within the impulse of modernism in its various forms has been the concentration on (which some have called a retreat, a withdrawal, or an escape into) art itself—on or into those aspects of art that may be governed by artistic imperatives rather than those contexts external to it. All of these issues, however plagued by self-contradiction, take on specific peculiarities when related to the example of Kafka and his work.

While the term "modern" and the more general German term *die Moderne* as they relate to literature were already current in the period in which Kafka lived and wrote, he did not explicitly identify with the term or express concern about what literary modernism should entail. He did not rush to join any of the programmatically avant-garde artistic circles current in his day, and his letters and diaries do not betray a preoccupation with the specific concern of how to modernize literature. Nonetheless, the texts he produced have earned him an undisputed place in the modernist canon. In fact the Habsburg Empire, of which Kafka was a subject until its dissolution at the end of World War I, was arguably a crucible for the literary, philosophical, and artistic forms of the modern. At the turn of the century in central Europe, the term was polemical and profoundly generationally inflected: urban artistic movements labeling themselves variously young (*Jung-Wien, Jung-Prag, das junge Deutschland, Jugendstil*, etc.) or secessionist actively rejected naturalism and academic realism for more aestheticist programs. For these writers and artists, by and large a half-generation older than Kafka and his cohort, "modern" was a battle cry, and one with which they explicitly identified. In Vienna, the essayist and critic Hermann Bahr was instrumental in articulating the program of a literary *Moderne* and has in fact been credited with introducing the term—as well as other linked terms such as "Secession" and "fin de siècle"—although research has borne out that it appeared earlier in print and was only popularized by him.¹

At first the college-aged Kafka, his friend Max Brod, and others of their generation of German-speaking Jewish Praguers demonstrated a strong identification with the aestheticist tendencies of these self-identified moderns, but their work soon departed from these styles. We know that several members of this cohort were organized in a reading group at the German university in Prague called the Lese- und Redehalle der Deutschen Studenten in Prag (Reading and Lecture Club of German Students in Prague), whose program at the time was markedly modernist and aestheticist while also respectful of the older generation of neoclassicist poets in Prague.² The literary and artistic section of the Halle, where Kafka befriended Brod and others of the so-called Prague Circle, at the time admired the work of German aestheticist poets, and Brod for a while after his university period imagined himself to be working along the lines of French writers Jules Laforgue and Flaubert. Kafka scholars have long noted the uncharacteristically florid style of the early work, particularly *Betrachtung*. In contrast to those who see this work as immature and underdeveloped, discontinuous with the crystalline, stripped-down style of work after the 1912 breakthrough, some scholars have appreciated the continuities of these equally modernist contributions.³

Kafka would generally not be identified under the labels of aestheticism, decadence, art for art's sake, and so on, and yet one could argue that his attitude toward writing was an extension and intensification of aestheticist positions. Certainly, life and art may seem for Kafka to have been opposing realms at times, as asserted by Max Brod early in the Kafka scholarship or assumed by readers of his letters to Felice Bauer.⁴ On the other hand, Kafka's more consistently held position was not the segregation of art and life but rather a view of art that was deeply connected to living or that promised or threatened to consume it. Chapter 7 mentions two salient examples: "Writing as a form of prayer," and the assertion in the letter to Felice Bauer that "I have no literary interests, I am made of literature, and can be nothing else."⁵ I argue that these apparently extravagant claims belong to Kafka's time and place.⁶ Attempting to understand how to take such statements seriously is as central to an understanding of Kafka's modernism as it is to an appreciation of his historical context.

Modern, Modernity, Modernism

While systematic explorations of the notion of literary modernity have traced the term "modern" (in the sense of innovation or break from antique models) to the medieval period and in the sense of a particular focus on artistic innovation to at least the eighteenth century, the category of literary modernism is historically situated in central European cultural history in the period from the 1880s to the 1920s.[7] The first use of the noun in this sense dates from 1886 and is associated with naturalism, although most of the central European movements identifying themselves as modernist were markedly antinaturalist in impulse, as witnessed by Hermann Bahr's influential programmatic work.[8]

Even taken in this narrower, historically specific sense, a catalogue of features of the literary modern is frustratingly difficult to produce. The questioning of received ideas about form and aesthetics as well as ambivalence about tradition and history characterize many accounts.[9] Some critics stress the thematics of modernity present in modernist works, particularly urban themes; in the case of central European modernism, some have stressed the topos of subjective crisis—crisis of self, crisis of consciousness, confusion or crisis of values, language crisis (see below), crisis of masculinity, and so on.[10] The relationship of the *Moderne* in its various meanings—the nature of the linkage between (artistic) modernism and (social) modernity, for instance—is itself an instrument of definition; whereas "modern" in the earlier usages suggested an adaptation or adherence to one's contemporary context, with the advent of fin-de-siècle modernism the relationship is sooner adversarial or oppositional.[11] The political implications of this artistic stance, even as it professed in its aestheticist (or *l'art pour l'art*) guise to be governed by purely aesthetic considerations, are the subject of other explorations of the institutional and political contexts of modernist movements.[12]

The ways that many people have thought about Kafka and *modernity* in the period since he has become widely known, after World War II, have often been less satisfying than those discussions of his place in the literary *Moderne*. Focusing in large part on the apparently dystopic worlds of the unfinished novels—*Der Process*, *Der Verschollene* (released under Brod's editing as *Amerika*), and *Das Schloß*—many readers have wanted to see in Kafka's work a metonym for modernity. In its most extreme forms, this interpretation becomes a belief that Kafka's dystopias presciently anticipated the catastrophic social and historico-political realities that would follow his death—namely, fascist dictators, communist apparatchiks, and the Holocaust. Others have presented a much more palatable version of this modernity thesis, that Kafka's works often seem to thematize the failure of modernity to fulfill the promises of enlightenment.[13] The patterns of life characteristic of Kafka's present—from bureaucratic structures to medial dimensions of modern forms of communication, to contemporary time-space compression and the modern experience of travel—run clearly throughout Kafka's writing, and as recent studies have shown, this need not be seen merely on the level of topos, or theme, but in the writing strategies he innovated.[14] Modernity may hence be less usefully seen as a theme on which Kafka's writings intend to expound as much as an alibi or an occasion for literary experimentation.

Language and Literary Modernism

Some of the discussion of modernism as aesthetic category has been clouded by its distinction not from what preceded it but from what some claim has followed it, postmodernism, although a catalogue of the characteristics of the latter often overlaps with more than distinguishes itself from the former. Underlying the (post)modern, in many accounts, is a fundamental skepticism about the representational capacity of language, or the reliability of its correspondence to anything like a reality external to itself. Such a skepticism about the competence of language to refer to things beyond itself is already apparent in the very earliest extant piece of writing by the author, the entry in a friend's memory book, entered in the first year of the twentieth century by a seventeen-year-old Franz Kafka:

> How many words in this book! Meant for remembrance! As if words could bear remembrance!
> For words make poor mountaineers and poor miners. They carry no treasures from the mountain peaks and none from the mountain depths.[15]

In the mature fictional writings of the author, many critics have identified their power precisely in the shift of linguistic operation away from allegory.

Some historians and critics have gone so far as to associate the innovations of modernism in its many cultural formations to the central European milieu of Freud, Wittgenstein, and Kafka, arguing that the heightened consciousness of language and its particular status in the Habsburg Empire gave its subjects privileged access to such a denaturalization of assumptions about language.[16] In turn-of-the-century Bohemia and Prague in particular, both the power of language and its contingency were apparent in a more explicit and literal way than elsewhere in the territory of modernism, although the relative importance of this fact is impossible to calculate.

The relationship of Kafka's historical context to the character of the language in his prose work that made such an important contribution to modernism has been the subject of some debate in the secondary literature. For some influential scholars of the first wave (after Brod) of Kafka studies, the alienated or otherworldly effects of Kafka's texts were linked to a sterility or artifice of the German spoken in Prague, which was in turn an effect of its demographic isolation from a larger landscape of German speakers or else of foreign (e.g., Czech) influences.[17] Ironically, these claims simply reiterated discussions of Prague German in the nineteenth and early twentieth centuries: while considered High German of the most exemplary kind before 1848, in the era of nationalism it came to be seen, as the existence of a polyglot city in a multinational empire itself, as something affected, unnatural, detached, in short, "alienated."[18] The very referent "Prague

German" (*Prager Deutsch*) is incidentally unclear: it sometimes refers to the German spoken in Prague (alternatively called *Kleinseitner Deutsch*, but the dialect spoken by the German nobility residing on the Prague Little Side of the Moldau [*Kleinseite*, or *Malá Strana*, in Czech] was only one variant of the German spoken in the city), or Bohemian German generally, or the various odd mixtures of Czech and German (*Kucheldeutsch* and *Kuchelböhmisch*, or kitchen German and kitchen Bohemian) spoken between servant staffs and their patrons.[19] The claims about the "impoverished German" inherited by Kafka hence have a strongly ideological character, not least because, as others have noted, all great contributors to German literature worked out of their own local dialects.[20] What is more, the debate about Prague German language and its relationship to Kafka's modernist contribution performs the tension between history and literature in the sense that it seems to pit those who identify in the crystalline precision of Kafka's prose the mark of a modernist aesthetic against a crop of literary historians armed with local knowledge of the Prague linguistic context. The latter identified the linguistic problem of the artificially isolated German-speaking bourgeois, separated from the organic language of a living dialect of the folk, as an atrophying limb. Hence, instead of a language deliberately engineered to be perfect and precise even as it was otherworldly and alienating, Kafka wrote in a language that was imperfect as a result of its unsalutary condition.[21] These two positions—somewhat lumpily reproduced here, for argument's sake—could also be read as either historical (a thesis focusing on the condition of Kafka's language determined by a degenerate relation of nation or territory) or literary (a reading of the literary language in terms of its aesthetic operations and effects).

A somewhat different problematic, also derived from questions relating to language, has emerged in relation to an influential essay on Kafka by French theorists Gilles Deleuze and Félix Guattari, which came to define a subfield of literary study—that is, the study of "minor literatures," sometimes rendered as "minority literature" (*littérateur mineure*).[22] In this slim volume, the French philosopher and psychoanalyst team established, on the basis of apparently scanty evidence, the structure of the political content of Kafka's writing. They based their analysis on a diary entry of Kafka's of December 25, 1911, and defined the language he had at his disposal as a "deterritorialized language, appropriate for strange and minor uses."[23] The diary entry to which they refer is indeed a fascinating fragment, outlining the special character of the literatures of small nations, such as the Czech or Polish-Yiddish, and cataloguing some of its salient features.[24] Importantly for our discussion, Kafka claims that the aesthetic projects of such literatures cannot be disentangled from their inherently political status. Scandalously, in what one critic has cleverly called a "flagrant but insightful misreading,"[25] Deleuze and Guattari understood Kafka to be speaking of his own literature and his own language (i.e., Prague German, see above) as *mineure*, and from this (false) premise they set out to construct an edifice of literature as politics based on an operation of (minor or minority) language. Their notion of deterritorialization entails the subversion of the major language, discourse, or culture from within, marking a "line of escape" from the majority discourse. *Kafka* therefore enables a critical reading of a specific potential political operation of literature, or writing working both with and against its given historical context.[26]

This idiosyncratic reading of Kafka has had an enormous impact on literary studies generally but has been met by Kafka scholars in particular with enormous skepticism. Many detractors have been satisfied simply to point out the "flagrant misreading" (that Kafka's diary entry refers to the Yiddish or Czech languages in the Polish or Bohemian context and not Kafka's German) rather than engaging the insight of the argument. Stanley Corngold has critiqued the French theorists in a way that defends Kafka's writing against a particular misuse of the notion of minor literature, since that writing is certainly not to be read as a polemical dialect or idiolect aimed against the standard language or canon of High German literature.[27] Yet there is evidence that Kafka did not see subversion (of the sort of Deleuze and Guattari describe) and the creation of great German literature as antinomies. The best example may be his discussion of "talking Jewy," or *das Mauscheln*, in the June 1921 letter to Max Brod on Karl Kraus, in which he seems to reclaim the offensive antisemitic term *mauscheln*, referring to the Jewish mutilation of German speech, as a gesture of power and also of art: he refers to "*mauscheln* taken in its broadest sense (in the only sense in which it should ever be taken)—namely, as the flagrant, or dead-silent, or self-pitying usurpation of foreign property that has not been earned, but stolen with a (relatively) fleeting grip, and that remains foreign property, even if not the slightest linguistic error could be detected" and says, "In German only the dialects and besides those only the most personal high German really lives, whereas all the rest—the linguistic middle class—is nothing but ashes that can be brought to a semblance of life only by the rummaging of surviving Jewish hands."[28] The tendency here belongs to a pattern that can be seen throughout Kafka's work. It is not so much that he falls prey to racist antisemitic assumptions about essential identity or other hostile historical discursive contexts as much as these become, as here, material for novel rethinking of the operative potential of literary language.

Kafka and History

Kafka's eccentric claim about the state of literary language in modernity brings us back to the general problem of literary modernity and indeed to the problem of the relationship of the modern to history. In chapter 2 I discuss in detail the complex relationship of these two, especially as they appear in de Man's reading of Nietzsche's *Untimely Meditations*. The two are bound together more than they were ever in opposition to one another, either in a dialectical tension or, as de Man would have it, as an aporia. There are arguably many references to history in Franz Kafka's extant ephemera, but a particularly apt one in relation to these questions was extracted from his notebooks by Hannah Arendt for use in the introduction to her *Between Past and Future*:

> He has two antagonists: the first presses him from behind, from the origin. The second blocks the road ahead. He gives battle to both. To be sure, the first supports him in his fight with the second, for he wants to push him forward, and in the same way the second supports him in his fight with the first, since he drives him back. But it is only theoretically so. For it is not only the two antagonists who are there, but he himself as well, and who really knows his intentions? His dream, though, is that some time in an unguarded moment—and this would require a night darker than any night has ever been yet—he will jump out of the fighting line and be promoted, on account of his experience in fighting, to the position of umpire over his antagonists in their fight with each other.[29]

This is a passage that maps spatial imagery onto the question of temporality, at least in the way Arendt has chosen to use it, as a metaphorical representation of an individual's place within history. There is in the passage an explicit reference to origins and destinations—but the subject is oppressed by his location between past and future. His fantasy moment of escaping from this condition, to be "promoted . . . to . . . umpire," is in this sense a hope beyond hope of escaping from the nightmare of history.[30] The relevant historical context here would be the conflict-rife atmosphere of competing nationalisms and the rise of racialist antisemitism in the last decades of the Habsburg Empire. This context is recalled here because of the possibility that the history metaphorically referred to in this passage could be interpreted to be not only history as such but a specific historical context. At least, some commentators have recognized in the conflict among three figures the potential allegory of Germans, Czechs, and Jews, the Jews after all sandwiched between the conflict of Czechs and Germans, wishing to take a neutral and liberal role of "umpire" between a German hegemony asserting itself from the past (or "block[ing] the road ahead") and an antagonistic Czech future. But such a reading is problematic at best. Like much other unpersuasive Kafka interpretation of this sort—let us call it historical allegory—it is too closed with regard to texts that seem defiantly open; overly deterministic, when Kafka's texts seem antideterministic; untrue to the texts as literature in its search for a historical referent.

It is hence prudent to resist the thesis that, to put it the way a Kafka scholar put it at a postperformance discussion of a dramatization of *The Trial* I once attended, "everything in Kafka's fiction can be traced back to something that occurred in his own life." This mode of Kafka interpretation is familiar: on the basis of sources such as the *Letter to His Father*, Brod's early Kafka biography, or the classic Kafka scholarship of Klaus Wagenbach and then Hartmut Binder and others, one produces a picture of an alienated and oppressed Kafka who conveniently corresponds to the protagonist K.[31] With this gesture, and other similar interpretive moves relating to other works, the first wave of Kafka critics (and many after them) "solved" an apparent tension between Kafka's imaginative works and the Kafka ephemera, the discrepancy between the very steady rumination on Jewish, German, and Czech identity in the letters and diaries and the virtual total absence of such reference in the fiction and literary fragments, published or unpublished in his own lifetime. The question of this connection, or forced connection, between Kafka's life experience and his literary work is central to an analysis of how his work contributes to literary modernism.

Allegory and Interpretation

The problem of history with relation to Kafka is remarkably similar to what might be thought of as the founding problem of Kafka interpretation generally, the one facing it from its very beginnings: the problem of allegory. Related to the figure of allegory is the term *Gleichnis*—"parable" is its most common translation—a term that was commented on explicitly by Kafka. Most poignantly perhaps, the slippery dynamics of the parable were put on display in the Kafka fragment appearing in translation under the title "On Parables."[32] Charles Bernheimer once produced an elegant reading of this fragment and the status of *Gleichnis* in Kafka's work generally, in which instead of allegory, literary reference to external reality, the *Gleichnis* (or "likeness") signals a moment of potential *gleich-werden*, "becoming like"—the dissolution of boundaries between language and referent, author and text, parable and life.[33] Another place where *Gleichnis* takes on importance is related to the publication history of two stories published by Martin Buber in the famous journal *Der Jude* in 1912. The two stories were "Jackals and Arabs" and "A Report to an Academy," both of which were seen by Buber and Max Brod as transparent parables representing the condition of Jewish life in the diaspora (the "Report" a parody of assimilation and "Jackals and Arabs" to a lesser degree as well). Buber wrote Kafka, suggesting that the two stories be published under a collective title, "Gleichnisse," to which Kafka hastily, pleadingly, and perhaps a bit pained, asked that they not be given the collective title "Gleichnisse" because "they aren't really *Gleichnisse*," offering instead the alternative title under which they did appear, "Zwei Tiergeschichten" (Two animal stories).[34]

Instead of relying on a symbolic structure in which literary figures (apes, jackals, Arabs, narrator) stand in for counterparts in historical reality, the stories operate on an allegorical grid that is always shifting, where apparent references to identity (whether Jewish, Czech, German, or other sorts of identity) are evoked only as they are subverted.[35] Historical referent in this sense is a trap in the stories, as other forms of reference to external reality are similar traps in other Kafka fiction and even nonfiction. Now, while Brod's master strategy of reading parable or allegory where Kafka explicitly rejected it might have had long-lasting effects, it is important to note that the alternative of reading these as multivalent and nonallegorical was noted very early by Walter Benjamin and Theodor Adorno.[36] Both of these critics rejected Brod's suggestion that Kafka's work was built on a fundamentally religious system of symbols and insisted instead on attention to the aesthetic effects produced by the uncanny literality or "wordliness" of the Kafka texts to follow the rule that says, as Adorno put it, "take everything literally; cover up nothing with concepts invoked from above."[37] But the hermeneutic mode of contextual allegory was to be dominant in the early Kafka reception and after.

The same thing can be said about the assimilations of antisemitic discourses in Kafka's writing, which are certainly numerous—one might even say innumerable if Sander Gilman had not so comprehensively catalogued them.[38] Yet in Kafka's hands, the laws of essentialist racism, antisemitism, degeneration theory, and so on, are pushed to such extremes that they become something else. Rather than standing as literary representations of immutable realities, they transform the latter into figures—and true to the form of figures in Kafka's writing, literary and otherwise, they are open rather than closed, indeterminate instead of fixed. This figurative status needs to be granted also to terms such as "Zionism" in works such as the letters to Felice.[39] Here, too, in spite of Kafka's consistent and puzzling play with networks of mutually alternating associations and counterassociations, some commentators insist on disciplining this free play into a trajectory—again, a historical development—from a position of liberal assimilationism to one of identification with a distinctly Jewish identity and the stabilization of its national life within a Jewish state. Of course, once again we see not only a mode of interpretation but also a story that was, from the beginnings of the Kafka reception, Brod's story.[40] And yet this should not imply that Brod's contribution is responsible for the tendencies I have been lumping together under the rubric of historical allegory. To the contrary, if anything, the practice is invited by the work itself. An assimilated ape in a central European Jewish journal, the (Slavic-sounding) name Odradek, a Count West-West, an animal in a synagogue, a half-breed (or *Kreuzung*)—if these are not codes for specific historical referents, then they must be traps laid for the reader with less than acute sleuthing capacities. For the real sleuths, of course, the index of historical referents is never ending. We can track them down in Kafka's library, in the lessons of his influential teachers, in the *Lebensreform* movement, in anarchist programs, in the Kabbalah or other Jewish writings he might (or even might not!) have come into contact with. But what do we do with this information, what does the recovery of such sources actually tell us if, instead of secret referents to be uncovered, they were for Kafka more like found objects used for the construction of entirely new, open, and evocative literary figures?

What does seem clear—and it echoes the point made above about national allegories, in fact it is a pattern—is that the typologies created by these historical contexts are consistently appropriated and instrumentalized by Kafka in all these cases. These questions lead us back to the problem of Kafka's place in (literary) modernity. Because there is a historical context for the emergence of this particular and difficult form of antireferentiality, of stripped-down language, of the resistance to historicity. The most honest historical work on Kafka in this sense would involve the recovery of the Prague and late Habsburg–early Czechoslovak contexts insofar as they produced conditions for the radical and imaginative emergence of a novel form of literary language. That is challenging work, to be sure, and it may be approached in very different ways. But the object of such work ought not to be the harmonious echoes of literary text and historical context in a case where these two are more often dissonant against one another. The light shed by certain forms of criticism may unwillingly take sides with the forces of an irretractable past and an unalterable future colluding to crush a subject who is really in search of a "night darker than any night has ever been yet," in which he can create a different present for himself, an aesthetic moment that cannot be touched by history.

Notes

1. See Fritz Martini, "Modern, Die Moderne," in *Reallexikon der Deutschen Literaturgeschichte*, vol. 2, ed. Werner Kohlschmidt and Wolfgang Mohr (Berlin: Walter de Gruyter, 1965), 409. This programmatic usage of modernism at the turn of the century did not originate with Bahr, as Bahr himself claimed and as was long held, but Martini attributes it to the 1886 appearance in print of E. Wolff's lecture "Die 'Moderne' zur Revolution und Reform der Literatur." The program in that lecture, however, differs quite substantially from Bahr's and those of the various movements of the *Jungen* around 1900.

2. The literary establishment in Prague was still controlled in large part by neoclassical tendencies represented by leading figures Hugo Salus and Friedrich Adler; the generation between that of these writers and Kafka and his cohort was more aligned with central European and western European modernist tendencies described variously as *Jugendstil*, symbolism, aestheticism, and so forth, and included writers such as Gustav Meyrink, Viktor Hadwiger, and Paul Leppin.

3. See G. Kurz, ed., *Der junge Kafka* (Frankfurt am Main, Germany: Suhrkamp, 1984). Particularly relevant is Mark Anderson's argument in *Kafka's Clothes: Ornament and Aestheticism in the Habsburg Fin de Siècle* (New York: Oxford University Press, 1992), in which the high

modernist and alienated, stripped-down style of the later Kafka is described as an unmistakably aestheticist self-fashioning of a different kind.

4. See Max Brod, *Franz Kafka: Eine Biographie; Erinnerungen und Dokumente* (Prague: H. Mercy Sohn, 1937); and Elias Canetti, *Der andere Prozeß: Kafkas Briefe an Felice* (Munich: Carl Hanser, 1969).

5. Franz Kafka, *Nachgelassene Schriften und Fragmente*, ed. Jost Schillemeit (Frankfurt am Main, Germany: S. Fischer, 1992), 2:354; Franz Kafka, *Briefe an Felice und andere Korrespondenz aus der Verlobungszeit*, ed. Erich Heller and Jürgen Born (Frankfurt am Main, Germany: S. Fischer, 1988), 444.

6. I have identified parallels in other early twentieth-century central European texts such as those of Georg Lukács in Scott Spector, "Beyond the Aesthetic Garden: Politics and Culture on the Margins of *Fin-de-Siècle Vienna*," *Journal of the History of Ideas* 59, no. 4 (1998): 691–710.

7. See Martini, "Modern, Die Moderne," 391–415; and Alfred White, "Die Moderne," in *Encyclopedia of German Literature*, ed. Mathias Konzett (Chicago: Fitzroy Dearborn, 2000), 2:709–712. An account with a strong sense of the centrality of Austrian modernism and of gender issues, which, however, oddly marginalizes Kafka, is Christine Kanz, "Die Literarische Moderne (1890–1920)," in *Deutsche Literaturgeschichte: Von den Anfängen bis zur Gegenwart*, 6th ed., ed. W. Beutin, K. Ehlert, W. Emmerich, C. Kanz, B. Lutz, V. Meid, M. Opitz, C. Opitz-Wiemers, R. Schnell, P. Stein, and I. Stephan (Stuttgart, Germany: J. B. Metzler, 2001), 342–386. An extremely helpful overview, albeit extending far beyond the notion of artistic modernism, is the conceptual-historical essay by H. Gumbrecht, "Modern, Modernität, Moderne," in *Geschichtliche Grundbegriffe: Historisches Lexikon zur politisch-sozialen Sprache in Deutschland*, ed. O. Brunner, W. Conze, and R. Koselleck, (Stuttgart, Germany: Ernst Klett 1978), 4:93–131. The noun appears in Brockhaus in 1902 specifically as "Bezeichnung für den Inbegriff der jüngsten sozialen, literarischen und künstlerischen Richtungen" (designation for the epitome of recent social, literary and artistic trends). *Brockhaus' Konversations-Lexikon: Neue Revidierte Jubiläums-Ausgabe*, 14th ed. (Leipzig: F. A. Brockhaus, 1902), 11:952. See also G. Wunberg, ed., *Die literarische Moderne: Dokumente zum Selbstverständnis der Literatur um die Jahrhundertwende* (Frankfurt am Main, Germany: Athanäum, 1971).

8. See Hermann Bahr, *Studien zur Kritik der Moderne* (Frankfurt am Main, Germany: Rütten and Loening, 1894); and Hermann Bahr, *Die Überwindung des Naturalismus: Als zweite Reihe von Zur Kritik der Moderne* (Dresden: Pierson, 1891). Bahr's polemic was at the same time aimed to distinguish the Viennese from the *Reichsdeutsch*, Berlin-based variety; see Peter Sprengel and Gregor Streim, *Berliner und Wiener Moderne: Vermittlungen und Abgrenzungen in Literatur, Theater, Publizistik* (Vienna: Weimar, 1998).

9. See, e.g., Andrew Sanders, "Modernism and Its Alternatives," in *The Short Oxford History of English Literature* (Oxford: Oxford University Press, 1994), 511.

10. See C. Kanz, "Die Literarische Moderne (1890–1920)"; and Jacques LeRider, *Modernité viennoise et crises de l'identité* (Paris: Presses Universitaires de France, 1990).

11. The point is made by Martini, "Modern, Die Moderne," 408. See also Scott Spector, "Introduction: Uneven Cultural Development? Modernism and Modernity in the 'Other' Central Europe," *Austrian History Yearbook* 33 (2002): 141–147. For an original interpretation, see Matei Calinescu, *Five Faces of Modernity: Modernism, Avant-Garde, Decadence, Kitsch, Postmodernism* (Durham, NC: Duke University Press, 1987).

12. Raymond Williams, *The Politics of Modernism: Against the New Conformists* (London: Verso, 1996); Peter Bürger, *Theorie der Avantgarde* (Frankfurt am Main, Germany: Suhrkamp, 1974); and Peter Bürger, *The Decline of Modernism* (University Park: Pennsylvania State University Press, 1992).

13. Elizabeth Boa, *Kafka: Gender, Class, and Race in the Letters and Fictions* (Oxford, UK: Clarendon Press, 1996), 23–44.

14. See, e.g., Wolf Kittler and Gerhard Neumann, eds., *Franz Kafka, Schriftverkehr* (Freiburg, Germany: Rombach, 1990); and John Zilcosky, *Kafka's Travels: Exoticism, Colonialism, and the Traffic of Writing* (New York: Palgrave Macmillan, 2003).

15. The original reads, "Wie viel Worte in dem Buche stehn! Erinnern sollen sie! Als ob Worte erinnern könnten! Denn Worte sind schlechte Bergsteiger und schlechte Bergmänner. Sie holen nicht die Schätze von den Bergeshöhn und nicht die von den Bergestiefen." Kafka, *Nachgelassene Schriften und Fragmente*, 2:8.

16. See, e.g., Allan Janik and Stephen Toulmin, *Wittgenstein's Vienna* (New York: Simon and Schuster, 1973); see also Scott Spector, *Prague Territories: National Conflict and Cultural Innovation in Franz Kafka's Fin de Siècle* (Berkeley: University of California Press, 2000), esp. 68–73. Besides Wittgenstein, the earlier language critique of Bohemian Fritz Mauthner is particularly relevant here; see Fritz Mauthner, *Beiträge zu einer Kritik der Sprache*, 3 vols. (Stuttgart, Germany: J. G. Cotta, 1913).

17. See, e.g., Klaus Wagenbach, *Franz Kafka: Eine Biographie seiner Jugend* (Bern: Francke, 1958), 81–96; Peter Demetz, "Noch einmal: Prager Deutsch," *Literatur und Kritik* 1, no. 6 (1966): 58–59; Emil Skála, "Das Prager Deutsch," *Zeitschrift für deutsche Sprache* 22, nos. 1–2 (1966): 84–91; Emil Skála, "Das Prager Deutsch," in *Weltfreunde: Konferenz über die Prager deutsche Literatur*, ed. Eduard Goldstücker (Neuwied, Germany: Luchterhand, 1967), 119–125; and Christoph Stölzl, "Prag," in *Kafka-Handbuch*, ed. Hartmut Binder (Stuttgart, Germany: Kröner, 1979), 1:83–85. The fallacy continues to hold sway, as in Joachim Neugroschel's introduction to his translations of Kafka stories, in which he considers the works monuments to the Prague German language! J. Neugroschel, introduction to *The Metamorphosis and Other Stories*, by F. Kafka (New York: Schocken, 1993), xi, cited in Stanley Corngold, *Lambent Traces: Franz Kafka* (Princeton, NJ: Princeton University Press, 2004), 142–143.

18. See August Ritschel, "Das Prager Deutsch," *Phonetische Studien* 6, no. 2 (1893): 129–133; see also E. E. Kisch, "Prager Deutsch," *Bohemia*, October 14, 1917, pp. 3–4; and Heinrich Teweles, "Prager Deutsch," *Bohemia*, October 21, 1917, p. 3; see also Spector, *Prague Territories*, 75–79.

19. See Marek Nekula, "Franz Kafkas Deutsch," *Linguistik Online* 13, no. 1 (2003), http://www.linguistik-online.de/13_01/nekula.html.

20. See Richard Thieberger, "Sprache," in *Kafka-Handbuch in zwei Bänden*, ed. Hartmut Binder (Stuttgart, Germany: Kröner, 1979), 2:177–203.

21. This issue is discussed in Spector, *Prague Territories*, 75–79.

22. Gilles Deleuze and Félix Guattari, *Kafka: Pour une littérature mineure* (Paris: Editions de Minuit, 1975); G. Deleuze and F. Guattari, *Kafka: Toward a Minor Literature*, trans. Dana Polan (Minneapolis: University of Minnesota Press, 1986).

23. Deleuze and Guattari, *Kafka: Toward a Minor Literature*, 17.

24. Franz Kafka, *Gesammelte Werke in zwölf Bänden*, ed. Hans-Gerd Koch, Michael Müller, and Malcolm Pasley (Frankfurt am Main, Germany: S. Fischer, 1994), 9:243.

25. Mark Anderson, ed., *Reading Kafka: Prague, Politics, and the Fin de Siècle* (New York: Schocken, 1989), 11.

26. Deleuze and Guattari, *Kafka: Toward a Minor Literature*, esp. 6–13, 20–27, 34–37, 59–61, 65.

27. Corngold, *Lambent Traces*, 142–157.

28. Franz Kafka, *Briefe, 1902–1924*, ed. Max Brod (New York: Schocken, 1958), 336–337 (translations mine).

29. F. Kafka, "'Er': Aufzeichnungen aus dem Jahre 1920," quoted in Hannah Arendt, *Between Past and Future: Eight Exercises in Political Thought* (New York: Penguin, 1968), 7. See also H. Arendt and M. Heidegger, *Briefe, 1925 bis 1975: Und andere Zeugnisse*, ed. Ursula Ludz (Frankfurt am Main, Germany: V. Klostermann, 1998), 162.

30. This is not an escape from the nightmare of history in the Marxian sense. The specific historical context in question is represented in Christoph Stölzl, *Kafkas böses Böhmen: Zur Sozialgeschichte eines Prager Juden* (Munich: Edition Text + Kritik, 1975). Ernst Pawel's biography, *The Nightmare of Reason: Franz Kafka* (New York: Farrar Straus Giroux, 1984), should be recalled here, although it has been criticized precisely for its removal of Kafka's work from its historical context within German literature.

31. Elsewhere I have questioned even this common assumption that the recurring character K in Kafka's fictions is meant to be associated with the author. See Scott Spector, "From Big Daddy to Small Literature: On Taking Kafka at His Word," in *Evolving Jewish Identities in German Culture: Borders and Crossings*, ed. Linda E. Feldman and Diana Orendi (Westport, CT: Praeger, 2000), 79–93.

32. The text is from 1922–1923 and is found in English as "On Parables," in *Parables and Paradoxes*, by Franz Kafka (New York: Schocken Books, 1961), 10–11.

33. See Charles Bernheimer, "Crossing Over: Kafka's Metatextual Parable," in *Flaubert and Kafka: Studies in Psychopoetic Structure* (New Haven, CT: Yale University Press, 1982), 45–55.

34. Martin Buber, *Briefwechsel aus sieben Jahzehnten*, ed. Grete Schaeder, vol. 1, *1897–1918* (Heidelberg, Germany: L. Schneider, 1972), 494.

35. My use of the term "allegory" is different from and arguably opposite that proposed by Stanley Corngold in *The Commentators' Despair: The Interpretation of Kafka's Metamorphosis* (Port Washington, NY: Kennikat, 1973), 31–38, although we agree with one another. Corngold proposed "symbolic interpretation" to refer to the dominant readings of Gregor's experience as standing for the alienated experience of the modern individual and insisting on its essential continuity, stability, and meaningfulness, whereas allegorical readings, after Benjamin's definition of allegory in *Origins of the German Tragic Drama*, take the text on more literal terms. Ibid., 37.

36. See, e.g., Walter Benjamin, "Franz Kafka: On the Tenth Anniversary of His Death," in *Illuminations: Essays and Reflections*, by Walter Benjamin, ed. Hannah Arendt, trans. Harry Zohn (New York: Schocken, 1968), 111–140; Walter Benjamin, "Some Reflections on Kafka," in Benjamin, *Illuminations*, 141–146; Walter Benjamin, "Franz Kafka: Beim Bau der Chinesischen Mauer," in *Gesammelte Schriften*, vol. 2, bk. 2, by Walter Benjamin, ed. Rolf Tiedemann and Hermann Schweppenhäuser (Frankfurt am Main, Germany: Suhrkamp, 1991), 676–683; and Theodor W. Adorno, "Aufzeichnungen zu Kafka," in *Prismen: Kulturkritik und Gesellschaft*, by Theodor Adorno (Frankfurt am Main, Germany: Suhrkamp, 1955), 302–342. Philip Rahv provides an insightful early assessment, in which he describes Kafka's narratives as "myths whose judicious, mock-scientific tonality at once dissociates them from the myth as an historical product," and therefore they are "experimental myths" or "myth as *procedure*," a "new mutation in the art of prose fiction." Philip Rahv, "Franz Kafka: The Hero as Lonely Man," *Kenyon Review* 1, no. 1 (1939): 62.

37. Theodor W. Adorno, *Prisms*, trans. Shierry Weber Nicholsen and Samuel Weber (Cambridge, MA: MIT Press, 1981), 247. Stanley Corngold offers a sophisticated reading of Adorno's notes on Kafka to show how the critic does not stay true to his own word in his actual reading of Kafka, but his insight was nonetheless closer to the mark than the rest of his generation and those that would follow. See Corngold, *Lambent Traces*, 158–175.

38. Sander Gilman, *Franz Kafka, the Jewish Patient* (New York: Routledge, 1995).

39. See Scott Spector, "'Any Reality, However Small': Prague Zionisms between the Nations," in *Kafka, Zionism, and Beyond*, ed. Mark Gelber (Tübingen, Germany: Niemeyer, 2004); and Spector, *Prague Territories*, 142–147.

40. See Max Brod, *Franz Kafkas Glauben und Lehre, Kafka und Tolstoi* (Winterthur, Germany: Mondial, 1948); and Max Brod, *Über Franz Kafka* (Frankfurt am Main, Germany: Fischer, 1974). For the debate on Kafka's Zionism, see Gelber, *Kafka, Zionism, and Beyond*.

9 The Law of the Letter
Kafka's Correspondence with Milena Jesenská

WHAT'S IN A LETTER? That is one way we might begin to interrogate the relationships among letters, correspondences, and translation in a packet of love letters such as those from Franz Kafka to his Czech lover Milena Jesenská. The letter is of course many things at once: it is the fundamental or irreducible component of words, languages, literatures—it makes a claim for language as itself, literal language, which demands transparency and refuses interpretation. This letter proclaims its own immediacy and resists mediation. The letter, though, is also the epistle, the mode of mediation par excellence: it should be a bridge between subjectivities, or the means of communication through which ideas, figures, and emotions are moved over (literally *übertragen*, translated) to another place and to another person.[1] The relationship of these two sorts of letters is not trivial—what is more, they both depend in some way on the tension created between them rather than cancel out one another.[2] There is a consciousness on some level of the utterly fictive character of both of these territorial images, the one standing its ground as confidently native, completely genuine, unambiguous, unshakable, and the other so blithely secure in its assumption that this writing, as a letter, will find its way into an envelope and, aided by the most advanced technologies and transportations, overseen by the most steadfast of national and international bureaucracies and loyal public servants, arrive in the hands of the intended recipient, who is sure to open and read it at once and, in this happy moment of reading, commune with the sender in an ecstatic unison of literary meaning. The implication of course is that this disingenuous dispute between two occupants of the word "letter" is precisely what takes place in translation theory, traditional and otherwise: the question of the literal and the figurative, or the problem of the mediation of the immediate. For the fact that perfect reproduction—or even adequate communication—may be impossible does not in any way guarantee the groundedness or authenticity of the original.

Kafka's correspondence with Jesenská begins with the Czech journalist's attempts to consult the author of the text she wishes to translate into her native tongue, "The Stoker."[3] Translation is thus struck as an inaugural figure in the love correspondence. A difficult logic of the ideology of mediation is pressured to the extremes in eight intensive months of letter writing to Jesenská, so that it is not in spite of but rather through the very laws of difference and mediation that the status of identity and the possibility of immediacy or authentic experience are put to the test.

While translation was the occasion for the initiation of the Kafka-Jesenská correspondence, Kafka was at once jealous of it, pointing out the paradox of the mediator, who establishes distance in order to bridge it or who opens dialogue even while standing in the way. In a few weeks in April 1920, Jesenská's initial inquiry regarding her translation of "The Stoker" had already become a deeply personal exchange. Receiving the draft manuscript at the end of the month, Kafka replied,

> When I pulled your translation out of the large envelope, I was almost disappointed. I wanted to hear from you and not the voice from the old grave, the voice I know all too well. Why did it have to come between us? Then I realized that this same voice had also come between us as a mediator.[4]

The figure of translation or mediation is already carefully manipulated in this early letter, where instead of the translator mediating between an original and translated text, the voice of the text stands between Kafka and Jesenská. Another important transgression in this brief passage is the subtle identification of the voice of the Czech text as the voice of the literary text "The Stoker"—not as a copy or as the mediated voice of the author, who stands apart from it and writes of it as an object without personal pronoun, but as the voice of the text, familiar and past, raised from the dead rather than lost in translation. The resentment in the passage is thus never directed at the translator's meddling with the authorial voice but, to the contrary, at that haunting voice itself, unexpectedly and without invitation returning in its original form from the netherworld. The mark of jealousy in this resentful response is directed at the fact that the caressing hands of the translator have veered away from the living body of Kafka's epistolary text to the corpse of his old story—the hidden arousal of the passage emanates nonetheless from the promise that Kafka's bodies and texts could appeal to those hands. The rest of this passage points in this direction:

> But apart from that it is inconceivable to me that you would take on such a troublesome task, and I am moved by your faithfulness toward every little sentence, up and down, a faithfulness I would not have thought possible to achieve in Czech, let alone with the beautiful natural authority you attain. German and Czech so close to each other?

What Kafka will not let pass is the intimacy effected by the act of translation, the real and physical closeness that has been created in the translated text.

Returning to the translations themselves, contemporary readers find them to be unprofessional and long on errors—"accuracy" was not at issue in Kafka's reading, even if "fidelity," in some sense or other, was.[5] The attention and care, the costly effort (*Mühe*) spent by Jesenská is felt by the author as her touch, as the closeness of the words *tief rührend* (deeply moving) to the verb *berühren* (to touch) and the image of the translator stroking the sentences imply. These very terms appeared in an even earlier letter regarding the forthcoming translation: "You are toiling [*mühn sich*] over the translation in the middle of the dreary Vienna world. Somehow I am both moved [es ist . . . *rührend*] and ashamed."[6] He is moved and shamed by this intimate touch of his text, up and down every little sentence ("tief rührend . . . Sätzchen auf und ab"). And the touching element is no less the virtue of the translation, its fidelity (*Treue*). Thus, it becomes clear that Kafka has transformed the business of this translation into an intimate intercourse that Jesenská has initiated. Further, by pointing up the correspondence between body and text, Kafka has invited Jesenská into an affair that can take place in writing, in letters, and attributed the invitation or seduction to her.

"Fidelity" in translation is never an innocent term and in all translation contexts belongs to an overdetermined set of gender relations aligning creative originality with male artists and mimesis with the feminine.[7] Lori Chamberlain has traced these gendered "metaphorics of translation" and pointed out the dual double standard of the translation and marriage relations: while the translation is subject to the test of fidelity, faithfulness remains a noncategory for the original.[8] In Kafka's letters, as we will see, translation does not serve to authorize the original, but rather it is the process that brings to light the inauthenticity of the original text—Jesenská's fidelity demonstrates Kafka's infidelity to himself and Kafka's text's infidelity to itself.[9] "Fidelity" was a heavily charged term in this correspondence with Jesenská, who had already confessed to Kafka the travails of her open marriage with Ernst Pollak (another German-speaking Prague Jew), saying of this arrangement, "I am the one who pays."[10] Kafka warns Jesenská, too, that he fears the Czechs will not forgive this literary fidelity of her translation of "The Stoker," the betrayal of the Czech language to which she belongs by the faithful attachment to the German (or German-Jewish) text or, in an antisemitic image Kafka plants later in the letters, the abduction of the Czech maiden by the German-Jewish rake.

The projection of this voice from the old grave into the Czech body, which revivifies it, is a black magic Kafka had not thought possible. But the magic that Kafka wishes to sustain is not the product, the resurrected voice of the text, but rather the act of translation—the moment in which difference still exists and yet in which the German text is absorbed into the body of Czech language. The closeness of German and Czech—a proximity beyond his dreams—depends on this retained difference. In the context of the correspondence, Kafka is resisting the closure that the completed text sealed in the large envelope threatens to represent. The erotics of translation seem at this point easily—too easily—to map themselves on the Prague milieu of Max Brod's novel *Ein tschechisches Dienstmädchen* (A Czech serving maid) and other chauvinist works of the period: the creative power of the German text faces the feminine Czech translation, reproductive and at the same time seductive, sexy in its exoticism and as a result of the exaggerated imbalance of power.[11] It is thus at this moment that Kafka seeks to sustain the creative and erotic tension of translation by asking Jesenská to write in Czech, not because she does not command (*beherrschen*) German, for she commands it astonishingly or, when she does not, it voluntarily yields or bows to her, thus remaining at her service. But this erotic tension is not the genuine encounter Kafka desires—Jesenská herself is lost in German translation, adapted to the dreary world of Vienna. He wants to read her in Czech because she belongs to it and not to German, because the whole Milena is there only in the Czech, and her translation is his evidence for this. And so he asks that she write in her native tongue.[12]

Hence the meeting with Milena will take place in letters, in Czech texts where "the whole Milena is," and in German writing, of which Kafka is made.[13] The transposition or translation of Milena's body (in)to the text of the letter is explicit in Kafka's responses to the Czech letters: "I see you more clearly, the movements of your body, your hands, so quick, so resolute, it is almost an encounter." Jesenská's textual presence supersedes Kafka's bodily presence in the spa in Merano so that consummation is still deferred: "And still I would be lying if I said I missed you: it is the most perfect, most painful magic, you are here, just as I am and even more so. . . . I occasionally imagine that you, who really are here, are missing *me* here and asking: 'Where can he be? Didn't he write that he's in Merano?'"[14] Within the framework of the correspondence exchange, bodies pass into texts and become more corporeal there than they are on the earth. At least that is the case for Kafka's ephemeral body, consumed by tuberculosis, unable to sleep, and barely alive until it is grounded in the earth of the letters:

> It is so wonderful to have received your letter, to have to answer it with my sleepless brain. I can't think of anything to write, I'm just walking around here between the lines, beneath the light of your eyes, in the breath of your mouth as in some beautiful and happy day which stays beautiful and happy even when the head is ill, tired and one departs Monday via Munich.[15]

So if the form and movements of Jesenská's body can only be touched on the page of her Czech letters, Kafka sets himself onto the page of his own letters in anticipation of her reading. If (as he wrote in the previous love correspondence to Felice Bauer, as I have discussed) he is not inclined toward but rather made of literature, his daylight radiates from her reading eyes, his air is her breath on the page. The image produced by writing and the sight evoked by reading are easier to arrange than the stopover in Vienna: "And so, *auf Wiedersehn* (but it doesn't have to be in Vienna, it can also be in letters)."[16] All this contact stands in for the physical encounter that is constantly deferred—here by returning from Merano to Prague over Munich rather than Vienna. In fact he would not be ready to return from his cure in Merano on Monday, and three more weeks of diligent letter writing would precede the revived conflict of whether and how to stop to see Milena.

Naturally, a love affair of letters can be enabled only by the deferral of physical meeting or distance from Vienna—the space between writer and reader is the prerequisite for writing to be produced.[17] The love affair was thus concentrated in letters, with Kafka's work and illness and Jesenská's marriage serving the useful function of keeping the lovers apart. In the course of the correspondence, Kafka and Jesenská met only twice: once for four days in Vienna and once for a single day at the Czech-Austrian border. Even here, the meetings retained a secondary function to letter writing rather than the letters having served as instruments to facilitate meeting. On June 25, 1920, a Friday, Kafka was still not sure whether he would travel over Vienna the following Tuesday; in a second letter that day he was ready to commit, but not to a rendezvous point: "[for] I would suffocate by then if I were to name a place right now and then have to see this place for three days and three nights, empty, waiting for me to arrive Tuesday at a certain hour."[18] Naming in the context of the letters brings the named into immediate and tangible existence—naming a future meeting place creates a physical space apart from the correspondence itself, which is painfully empty and impossible to bear. The next line has a confusing syntax and frugal punctuation: "Gibt es überhaupt Milena auf der Welt soviel Geduld, wie für mich nötig ist?" (Is there Milena anywhere in the world as much patience as I need?)[19] It seems at first to ask, is Milena in the world at all (is she not really bound to the territory of letters?) and then reveals that the direct object is "patience." And yet even this more pedestrian meaning of the sentence is strange, depending as it does on the assumption that corresponding with Milena in letters over three months has not required the patience demanded by making an arrangement to see her on Tuesday. He did in fact take the train to Vienna on Tuesday. Arriving at the South Station, he sat down with a cup of chocolate and wrote Milena a letter. The question of the arrival of this letter is more his concern than his own presence in Vienna:

> This letter won't likely arrive by noon, or certainly won't, it is already 10:00. Then not before tomorrow. Perhaps it is better that way, since although I am in Vienna . . . I am not completely here.[20]

It is almost as though, instead of this correspondence mediating their meeting, Kafka's presence in Vienna is another excuse to write a letter—at least in this case it is clear that the letter does not facilitate their physical contact as much as it does defer it another day.[21] In this day a ghostly Kafka will pass through Vienna, "as invisible as possible,"[22] until Jesenská receives his letter and finds his hotel. It is certainly not insignificant that they did meet, that there is reference to a successful copulation, and that they did write endlessly about the possibility of meeting again. But even then it is arguable that, just as letters are assumed to reflect on and anticipate experience, in this case the reverse seemed to be true. The record of what transpired during the brief Vienna tryst includes Jesenská's description of a lengthy visit to the post office as well as Kafka's note on July 27: "You see, you need a new pen nib, why didn't we make better use of our time in Vienna? Why didn't we spend the whole time in the stationer's shop, for example; it really was so beautiful inside and we were so close to one another."[23]

The tension between life and writing and the deferral of physical trysts to write letters have long been recognized in Kafka's earlier letters to Felice Bauer in Berlin (1912–1916), in which "life" or "happiness," being with Felice, was explicitly identified as a cancellation of the possibility of writing.[24] In the correspondence with Milena, though, the dichotomy of life and writing is intensely refracted by the element of (un)translatability—Milena is physically present in the letters in a way that Felice could not be, and Franz then surrenders himself to the textual Milena in a manner neither ascetic nor renouncing. Yet even Milena needed to be schooled in this art of correspondence, in which letters do not mediate experiences and identities but rather take their places. She might have been flattered by the volume of correspondence coming from Prague but was doubtless puzzled at the currency of letters within this dialogue. Kafka's obsessive accounting of the number of letters he had received and sent, his recurring anxiety about the possibility of letters being lost in the postal system, his descriptions of how her letters and his to her ruled over his daily life were noted by Milena, who could not understand. Kafka wrote,

> You once asked how it happened that I made my stay here dependent on one letter, and then you immediately answered your own question: *nechápu* [I don't understand]. A strange word in Czech and even in your mouth it is so severe, so callous, cold-eyed, stingy, and most of all like a nutcracker, pronouncing it requires three consecutive cracks of the jaw or, more exactly, the first syllable makes an attempt at holding the nut, in vain, the second syllable then tears the mouth wide open, the nut now fits inside, where it is finally cracked by the third syllable, can you hear the teeth? Particularly this final, absolute closing of the lips at the end prohibits the other person from expressing anything to the contrary, which is actually quite good at times, for instance when the other person is babbling as much as I am now.[25]

It is not for nothing that these complex effects are attached to the brittle word expressing the lapse of mutual comprehension, a closing off or cracking of the hope of translatability. It is a foreign word in Czech, Kafka claims, and so even in or on Milena's tongue does not seem to belong to her or her to it: "callous, cold-eyed, stingy." While excusing himself for babbling, Kafka is also warning Jesenská to defend the letters against foreign interventions, which will destroy the delicate mechanisms that make these letters a mutual territory of the two languages and two genders. Chief among these mechanisms is precisely the primacy of letters, which is challenged by Jesenská's reply: *nechápu*.

The interesting focus on the physical effects of words, the effects performed not by their referentiality but by their "wordliness," belongs to the kabbalistic science, as Kafka knew. Interestingly, the phenomenological magic of this word and others is inaccessible to the Czech native speaker—Kafka speaks of these performances as side effects the Czech language has for German ears. The examples he offers of such effects are violent. In the same early letter he responds to Jesenská's question "Are you a Jew?"

> And on top of that Milena is still going on about anxiety, striking my chest or asking: *jste Žid* [are you a Jew]? Which in Czech has the same movement and sound. Don't you see how the fist is pulled back in the word "*jste*," so as to gain muscle power? And then in the word "*Žid*" the happy blow, flying unerringly forward?[26]

From this point forward, "Jew" and "Jewishness" remain important textual figures in the letters, and the dynamics aligning them from within with *Ängstlichkeit* and *Angst*, fear and anxiety, and from without with rejection and violence never subsides. A reading of the valence of fear in the letters would alone take up the full space of an analytic essay on this correspondence. In shorthand I suggest that it serves a function parallel to the complex operation of the trope of size and inferiority in the letter to his father—he writes Milena that his fear represents a "retreating from the world."[27] In fact, at several points where Kafka discussed this fear in the correspondence he promised to send her the letter to his father, which he finally did. This gesture reinforces the primacy of letters, since it identifies referents for the letter, a space outside the letter text, chiefly in another letter. Similarly, the play with presence and absence in the letters to Milena covertly work through the set of concerns established in the letters to Felice. Even the real-life relations of Kafka and Jesenská in this period are compelled within the boundaries of the correspondence: leaving Julie Wohryzek for Jesenská is a process enacted by showing the former Jesenská's letters, writing her letters, and most important mediating an exchange of letters between the two women. Wohryzek in turn sent Jesenská's letter to her back to Kafka, full of angry underlinings and notations, which he in turn sent on to Jesenská with his own commentary. At Kafka's suggestion, Jesenská also began a correspondence with Max Brod that continued as a subtext to the primary text of the correspondence with

Kafka—she asked Brod to keep to himself her questions about Kafka's true state of mind and of body, which she felt he represented deceptively in his letters to her.

This traffic of letters seems in this retrospect to have been implicated in the drive within the correspondence to subvert the hierarchy that privileges unmediated experience in the world over the allegedly mediate function of writing, the authentic over the copy, the original over the translation. While Kafka's letters were gravely engaged in a confrontation with the problems of mediation, communication, and the meeting of souls, they also work toward hermetically sealing the world of the letter texts from the pollution of outside air, even as they exist only to be opened, to be read. Correspondence, of course, like translation, like mediation, is not supposed to close itself off but rather to make connections of various kinds. *Korrespondenz*, from the Latin *correspondentia*, has connection as its first connotation, as in social connection, the traffic of letters, or reportage, such as that in letters or that reported to a public by a journalistic correspondent. The correspondence that is an exchange of letters aspires to one of its homonyms as an ideal: "correspondence" is the perfect agreement of two voices, responding in unison with another. And then there is the moment of correspondence connecting a word or image, a historical moment or a spatial coordinate, with (an)other, a co-incident. The task of translation, to borrow from Walter Benjamin's famous essay (roughly contemporary to Kafka's exchange with Jesenská), is to resist the trap of this sort of correspondence, for the aura of the work does not rest in its apparent referents but in the moment that is free from such correspondences, when it is closest to a perhaps unattainable true language. And yet this linguistic purity can be pointed to first with the true translation, transparent, a specular arcade or passage instead of an opaque linguistic wall.[28]

By delivering himself as object of translation, by surrendering to his own absorption into the Czech and feminine body of Jesenská's text, the Kafka who was "made of literature" broke free from the tenuous mooring that was left even to him: that of German literary territory. Benjamin sheds light on this territorial displacement, too, when he writes,

> Unlike a work of literature, translation does not find itself in the center of the language forest but on the outside facing the wooded ridge; it calls into it without entering, aiming at that single spot where the echo is able to give, in its own language, the reverberation of the work in the alien one.[29]

Hence this "reverberation" is an echo of what Benjamin names "pure language," ahistorical or aterritorial precisely because of the irretractable historicity and territoriality of the literary text. The translation points the way to a momentary and inconsumable promise of antiterritorial purity: "The text rises into a higher and purer linguistic air."[30] It is not that the original is technically untranslatable into another language but rather that even on its native ground it immediately begins to grow distant from itself and irrecoverable. Thus, through an orthodox concentration on the laws of linguistic territoriality one finds oneself pushed from the centered discourse of author-language-territory to the extremity, where the text is not even identical to itself but where an echo of the voice of the text, the gesture toward the moment of "true language," can be listened for in the translation.

In the postwar period, in this correspondence with a Czech woman in Vienna (Milena) rather than a German Jew in Berlin (Felice), the boundaries between art and life, writing and happiness, and subjectivity or identity and mediation are subject to thoroughly radical critique: the original is secondary to translation, Franz defines himself through Milena, but "Milena," too, is an ungrounded and mediated figure. The name into which he is absorbed, "Milena," "so full it is hard to lift" (*vor Fülle kaum zu heben*) seems to him itself a Greek or Roman translated or moved over to Bohemia, "violated" (*vergewaltigt*) by Czech, "betrayed" (*betrogen*) by the unfaithful Czech stress on the first syllable—and this unbearable object is yet "in color and form a woman to be carried out of the world in ones' arms . . . and she presses herself into your arms willingly and full of trust, except the strong accent on the 'i' is bad, doesn't the name jump right back away from you? Or might that just be a leap of joy, which you yourself perform with your burden?"[31] This dense parenthetical reflection on "Milena" thus effects a set of contradictions that may be seen as dialectical oppositions: "so full it is hard to lift" yields to "to be carried out . . . in one's arms"; then, conversely, "she presses herself into your arms willingly" leads directly to a spring away suggested by the Czech intonation: "doesn't the name jump right back away from you?" Or else it is the bearer's joyful leap, weighed down by this heavy burden.

This tragicomic image of Milena's name is to be given serious weight, since it is to become the vehicle for the disappearance of Kafka's own signature from the letters. Its gravity should become clear in another passage from the letters that I read closely, a paragraph on a single sheet of paper of July 14, 1920, responding to a single line of a previous letter from Jesenská:

> You write: "Ano máš pravdu, mám ho ráda. Ale F., i tebe mám ráda [Yes you are right, I am fond of him. But F., I am also fond of you]—I am reading this sentence very precisely, pausing in particular at the i [also]—it is all correct. You would not be Milena if it were not correct and what would I be if you weren't, and it is also better that you write it from Vienna than say it in Prague. All this I perfectly understand, maybe better than you and yet out of some weakness I cannot get over the sentence, it reads endlessly, and finally I am transcribing it here for you to see as well and for us to read together, temple to temple.[32]

In a single line of Jesenská's, Kafka finds a diagram for the circular relations of territorial translation, and he offers it as a primer. The condition of their correspondence is not only their emotional attachment to one another, as I have mentioned, but also their physical detachment: this tension between Vienna and Prague, between Milena's physical presence with Ernst Pollak and the distance from Kafka and Prague that calls for letters. Milena's dual affirmation ("Yes, I love him,"—as Philip Boehm's translation goes—"but F., I also love you")[33] guarantees both conditions. Kafka here, as throughout the letters, does not translate Jesenská's Czech but transcribes it directly, inserted within his German text; he then takes her through a reading of it to create reciprocal conditions of writing and reading (as he tells her at the end of the passage—so they can read together, temple to temple). Reading this simple, fairly musical sentence requires the ruthless precision he has offered glimpses of before: instead of speaking of contents and referents, the active function of reading reverberates around the sound of the words, the rhythm of clauses, the shape and relation of letters. To return to the terms of Benjamin's discussion of translation, rather than gleaning meanings (*Bedeutungen*) that can be transmitted (*vermittelt*) by German correspondents to the Czech words, the sense (*Sinn*) of the sentence comes to Kafka by standing in its middle—pausing at the "i" of the phoneme "i-tebe," pronounced in Czech as a single word.

The perfect symmetry of the sentence is first exposed by Kafka's reiteration of it, even as its rightness proceeds from its attachment to "Milena," paralleling "i-tebe," "you-too," performing (as Kafka wrote before) simultaneous yielding and resistance, or a leap with a burden. We see that this double movement of yielding and resistance is severalfold: it is in the "you, too" of "i-tebe," it is in the name "Milena," and it is in the melodic sentence as a whole, teetering from Pollak to Kafka, weighted on each end by the repeated "mám ráda–mám ráda." The sentence is Milena's because it is *Milena*, as Kafka writes: "Es ist alles richtig. Du wärst nicht *Milena* wenn es nicht richtig wäre," reiterating that the double movement is contained in the name that covers the passage. Thus, the parallel musical counterpoint of Milena's name and her sentence allows "F." to read one as the other, so that when he comes to a standstill at the "i" he finds himself again in the midst of "Milena," and as he reveals this correspondence we find the tall thin figure "l" "remaining standing" at her center ("beim i bleibe ich stehn").

And what would he be if she were not, he asks? Kafka lays a trap here, too—indeed, throughout the correspondence—for the reader is tempted to see in this repeated gesture the neat assimilation of the authorial subject into Milena. Mark Anderson, who has done the most to flesh out this question of absorption in the letters to Milena, productively brings his essay on Kafka's unsigned letters in the correspondence back to his own exemplary readings of "Josephine, the Mouse Singer" and "The Hunger Artist," suggesting that the erasure of the authorial name was more at stake than its "merging" into the name or body of Milena.[34] Indeed, the double movement I have been describing asserts the impossibility of such a closure. For Kafka does not "remain standing" at rest in this passage, but (as Boehm's translation would have it) pauses for a moment in the midst of "Milena," while the tension effected by his reading puts it into motion again. As in Kafka's reading of the name "Milena," motile contradictory alternations are effected by inversions pertaining to existence and identity and lack and difference, described as following from one another:

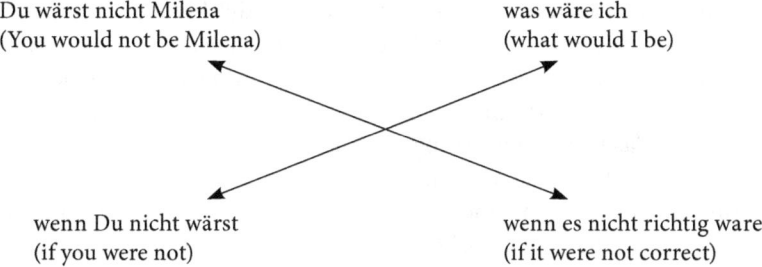

The last term, "wenn Du nicht wärst," begins the cycle again (with "Du wärst nicht Milena").[35] Thus, it is through the power of Kafka's reading, appearing as "some weakness" in the above passage, that the machine is put back into motion: "I cannot get over the sentence, it reads endlessly," and so, as his own sentence is beginning to seem endless, he offers it back to Milena, "mám ho ráda . . . i tebe mám ráda . . . mám ho ráda . . . i tebe mám ráda" an endless circle of translation and correspondence that points to a utopian moment of identity and union only as it utters its necessary impossibility. *Volvitur in rota*—turned on the wheel, torture on the wheel (in German, *Foltern auf dem Rad*).[36]

Kafka does offer Jesenská an image of a torture machine similar to the wheel a couple of months later (see figure 6). But September 1920 was worlds apart from July 14, 1920, according to Kafka's own periodization of the correspondence: "The person writing to you now [October 27, 1920] is the person you know from Merano. After that we were one, there was no more talk of knowing one another, and then once again we were split" (Dann waren wir eines, da war vom Sichkennen keine Rede mehr und dann sind wir wieder gespalten worden).[37] The brief period of correspondence (in the sense of overlaid voices) in the correspondence, or the moment of unison of the echo of the text and of the translation, falls between the consummation of the affair in Vienna and the failed connection in Gmünd. But by this I would not want to suggest that the above rhetorical figures of union ("waren wir eines") and disunion ("sind wir wieder gespalten worden") in the letters reflected respective successful consummation and impotence in the hotel rooms—it is clearly the reverse that is the case, with this letter constructing sexual performance as a metaphor for the dynamics of the correspondence. In the latter period of division, or *Spaltung*, Kafka drew the image in figure 6 and sent it to Jesenská.

The "delinquent's" hands and feet are fastened to poles running through four posts; the poles are "slowly pushed outward until the man is torn apart in the middle," according to Kafka's explication of the drawing. But two figures are in the illustration: the "delinquent" and the "inventor" of the machine, leaning against a column on the right, arms and legs crossed.[38] The inventor is inflected as masculine in the written description, but the figure in the drawing is of ambiguous gender, with a wide rectangle ending at the pelvis that could be either a long, wide shirt or a short skirt or dress, with dandyishly delicate crossed legs and hooflike pointed toes and with the doubled V shape of the unnaturally high crossed arms suggesting a woman's bust. This feminine posture is associated with putting on airs, in the very specific sense of the copycat claiming the originality of his creation: "as if the whole thing were his original invention, whereas all he really did was watch the butcher in front of his shop, drawing out a disemboweled pig."[39] Thus, the torture machine is not an expression of creative originality but a copy claiming the status of an original—what is more, it is not the translation of a great work but rather of the commonest brutality. The ambiguity of the inventor figure suggests a fluidity of roles and identities in the drawing: she or he is clearly a spectator, not in immediate control of the spectacle (the person or mechanism driving the poles is invisible, just as the empowered subjects in *The Trial* and *The Castle* are unseen and somehow beside the point). Inasmuch as the inventor is revealed to be the translator, the figure must remain open for Jesenská; and yet we know that it is Kafka who has "invented" this torture, who has conjured up both figures, and that both must also be open to stand in for him. This busyness (the illustration is sent as evidence of how he has been keeping himself busy, his "occupation," "Damit Du etwas von meinen 'Beschäftigungen' siehst") is a dark reflection on the possibility of writing that comes after the hope offered earlier by the translation relationship has passed. Responding to Jesenská's translation of a torture scene from Upton Sinclair's *Jimmie Higgins*, Kafka comments on their shared tastes: "Yes, torture is extremely important to me—I occupy myself solely [ich beschäftige mich] with torturing and being tortured." Both subject and object positions, torturing and being tortured, are pathetic (*kläglich*), illusory, opposed to real action, and identified with this occupation of writing. Kafka is occupied by torture for the reasons other torturers are: "um aus dem verdammten Mund das verdammte Wort zu erfahren" (to get the damned word out of the damned mouth).[40]

The dark picture of their narrowing common territory emerging here ("den schmalen, uns gemeinsamen . . . Boden") is symptomatic of the September letters, indeed of the letters through the autumn of 1920 until the interruption of the correspondence in November.[41] Just as Jesenská wrote of their future life together, of the promise of being together sooner than Kafka expected, the tangibility of their relationship seemed to evaporate in the correspondence. Losing her will mean losing even every illusion of territoriality, as Kafka writes—he will be Robinson Crusoe, even more so than Robinson himself, who at least had an island, whereas Kafka had surrendered even his name (September 5); his relative independence of Jesenská is established by the "boundlessness" of his dependency on her ("eben weil die Abhängigkeit so über alle Grenzen geht"); he is resigned to the "insurmountably high waves" of the "sea" between Prague and Vienna; he is an animal she had drawn out into the open where it did not belong; he was groundless. By November she had come to describe this darkness as an illness—all such illnesses, he replied, are "matters of faith" ("Glaubenstatsachen"), "anchorages" of needy humanity in "some maternal ground or other" ("Verankerungen des in Not befindlichen Menschen in irgenwelchem mütterlichen Boden").[42] Thus, the narrow, shared ground of mediation is lost in the letters to this illness, a grounding he compares to what used to be religious communities, while such community was possible. The suffering subject is described here with an image of concentric circles, but they are no longer communal or shared territories. Jesenská sees but does not want to accept that his circle is humanly uninhabitable.

It is thus with no small degree of violence ("even if the tongue that wants to speak must be bitten through") that the correspondence must be cut off: letters are torn up or burned, sent back unopened, or lie about in their envelopes. The "decisive thing," Kafka concludes, has been "my increasing (letter by letter) inability to go beyond the letters" and "the *irresistibly strong voice, literally your voice* calling on me to be silent," followed by words stricken beyond recognition.[43] In the final diagnosis, the letters are only symptoms of an incurable illness opposed to life but inseparable from Kafka's circle of living—they leave no space for rest or peace but "are pure anguish, *they are caused by incurable anguish and they cause incurable anguish.*"[44] Moreover, Kafka says of this illness, the condition is worsening—and the descent of the letters from September through November would seem to confirm this—and how could it survive winter? Indeed, this November letter is the last, or nearly the last, for at the end of March two years later there is another letter to Jesenská, this time using the formal *Sie* as he had early in Merano. He does not feel the need to apologize for his silence, since

> after all, you know how much I hate letters. All my misfortune in life... derives, one might say, from letters or from the possibility of writing letters. People have hardly ever deceived me, but letters always have, and as a matter of fact not those of other people, but my own.... The easy possibility of writing letters—from a purely theoretical point of view—must have brought wrack and ruin to the souls of the world. Writing letters is actually an intercourse with ghosts and by no means just with the ghost of the addressee but also with one's own ghost, which secretly evolves inside the letter one is writing or even in a whole series of letters, where one letter corroborates another and can refer to it as witness. How did people ever get the idea they could communicate with one another by letter![45]

And so, finally, the writing that is Franz's affair with Milena and is "Milena," his escape from Prague into the hands of the Praguer Milena in Vienna, circles again around to Prague, the city of ghosts. Kafka's letter circles in on itself and surrenders even the intention to communicate, to mediate, to move. This circularity has a history, even as it can be found embodied in the figures of friendship and walking in the very first surviving Kafka correspondence, that with Oskar Pollak.[46] Similarly, while the tension between writing and living was melodramatized to be collapsed in the letters to Felice Bauer, the correspondence with Milena Jesenská works through this issue of correspondence with even more pained intensity; in the former he articulated the correspondence of writing and his life, living and prayer—but in the latter the prayer of writing was clearly now the "pure anguish" of an incurable disease, which can only end in death.

But this illusion of closure, or the representation of the correspondence as an evolution from promise to despair and to death, is a misleading guide for the reader of the correspondence.[47] For Kafka's letters began with sickness from the spa at Merano and with the "old grave" of his own literary text; the whole postal exchange, rather than the postscript, has been an "intercourse with ghosts." The last trace we possess of Kafka's written correspondence with Jesenská, almost certainly the last item he sent to her, is not a letter, but a postcard, the stamp canceled at Berlin-Steglitz on Christmas 1923.[48] It reports that Kafka had changed his address.

Notes

A version of this chapter was previously published as Scott Spector, "Middle Ground: Translation, Mediation, Correspondence," in *Prague Territories: National Conflict and Cultural Innovation in Franz Kafka's Fin de Siècle* (Berkeley: University of California Press, 2000), 195–233. The University of California Press has graciously permitted the reprint of portions of this chapter.

1. In Jacques Derrida's *La carte postale*, the German term *Übertragung* frequently serves to remind the reader of certain linked functions: the material conditions of transmission by post (transport, carrying) and the reciprocal relations between precursors and their legacies, texts and their translations. See Jacques Derrida, *The Post Card: From Socrates to Freud and Beyond*, trans. Alan Bass (Chicago: University of Chicago Press, 1987).

2. In an essay on this particular exchange of letters, Mark Anderson traces the valences of the Latin terms *littera* (in the singular, a letter of the alphabet) and *litterae* (plural, meaning either epistle or literature in general) and suggests that this common source for the often-opposed terms "literal" and "literary" (or figurative) is not an accidental ambiguity: "For precisely the ambivalence of the 'littera,' its hovering status between the material signs of the alphabet and their figurative use, between 'litteralis' and 'litterarius,' is what makes literature possible." Mark M. Anderson, "Unsigned Letters to Milena Jesenská," in *Reading Kafka: Prague, Politics, and the Fin de Siècle*, ed. Mark Anderson (New York: Schocken, 1989), 243.

3. Other essays on the Kafka-Jesenská correspondence include Werner Vordtriede, "Letters to Milena: The Writer as Advocate of Himself," in *Franz Kafka Today*, ed. Angel Flores and Homer D. Swander (Madison: University of Wisconsin Press, 1958), 239–248; Hartmut Böhme, "Mutter Milena: On Kafka's Narcissism," in *The Kafka Debate*, ed. Angel Flores (New York: Gordian, 1977), 80–99; and Kurt Krolop, "Franz Kafkas *Briefe an Milena*," in *Allemands, Juifs et Tchèques à Prague de 1890 à 1924*, ed. Maurice Godé, Jacques Le Rider, and Françoise Meyer (Montpellier, France: Université Paul-Valéry-Montpellier III, 1996), 253–272. See also Elizabeth Boa, *Kafka: Gender, Class, and Race in the Letters and Fictions* (Oxford, UK: Clarendon, 1996).

4. Franz Kafka, *Briefe an Milena: Erweiterte Neuausgabe*, ed. Jürgen Born and Michael Müller (Frankfurt am Main, Germany: S. Fischer, 1983), 8–9. All English translations adapted from Franz Kafka, *Letters to Milena*, trans. Philip Boehm (New York: Schocken, 1990).

5. Jaroslav Dresler's comments on these errors are cited in Ota Filip, "Wer war Milena?" *Die Zeit*, January 14, 1983, p. 21.

6. Kafka, *Letters to Milena*, 5.

7. See, especially, Lori Chamberlain, "Gender and the Metaphorics of Translation," *Signs* 13 (1988): 454–472. See also Barbara Godard, "Theorizing Feminist Discourse/Translation," in *Translation, History and Culture*, ed. Susan Basnett and André Lefevere (London: Frances Pinter, 1990), 87–96.

8. Chamberlain, "Gender and the Metaphorics," 454.

9. The commonplace of contemporary translation theory to stress the diacritical function of translation or to foreground the impossibility of linguistic equivalence has sometimes had the strange effect of reifying the category of identity through the back door, more powerfully than more naive approaches to translation could ever do. George Steiner's classic study of translation demonstrates this in a revealing way when he concludes that semantic contrast or difference "defines conversely": "To experience difference, to feel the characteristic resistance and 'materiality' of that which differs, is to reexperience identity. One's own space is mapped by what lies outside." George Steiner, *After Babel: Aspects of Language and Translation* (London: Oxford University Press, 1975), 362. While Steiner's comments are inspired by his reading of Derrida's *Margins of Philosophy*, he seems to have come out at a position completely at odds with it. See Joseph F. Graham, ed., *Difference in Translation* (Ithaca, NY: Cornell University Press, 1985).

10. Kafka, *Briefe an Milena*, 18.

11. Max Brod, *Ein tschechisches Dienstmädchen: Kleiner Roman* (Berlin: A. Juncker, 1909). Cf. Pavel Eisner, *Milenky: Německý Básnik a česká žena* (Prague: Helios, 1930).

12. The foundations of an image of translation, in which a native language is transposed to foreign literary ground, are somewhat disturbed by the situation created here, with Kafka's German letters emanating from Italian Merano and then from Czechoslovak Prague, while Jesenská and her Viennese letters are located "in" Czech language. Jesenská's letters have not been preserved, except for the passages smuggled into Kafka's own letters to Jesenská and sent back to her. This one-way passage is mirrored in Jesenská's inability to visit Kafka in Prague: because of the status of her visa, she was unable to cross the border (or rather, would not have been able to return to Vienna if she did so). Thus, their second—and disastrous—meeting since beginning the correspondence relationship was to be on the very boundary of Austria and Czechoslovakia, in the border town of Gmünd.

13. The well-known assertion appears in a letter from Kafka to Felice. See Franz Kafka, *Letters to Felice*, ed. Erich Heller and Jürgen Born, trans. James Stern and Elisabeth Duckworth (New York: Schocken, 1973), 304.

14. Kafka, *Briefe an Milena*, 45.
15. Ibid., 34.
16. Ibid., 77.
17. As Mark Anderson has noted, "The 'condition of possibility' structuring the letters is Kafka's isolation." Anderson, "Unsigned Letters," 244. The same point holds for his earlier correspondence with Felice Bauer, as several commentators have noted.
18. Kafka, *Briefe an Milena*, 80.
19. Ibid.
20. Ibid., 81.
21. In the correspondence with Felice some seven years earlier, a similar set of circumstances, in this case contradictory letters about whether he would be able to come to Berlin on Easter Sunday 1913, led to a botched meeting at the Askanischer Hof Hotel. The day before the rendezvous he mailed a letter reading only, "Still undecided. Franz," and arriving at the Askanischer Hof the next day, he sent a note reading, "But what has happened, Felice? . . . I am sitting at the Askanischer Hof—waiting." Kafka, *Letters to Felice*, 225–228.
22. Kafka, *Briefe an Milena*, 81.
23. Ibid., 151. Jesenská's report on the post office visit is in her letter to Max Brod of August 1920, first published by Brod in his Kafka biography and since in a number of volumes, including Kafka, *Briefe an Milena*, 363–367.
24. See Scott Spector, "'Any Reality, However Small': Prague Zionisms between the Nations," in *Kafka, Zionism, and Beyond*, ed. Mark H. Gelber (Tübingen, Germany: Max Niemeyer, 2004), 19–22.
25. Kafka, *Briefe an Milena*, 28.
26. Ibid., 28.
27. Ibid., 60. See Spector, "From Big Daddy to Small Literature: On Taking Kafka at His Word," in *Evolving Jewish Identities in German Culture: Borders and Crossings*, ed. Linda E. Feldman and Diana Orendi (Westport, CT: Praeger, 2000), 79–93.
28. See Walter Benjamin, "Die Aufgabe des Übersetzers," in *Gesammelte Schriften*, vol. 4, bk. 1, by Walter Benjamin (Frankfurt am Main, Germany: Suhrkamp, 1980), 9–21. Translations are from Walter Benjamin, "The Task of the Translator," in *Illuminations: Essays and Reflections*, by Walter Benjamin, ed. Hannah Arendt, trans. Harry Zohn (New York: Schocken, 1968), 69–82.
29. Benjamin, "Task of the Translator," 76; Benjamin, "Die Aufgabe des Übersetzers," 16.
30. Benjamin, "Task of the Translator," 75.
31. Kafka, *Briefe an Milena*, 59.
32. Ibid., 112.
33. Kafka, *Letters to Milena*, 87.
34. Anderson, "Unsigned Letters."
35. This constellation seems provocatively comparable to Benjamin's "dialectical image," although it is posited in spatial terms (self and other, here and there) rather than temporal or historical terms (the "been" and the "now"). The oppositions do not operate in a narrative sequence that moves dialogically forward but offer a moment in which difference and identity "blitzhaft zu einer Konstellation zusammentritt": what Benjamin has called dialectics at a standstill. See Walter Benjamin, *Gesammelte Schriften*, vol. 5, bk. 1 (Frankfurt am Main, Germany: Suhrkamp, 1982), 566–567; see also Benjamin, *Gesammelte Schriften*, vol. 5, bk. 2, 1034–1035.

36. This passage evokes a verse from section 4 of the *Carmina Burana*:

> sum presentialiter   I am with you
> absens in remota,   even when far away.
> quisquis amat taliter, Whosoever loves this much
> volvitur in rota.   knows the torture of the wheel.

37. Kafka, *Briefe an Milena*, 285.
38. Ibid., 271.
39. Ibid., 272.
40. Ibid., 290.
41. Ibid., 277.
42. Ibid., 252–253, 276, 292.
43. Ibid., 299–301 (emphasis in original).
44. Ibid., 300–301 (emphasis in original).
45. Ibid., 301–302.
46. See Spector, *Prague Territories: National Conflict and Cultural Innovation in Franz Kafka's Fin de Siècle* (Berkeley: University of California Press, 2000), 1–25.
47. The Fischer edition of the correspondence seems to fall into this trap by juxtaposing the sequenced letters to certain appendices: "Milenas Nachruf auf Franz Kafka," which appeared in the *Národní listy* in 1924, and a timetable beginning with Jesenská's 1919 request for permission to translate Kafka's writings and ending with Kafka's burial in 1924. See Kafka, *Briefe an Milena*, 379–381, 402–407.
48. Ibid., 321–322.

Index

Page numbers in italics indicate material in figures.

Abraham, Karl, 90–91
Adler, Friedrich, 125, 146n2
Adorno, Theodor W., 10, 34–35n5, 41–42, 48, 103, 145
aesthetic autonomy and modernism, 28, 37n34
aestheticism, 28, 37n37, 87, 125–126, 137–139
Agamben, Giorgio, 40
agency-structure dichotomy, 6
Ahad Ha'am, 16n12, 26, 130
allegory and interpretation, 144–146
Alt, Peter-André, 136n40
Altneuland (Herzl), 27
analogon, photograph as, 70, *83*
Anderson, Mark, 160, 164n2, 166n17
Andreas-Salomé, Lou, 92
Anne, Saint, 93
antiliberalism, 27, 48
antisemitism: Arendt and, 143; Brod and, 123, 130–131, 142; categories of antisemites, 3; Celan and, 114; contemporary, 27–28; and critical and historical literature, x, 7–9; de Man and, 31, 33; Freud and, 87–88, 91; and German Jewishness, 10; and the Halle, 123; and Jewish identity, 11, 12; and Jewish integration, x; and Jewish modernism, xiv, 9, 19–20, 22–25, 27, 29, 109; Kafka and, 142, 145, 153; Masaryk and, 91; and populist politics, 102, 143; Schmitt and, 49–50; and self-identity, 10–12; and sexism, xii; Stein and, 64–65, 71–73, 78–79n14; stereotypes regarding laws and science, 91; Wagner and, 19–22, 34n3, 34–35n5
Antschel, Paul (Paul Celan), 113–114
aporia, 29–31, 38n45
Arendt, Hannah, xi–xii, xvii, 14, 41, 49–51, 70, 143
Asad, Talal, 52n6
Aschheim, Steven E., 7, 14, 15–16n10, 17n29

assimilation, German-Jewish: and Arendt on Rahel Varnhagen, xi–xii, 11, 49; Beller and, 36n19; Birnbaum and, 26; Buber and, 13; as delusion, 46; emancipation-assimilation pact, 5–6, 10, 50; Goldstein and, 18n41; and identity, 4–5, 9–10, 36n19; ideology of, 6; and Jewish Austrians, 17n30; Kafka and, 145, 160; Löwith and, 44; as relative, not zero-sum, 5, 12, 14, 15n5; and "A Report to an Academy," 144; Scholem and, 3–4; as term of analysis, x, 4–6; and *Vom Judentum*, 130; Zionist critiques of, 28. *See also* postassimilationism; Stein, Edith
Ausländer, Rose, 112
Austria. *See* central Europe

Bahr, Hermann, 25, 28, 105, 137, 139, 146n1
Bakan, David, 88
Barash, Jeffrey Andrew, 44, 53n12
Bar-Kochba Association, 13, 129
Barthes, Roland, 39n58, 70
Batnitzky, Leora, 52n6
Bauer, Felice, Kafka's letters to, 124, 157, 166n21; Kafka as "made of literature," 124, 126, 138, 154; Kafka's use of term "Zionism," 145; as opposed to Milena Jesenská, 159; writing versus life or happiness, 156, 164
Baum, Oskar, 123
Beaujour, Michel, 61
Beim Bau der Chinesischen Mauer (Kafka), 109
Beller, Steven, 24–25, 32, 36n19, 109
Benjamin, Walter, xv, 30, 38n46, 50, 145, 158, 160, 166n35
Ben-Shammai, Haggai, 121–122, 127–128
Bergman, Hugo, 114, 123, 130
Bergman, Ingrid, 94, 96
Berlin antisemitism debate, ix
Berlin literary scene, 105, 126

169

Bernheimer, Charles, 144
Betrachtung (Kafka), 138
Bettauer, Hugo, 21–24, 28, 31, 35n11
Between Past and Future (Arendt), 143
Bhabha, Homi, 109
Biale, David, 32
Binder, Hartmut, 144
Biran, Sigmund, 112
Birnbaum, Nathan, xv, 26–27, 36n27
bisexual/intermediate figures, 69–70
Bloch, Ernst, 48
blood, metaphors of, 13, 64, 73
Blum, Klara, 113
Blumberg, David, 127
Blumenberg, Hans, 41–42, 46–51, 54n25, 54n28, 54n36, 103
Blumenfeld, Kurt, xi
Boehm, Philip, 160
Brenner, Michael, 8
Breslauer, Hans Karl, 21–22
Brient, Elizabeth, 49, 54n27
Brod, Max, xv, 10; birth and early life of, 122–123; and early commitment to Zionism, 122, 129; *Ein tschechisches Dienstmadchen*, 154; flight to Palestine by, 121–122; as "Jewish writer of German tongue," 110, 131; and Kafka, 127, 138, 142, 157; and Milena Jesenská, 157–158; as "odd duck" in Tel Aviv, 128; and posthumous dispute over Kafka manuscripts, 121–122, 127–129; as preferring Berlin to Vienna, 126; and preservation of Kafka manuscripts, 131–134; *Streitbares Leben*, 131; as student of culture, 123–125; and "supranationalism," 131
Brulov, Dr., 96–97
Buber, Martin: as eastern European Jew, 111; and Jewish dualism, 17n37; on Jewishness as matter of choice, 13; and "Jewish Renaissance," 26; on "personal Jewish Question," 11; Prague lectures, 13, 129–130; and reconceptualization of spirituality, xv; stories in *Der Jude*, 144
Bukovina, 104, 112; Jewish writers from, xv, 104, 112–113
Burckhardt, Jacob, 40, 43
Butler, Judith, 71, 81n42, 81–82n48, 82n53, 127, 135n21

"The Calling of Man and Woman According to the Orders of Nature and Grace" (Stein), 69
Carmina Burana, 167n36
The Castle (Kafka), 162
Celan, Paul (Paul Antschel), 113–114
census form, Habsburg Empire, 129
central Europe: and modernism, 105–107; myth of, 106–109; Prague and central Europe effect, 114–115
Chamberlain, Lori, 153
Charcot, Jean-Martin, 89
Chekhov, Mikhail, 96
chol and *kadosh* (profane and holy), xiv
Christianity: Catholicism and Schmitt, 50; Christendom as led by Jews, 19–20; and meaning of "secular," xiv. *See also* Stein, Edith
Christian Social Party (Austria), 23–24
Cioffi, Frank, 98n3
The City without Jews (*Die Stadt ohne Juden*; Bettauer), 21, 22–24
Cohen, Hermann, 44–45, 53n14
Corngold, Stanley, 142, 149n35, 149n37
counterfactual history, 32, 39n55
counterhistories of Jewish modernism, 31–34
Crusoe, Robinson, 163
cultural hybridity, 109
Czechoslovakia, 91, 110; Prague, 110, 121–125, 140–141; Prague Circle, 123, 138; Prague German (*Prager Deutsch*), 140–141; sound of Czech language, 156–157; translations to and from Czech language, 152–154, 158–161
Czernowitz, 103–105, 107, 112–114

Das Schloß (Kafka), 139, 162
Death to the Dead! (Brod), 125
decisionism, 44, 53n12
degeneration, 90, 145
Deleuze, Gilles, 141
de Man, Paul, 29–31, 33, 39n58, 142–143
Dembitzer, Salamon, 112
Der Fall Bettauer (Hall), 23
Der Golem (film), 37n31
Der Jude (Buber), 13, 144
"Der jüdische Dichter deutscher Zunge" (Brod), 110
Der Process (Kafka), 139

Derrida, Jacques, 30, 164n1
Der Verschollene (Kafka), 139
Der Weltkampf (Rosenberg), 23–24
"destructive dialectic," 14
deterritorialization, xii, 110, 141–142
"Deutsch-jüdischer Parnaß" (Goldstein), 18n41
dialectical image, 30, 38n46, 166n35
dialectics: versus aporia, 30, 143; versus dialectical image, 38n46; of Enlightenment, 42; of German-Jewish assimilation, xii, 5, 12–14, 15n5; as historical concept, 30; of Jewish presence and absence, 20, 27–28, 42; in Kafka's letters to Jesenská, 159; of subjectivity and history, 73–74
"The Dialectics of Assimilation" (Funkenstein), 5
Die Fackel (Kraus), 104
"Die jüdische Moderne" (Birnbaum), 26
Die Stadt ohne Juden (*The City without Jews*; Bettauer), 21, 22–24
Dilthey, Wilhelm, 68, 80n34
displacement, 87; Benjamin on, 158; central European, 103, 106–107, 110, 114; of Joseph Roth, 104–106; mystique of, 113; of theology with science, 42
"dissimilation," 4, 15n5
dualism in each Jewish life, 11
Dufresne, Henry, 21
Dvořák, Max, 25

Echt Carmel, 73
Edwardes, Anthony/Ballantyne, 95–97
Einstein, Albert, 90
Ein tschechisches Dienstmadchen (Brod), 154
emancipation, Jewish: emancipation-assimilation pact, 5–6, 10, 50; and "final solution," 42; in Habsburg and German Empires, ix; and imaginary "subculture," 6; and Jewish question, 41; and modernism, 20, 28; and passing, 72; and reflections on minority identity, ix; and secularization, x, 20, 28, 50
"emotional confusion" of German Jews, 3–4
empathy (*Einfühlen*): as associated with the feminine, Jewishness, 69, 96; Dilthey and, 68, 80n34; excess of, among historians, 4; portraits based on, 62, 71–74; relation of, to sympathy, 65, 67; Stein's dissertation on, 61–63, 76
Endlösung (final solution), 42
Enlightenment, xii, xiii, xv, 28, 40, 42, 43, 47–48, 50, 92, 94, 109
An Ermine in Czernopol (Rezzori), 104
erotics of translation, 152–156
Er und Sie (Bettauer), 24, 36n16
eschatology, xiv, 40–44, 47–48, 52n5, 53n12
The Eternal Jew (Hippler), 22, 72
Ethical Seminar (University of Czernowitz), 113
expressionism, 123, 126

femininity as masquerade, 71
feminism, 12, 59–61, 65, 76, 78n8, 80n39
Ferenczi, Sándor, 93
"fidelity" in translation, 153
"final solution" (*Endlösung*), 23, 42
fin-de-siècle thesis, 101, 115n1, 116n13, 138
Fin-de-Siècle Vienna (Schorske), 116n13
"Fin de Siècle Vienna and Its Jewish Cultural Influences" (Gombrich), 25
Flaubert, Gustave, 125, 138
formalism, 28–30, 38n38
Foucault, Michel, 39n58
Franzos, Karl Emil, xiii, 111–112
French Revolution, ideas of, 92
Freud, Sigmund, xv, 101, 140; anxieties of, about acceptance, 87; on Jung, 90–91; on love, 94; self-identifying as scientist, 86. *See also* psychoanalytic science
Fuchs, Rudolf, 115
Funkenstein, Amos, 5, 38n53

Galicia, xv, 104, 111–112, 114
Gay, Peter, 87–88
gender: and Constance Petersen in *Spellbound*, 94–96; and Edith Stein, 65, 69–73, 77–78n5, 80n38, 81n46, 82n53; in Kafka-Milena correspondence, 157; and "metaphorics of translation," 153; performance of, 71
Genealogy of Morals (Nietzsche), 33
German-Jewish identity: crisis of, 4, 7; Goldstein on, 18n41; historical understandings of, 6; nationalism as excluding Jews, 129; Wassermann on, 7

German language in Prague, 140–141
Geschlecht und Charakter (Weininger), 80n38
Gilman, Sander, 87, 145
Glatzer, Nahum, 112
Gleichnis (parable), 144–145
Gogarten, Friedrich, 53n12
Goldstein, Moritz, 18n41
Goll, Claire, 114
Gombrich, Ernst, 25
Gong, Alfred, 113
Gordon, Peter Eli, 51
Grillparzer, Franz, 104–105
Gross, Raphael, 49–50
Guattari, Félix, 141
Gumbrecht, Hans-Ulrich, 37n35

Habermas, Jürgen, 48, 89
Habsburg Empire: as central Europe, 105; dissolution of, 131; Germanization efforts in, 112; language in, 103, 140; and loyalty of Jews, 20, 108; and modernism, 107, 137, 140; national conflict in, 143. See also central Europe
Habsburg modernism, 101–106, 109, 113, 137. See also Bukovina, Jewish writers from
Hadwiger, Viktor, 146n2
Halle (Lese und Redehalle der Deutschen Studenten in Prag), 123, 138
Hamann, Brigitte, 34n2
Heath, Stephen, 81n42
Hebrew-language writings, 115
Hegel, G. W. F., 40, 48, 71
Heidegger, Martin, 44, 47, 53n12
Heine, Heinrich, 103
"herostratic deed," 133
Herzl, Theodor, 26–27, 37n32, 130
hidden life, 71; *The Hidden Life* (Stein), 73; "The Hidden Life and the Epiphany" (Stein), 75–76
Hilsner, Leopold, 91
Him and Her (Bettauer), 24, 36n16
Hippler, Fritz, 22, 72
historicism, 44; German, 45; and humanism, 91; versus modernism, 30; versus philosophy of history, 43
history: allegory and interpretation in, 144–146; ancient, 86; central European, 114, 139; counterfactual, 32; cultural, ix, 33, 60, 87, 101, 107, 109; feminist, 60; German-Jewish, ix–x, xii, 3, 8, 14, 60, 63, 69; and Habsburg Empire, 105, 106; individual's place in, 143; versus literature, 141; and modernity, 29–30, 42, 142; orthodox view of, 3; philosophy of, 42–44; and secularization process, 40–42, 47–48; versus spirit, 76
Hitchcock, Alfred, 94, 95, 97
Hobbes, Thomas, 45
Hoffe, Ilse Esther (Ester), 121, 127–128, 134n2, 134n6
Hofmannsthal, Hugo von, 9, 101–102
Holocaust, x, 9, 10, 40, 59, 60, 76, 77–78n5, 109, 113, 114, 139
holy and profane (*kadosh* and *chol*), xiv
homeland and patrimony, 122
homosexuality, 24, 70, 81n42
Horkheimer, Max, 42
The Human Condition (Arendt), 49
humanism, 91
"The Hunger Artist" (Kafka), 160
Husserl, Edmund, 44, 59, 62
"A Hybrid" (Kafka), 109–110
hysteria, 89–90

identity: as given, 6; identity crisis of German Jewry, 4; as performance, 71; public versus private, 13
ideology: of assimilation, 6, 8; and defining Jewishness, 15–16n10; of emancipation, 6; and false consciousness, 6; and "Jewish physics," 90; of Marx, 43; of mediation, 152; of modernity, 29, 88–89; and myth of central Europe, 106, 114; of nationalism, 129; and subjectivity, xiii, 17–18n39
Ifergan, Pini, 48, 52n5, 54n25
indifferentism, 125
Isenberg, Noah, 37n31
Israel, State of, 3, 121, 127

"Jackals and Arabs" (Kafka), 144
Janáček, Leoš, 124
Janik, Allan, 88
Janowitz, Franz and Hans, 123
Jaspers, Karl, xi–xii, xvii
Jay, Martin, 54n29, 54n36
Jesenská, Milena, xv–xvi, 85, 124, 151–164, 165n12
Jewish modern (*jüdische Moderne*), xv, 20, 26–27, 32, 34n2, 42

Jewishness: in Austria and Central Europe, 17n29, 108; consciousness of, 9; dialogue within, 17n38; as elective, 13; Habsburg, 107–109; in Kafka-Jesenská relationship, 157; as masquerade, 69–73; Stein and Jewish self-hatred, 64
"Jewish physics," Einstein's relativity as, 90
Jewish question (*Judenfrage*), x–xi, xiv, 7, 11, 28, 31, 33, 41–42, 46, 48–50
Jewish Renaissance, 10, 13, 26–27
"Jewish type," Arendt on, xii
"Jews and Germans" (Scholem), 3–4, 9
Jimmie Higgins (Sinclair), 162
John of the Cross, 59, 81n46
John Paul II, 59, 77n1
Jonas, Hans, 46, 52n4
Jones, Ernest, 81n41
Jonnson, Stefan, 107
Joseph II, 112
"Josephine, the Mouse Singer" (Kafka), 160
"Judaism in Music" (Wagner), 19–20
Judenfrage (Jewish question), x–xi, xiv, 7, 11, 28, 31, 33, 41–42, 46, 48–50
Judenzarathustra, 14
jüdische Moderne (Jewish modern), xv, 20, 26–27, 34n2, 42
Jugendstil, 105, 146n2
Jung, C. G., 90–91
Junker, Axel, 126

kadosh and *chol* (holy and profane), xiv
Kafka, Franz, xv; and aestheticism, 126, 137–138; and allegory, 144–146; Arendt on, 143; and attachment to Prague, 124–125, 140; birth and early life of, 122–124; Brod and posthumous dispute over manuscripts of, 121–122, 127–129, 131–134, 136n38; Brod's reading of, 144–145; Butler on, 127; and *die Moderne*, 137–139, 141; on fear, 157; and history, 142–144; "A Hybrid," 109–110; and instruction to burn documents, 132–134, 136n38; on literatures of small nations, 141–142; and Milena Jesenská, xv–xvi, 85, 124, 151–164, 165n12; and Prague German, 140–141; relationship of, to Judaism/Zionism, 10, 17n30, 127–130, 145; torture machine drawing by, 85, 161–162; wills and testaments of, 132–134, 136n38, 136n40; on words, 140; on writing, 17n32, 126, 138

Kantianism, 51
Kantorowicz, Ernst, 41, 51
Katz, W. H., 112
The King's Two Bodies (Kantorowicz), 51
Kisch, Egon Erwin, 123–124
Kittner, Alfred, 113
Kleinseitner Deutsch (Prague German), 141
Klemperer, Victor, 12, 14
Klimt, Gustav, 101
Kokoschka, Oskar, 101
Kollwitz, Käthe, 77–78n5
Kornfeld, Paul, 123
Körper versus *Leib*, 68
Korrespondenz, meanings of, 158
Krafft-Ebing, Richard von, 89
Kraus, Karl, 9, 17n32, 104–105, 142
Kuchelböhmisch (kitchen Bohemian), 141
Kucheldeutsch (kitchen German), 141
Kundera, Milan, 106, 115
Kunstwart debate, 12, 18n41

Laforgue, Jules, 125, 138
Langer, Jiří, 114
language and literary modernism, 140–142
Lasker-Schüler, Else, xv
Lassalle, Ferdinand, 9
La Vopa, Anthony, 6
League of Truthful Christians, 21, 23
Legend of the Baal-Shem (Buber), 13
The Legitimacy of the Modern Age (Blumenberg), 41, 46, 48
Leib versus *Körper*, 68
Leonardo da Vinci, 92–93, 145
Leonardo da Vinci and a Memory of His Childhood (Freud), 92–93
Leppin, Paul, 146n2
letters and translation theory, 151–154
Letter to His Father (Brod), 133, 144
Leviathan (Hobbes), 45
Lévinas, Emmanuel, 92
Life in a Jewish Family (Stein), 12, 62–64, 71
linguistic territoriality, 159
Liquornik, Alfred M., 113
"Literary History and Literary Modernity" (de Man), 29–30
literary self-portrait genre, 61
Lives of the Saints (Butler), 74
The Location of Culture (Bhabha), 109
logic, 93

Loos, Adolf, 101
love in *Spellbound*, 94–97
Löwith, Karl, 12, 40–44, 46–48, 50–51, 52n5, 52n10
Löwy, Michael, 54n35
Luther, Martin, 13

Machiavelli, 45
Magris, Claudio, 106–107, 115
Mahler, Gustav, 9, 101
Maimon, Salomon, 37n36
Mann, Thomas, 131
Mansfield, Nick, 17–18n39
Margul-Sperber, Alfred, 103–105
Marie-Aimée de Jésus, 73
martyrdom, 12, 59–61, 74, 77n1, 78n6, 81n46. *See also* Stein, Edith
Marx, Karl, 9, 40, 43
Marxism, 89
Mary, Saint, 93
Masaryk, Tomáš Garrigue, 91
masks and masking, xi–xii, 70–71, 81n47
Matysik, Tracie, 54n28
Mauscheln ("talking Jewy"), 142
Meaning in History (Löwith), 43, 46
Meerbaum-Eisinger, Selma, 113
Mendelssohn, Moses, 37n36
Mendes-Flohr, Paul, 17n38
"Meridian" (Celan), 114
messianism in Marx, 43
"metaphorics of translation," gendered, 153
methodological problems with subjectivity, xii, xiii–xvi, 11–14
Meyerbeer, Giacomo, 19, 34–35n5
Meyrink, Gustav, 146n2
minority: Germans in Prague as, 123; Jews as, ix, 108, 113, 131; modern conceptualization of, xii
minor literatures, 141–142
mirrored images: Arendt and Rahel Varnhagen, xi–xii, xvii; Nietzsche and Benjamin, 30; and "reiterated empathy," 68; and Stein, 73–75
Mode (fashion) and modernity, 19
modern, Jewish (*jüdische Moderne*), xv, 20, 26–27, 34n2, 42
Moderne (the modern), xiii, xv, 20, 27, 28, 31–32, 35n7, 42, 137, 139, 146n1, 147n7

modernism, ix, xiii–xv, 89, 107–109; association of, with Jews, x, 19–21, 26–29; counterhistories of Jewish, 31–34; Freud and, 87; Habsburg, 101–102, 107; Kafka and, 110, 137–150; language and literary modernism, 140–142; versus modernity, 28, 29, 139; "new culture" as, 19; Romantic, 48; Roth and, 105, 111; secularization as, xv, 42; Snow and, 88–89; and "two cultures" of educated society, 88
Modernist Form and the Myth of Jewification (Levi), 36n19
modernity: legitimacy of, 42, 50; and self-deception, 47; without Jews, 21–24, 29–31
modernization, xiv, 23, 30, 46, 137
modern Judaism, xv, 20, 26–27, 32, 34n2, 42
moral relativism, 30, 44–45
Morgenstern, Soma, 112
Moyn, Samuel, 6, 49
Mufti, Aamir, xii
"muscle-Jew," 32, 39n54
Musil, Robert, 105, 107, 111
Mut (goddess), 92–93
Mutter mit Sohn (Kollwitz), 77–78n5
My Life as German and Jew (Wassermann), 7
mysticism, 68, 91
mystique of central European displacement, 103

nationalism: Brod's and Kafka's reactions to, 129; culture as retreat from, 123, 129; era of, 140; as essentialist ideology, 13; German antisemitic, 14, 91, 123; German cultural, 67, 111, 129; and Habsburg Empire, ix, 109, 129, 143; Jewish, 4, 7, 9, 122, 129, 131
naturalism, 139
Natural Right and History (Strauss), 44
natural right theory, 44–45
Negative Dialectics (Adorno), 10
neoidealism, 113
Neugroschel, Joachim, 148n17
New Criticism, 28
"new culture," 19
Nicholl, Donald, 79n20
Nietzsche, Friedrich, 14, 29–30, 33, 89
nonessentialism, 48
nonidentity, Jewish, 10
Nornepygge Castle (Brod), 125

nostalgia, misplaced, 106
Nuremberg decrees, 41, 46

observer effect, 108
Occidental Eschatology (Taubes), 41
"On Parables" (Kafka), 144
On Revolution (Arendt), 49
On the Problem of Empathy (Stein), 64–68
Outline of Psycho-Analysis (Freud), 87

Palestine as homeland, 121
pan-Germans, 22–23
parable (*Gleichnis*), 144–145
"pariah qualities," xvii
passing, 22, 61, 65, 69, 70, 72, 80n39, 82n53
patrimony, 122
Peck, Gregory, 95
Petersen, Constance, 94–96
philosemitism: antisemitism and, x, xiv, 28, 36n19; Masaryk and, 91; modernism and, 20, 22
philosophy of history, 42–44
photographs of Stein family, 70–71, 82n52, 83
Piehowicz, Karl, 103–104
"Pietà without the Christ," 60, 77–78n5
pluralistic liberalism, 45
poetry: of Bukovina Jews, 113–114; and comment in *Spellbound*, 95; of Else Lasker-Schüler, xv; of Franz Werfel, 123–124; of Jules Laforgue, 125; of Karl Emil Franzos, 111; of Karl Piehowicz, 103–105; of Prague German-speaking Jews, 114–115, 130–131, 138; Wagner's dismissal of Jewish, 20
political authority, locus of, 45
political theology, 40, 42, 45, 48, 49, 51n1
Pollak, Ernst, 153, 160
Pollak, Oskar, 124, 164
postassimilationism, 7–11
postmodernism, 140
Prager Deutsch (Prague German), 140–141
Prague, 110, 121–125, 140–141
Prague Circle, 123, 138
Prague German (*Prager Deutsch*), 140–141
Prague lectures (Buber), 13, 129–130
progress as eschatological, 41
Protestantism, xiv
pseudoscience, 86–88, 98n3

psychoanalytic science, xv; in film, 94–97; intersubjectivity in, 94; labeled as Jewish science, 90–91; validity of, as science, 86–87, 89–90; Viennese context of, 88. *See also* Freud, Sigmund
pure and impure (*tahor* and *tamay*), xiv
"pure language," 158

Radetzky March (Roth), 104–106, 111
Rahv, Philip, 149n36
Ratmoko, David, 52n5
"reiterated empathy," 68
relative assimilation spectrum, 4–5
Renaissance, 26, 40, 64, 82n54, 92–93
Rentschler, Eric, 35n9
reoccupation of sacred positions, 47–48
"A Report to an Academy" (Kafka), 144
resacralization, 48, 50
"residual Jews," 52n5
revelation, religious, 45, 64, 66, 68, 75
Rezzori, Gregor von, 104, 110–111
Riegl, Alois, 25
Riviere, Joan, 69–70, 81n41
Robert, Marthe, 88
Roda Roda, Alexander Friedrich, 110–111
Romm, May, 95, 97
Rorty, Richard, 47
Rosenberg, Alfred, 23
Rosenkranz, Moses, 113
Rosenthal, Michael A., 45
Rosenzweig, Franz, 4, 15n5, 32, 48, 88
Roth, Joseph, 104–106, 111–112
Rothfels, Hans, 51, 55n44
Rothstock, Otto, 24
Rugg, Linda Haverty, 70, 81n45

Sacher-Masoch, Leopold von, 112
sacralization, xiv–xv, 50, 55n44, 62, 68, 70, 126
Salamon Dembitzer, 112
Salus, Hugo, 125, 146n2
scapegoat (*Sündenbock*), Jews as, 66
Scheler, Max, 79n23
Schiele, Egon, 101
Schlosser, Julius von, 25
Schmitt, Carl, 40–42, 44–45, 48–51, 52n5, 52n10, 53n12, 54n25
Schnitzler, Arthur, 101
Schoenberg, Arnold, 101

Scholem, Gershom, 16n23; Aschheim's study of, 14; Biale's study of, 32; and emancipation-assimilation pact, 5; and German-Jewish identity crisis, 4, 11; "Jews and Germans," 3–5, 7, 9, 12, 14; and *Judenzarathustra* concept, 14
Schopenhauer, Arthur, 125
Schorske, Carl, 29, 87–88, 106, 116n13
scientism and humanism, 92–94
Secession, 25, 101, 102, 137, 138
secularization, 50–51; Arendt and, 49; Blumenberg and, 46–48, 54n28, 54n36; Cohen and, 44; debates about, 49–51; different meanings of, xiv–xv, 45; as Jewish history, 40–42; and the Jewish question, 42; Kafka and, 126; legitimacy of, 46–51; Löwith and, 42–44, 48, 52n5; Lupton on, 82n54; and Nazi sacralization program, 55n44; pathologization of, 6; Schmitt and, 49; Stein and, 65–66; Strauss and, 44–45; thesis of, xiv, xv, 40, 42, 44, 45, 47, 48, 50, 51, 82n54, 89
secular Jew(s), 4; Aschheim on, 15–16n10; Christendom as led by, 19–20; Freud as, xv; as paradox, 5, 8; Scholem on, 9
Selbstwehr weekly, 108
Self, Will, 128
self-assertion as modern, 47
self-conscious assimilation, 5
self-identity, 9–10, 61
self-mythology of modernism, 29
Self-Portrait in Letters (Stein), 73
Selznick, David O., 95
Sigmund Freud and the Jewish Mystical Tradition (Bakan), 88
Simmel, Georg, 9
Simon Dubnow Institute for Jewish History and Culture, 103
Sinclair, Upton, 162
"Slavery within Freedom" (Ahad Ha'am), 16n12
Snow, C. P., 88
Sorkin, David, 6, 46
spectrum model of gender, 69–70
spectrum of relative assimilation, 4–5
Spellbound (film), 94–97
Sperber, Manès, 112
Spinoza, Baruch, 45
Srámková, Barbora, 125

Star of Redemption (Rosenzweig), 32
Steigmann-Gall, Richard, 55n44
Stein, Arno, 71
Stein, Auguste Courant, 63–65, 67, 72
Stein, Edith, xiii, xv, 83–85; as Aryan double of sister, 72; and assimilation, 12, 60, 66; canonization of, 12, 59–60, 77n1; and contextuality, 76–77; on empathy, 64–65, 68, 73; essentialism of, 78n8, 80n39; as feminist, 12, 60–61, 65, 76, 78n8, 80n39; and gender spectrum, 65, 69, 80n38; Germanness of, 13, 66–67; and identification with crusades, 75; interiority-exteriority dialectic of, 73–76; as Jew and Christian, 60–61, 65–66, 77n2, 77–78n5, 78n9, 78–79n14; life and death of, 59–60, 62–64; on mother's life, 72; as Teresa Benedicta of the Cross, 59, 81n46; and Teresa of Ávila, 62, 74; on train to Auschwitz, 59, 62, 73. *See also Life in a Jewish Family* (Stein)
Stein, Erna, 72–73, 85
Steinberg, Michael P., 17–18n39
Steiner, George, 25, 109, 165n9
"The Stoker" (Kafka), 151–153
Strakosch, Leo, 21–22
Strauss, Johann, 105
Strauss, Leo, 41, 44–46, 50–51
Streitbares Leben (Brod), 131
structure-agency dichotomy, 6
subjectivity: democratic, 51; gendered, 71; German-Jewish, xiii, xv, 10–14; and historiography, xii; as illusive category, xiii, 11, 17–18n39, 60, 71; and mediation, 159; and methodological problems of analysis, 11–14; versus political contexts, 76; as process, xiii; versus scientific objectivity, 96; as self-experience, xiii, 17–18n39; in social context, xiii; spiritual, 74; versus structure, 6; as troubled, 5
Subject without Nation (Jonnson), 107
supranationalism, 131
symbolic interpretation, 149n35
sympathy (*Mitfühlen*), 65

tahor and *tamay* (pure and impure), xiv
Tales of Rabbi Nachmann (Buber), 13
"talking Jewy" (*Mauscheln*), 142
Taubes, Jacob, 41, 46, 51, 52n5

teleology, 43, 47, 131
Teresa Benedicta of the Cross. *See* Stein, Edith
Teresa of Ávila, Saint, 62, 73–75
territorial ideology, 128–130
territorial translation, 159
textuality of history, 29
theologico-political predicament, 45–46
theology, 40, 42, 50, 59, 60. *See also* political theology
Tildy, 104–105
Todorova, Maria, 106
torture machine drawing by Kafka, 85, 161–162
Toulmin, Stephen, 88
"The Tragedy of Central Europe" (Kundera), 106
transference and countertransference, 94
translation: as intercourse, 152–158, 161; theory of, 151–154, 165n9. *See also* Jesenská, Milena
transposition of sacred positions, 47
The Trial (Kafka), 127, 143–144, 162
"two cultures" of educated society, 88
"two vultures," science and humanism as, 89

universality and natural law, 92
Untimely Meditations (Nietzsche), 29, 142
"Unzeit" (Fuchs), 115
utopianism, 22, 24, 28, 32, 161

Varnhagen, Rahel, xi–xii, xvii, 49
Varnhagen von Ense, Karl August, xi
Verjudung (jewification), 20, 26
Vienna: in *Vienna and the Jews*, 24–25, 32; Vienna thesis, 101; in *Wittgenstein's Vienna*, 88
Voegelin, Eric, 52n4
völkisch (racialist) language, 13
Volkov, Shulamit, 15n4
Voltaire, 43
Vom Judentum, 130
von Trotta, Baron, 104–105

Wagenbach, Klaus, 144
Wagner, Otto, 101
Wagner, Richard, 19–20, 22, 27–28, 31, 34nn2–3, 34–35n5

Wassermann, Jakob, 7, 9, 11, 16n23
Weber, Alfred, 131
Weigel, Sigrid, 77–78n5
Weil, Simone, 79–80n26
Weimar Republic, 21, 23–24, 32, 40, 45–46, 67
Weininger, Otto, 69, 80n38
Weissglas, Immanuel, 113
Weltsch, Felix, 123, 130
Werfel, Franz, 123, 124, 126
"Who Owns Kafka?" (Butler), 127
Wickhoff, Franz, 25
Wiener, Jon, 30, 38n47
wissenschaftlich (scientific), 86
Wittgenstein, Ludwig, 9, 101, 103, 140
Wittgenstein's Vienna (Janik and Toulmin), 88
Wohryzek, Julie, 157
Wolff, Kurt, 126
"Womanliness as a Masquerade" (Riviere), 69–70
"The World Friend" (Werfel), 126
The World of Yesterday (Zweig), 101–102
World War I, 13, 67, 113, 114, 126, 131, 137
World War II, 30, 40, 139
"writing as a form of prayer," 126, 138

Yerushalmi, Yosef Hayim, 5
Yiddish-language writings, 115; Kafka and, 130
The YIVO Encyclopedia of Jews in Eastern Europe, 102
Yom Kippur, 66

Zank, Michael, 53n14
Zionism, 26–28; Birnbaum and, xv, 26, 36n27; Brod's early commitment to, 122, 129, 132; cultural, 26, 130; versus German nationalism, 7, 129; Kafka's relationship to, 10, 128, 145; as postassimilationism, 7–9; Strauss and, 44
Žižek, Slavoj, 71, 81–82n48
Zohn, Harry, 24
Zweig, Stefan, 25, 101–102, 109, 116n6
Zweistromland (land of two streams), 88
"Zwei Tiergeschichten" (Kafka), 144

SCOTT SPECTOR is Professor of History, German Studies, and Judaic Studies at the University of Michigan, Ann Arbor. He is the author of *Prague Territories: National Conflict and Cultural Innovation in Franz Kafka's Fin de Siècle* and *Violent Sensations: Sex, Crime, and Utopia in Vienna and Berlin, 1860–1914*.

www.ingramcontent.com/pod-product-compliance
Lightning Source LLC
Chambersburg PA
CBHW050109170426
43198CB00014B/2512